BILL SEVERN'S
GUIDE TO MAGIC
AS A HOBBY

To Rick with love
from mama

Lancaster, March 1982

BILL SEVERN'S GUIDE TO MAGIC AS A HOBBY

by

Bill Severn

David McKay Company, Inc.

New York

Library of Congress Cataloging in Publication Data

Severn, William.
Bill Severn's Guide to magic as a hobby.

Bibliography: p.
Includes index.
SUMMARY: Chapter titles include: "Performing Magic,"
"Women in Magic," "Books and Magazines," "Collecting
Magic," "Showplaces of Magic," "Clubs and Conventions,"
"The Dealers," and "A Short Dictionary of Magic."
1. Conjuring. [1. Magic tricks] I. Title.
II. Title: Guide to magic as a hobby.
GV1547.S485 1979   793.8   79-17155
ISBN 0-679-51201-2
ISBN 0-679-51202-0 pbk.

Book design: Arlene Schleifer Goldberg

1 2 3 4 5 6 7 8 9 10

Manufactured in the United States of America

CONTENTS

INTRODUCTION

Magic, more than anything else, *is* a hobby. In all the world, there probably are not five thousand full-time professional magicians who earn their living entirely by performing magic. There are many more who perform part-time professionally, some of whom earn a considerable part of their income from it.

The professionals set the pace, make good the dream, give the hobby of magic its meaning and reason to be. But it is mainly the amateurs, however professionally they may perform in their spare time, who support the magic clubs, societies, conventions, books, magazines, dealers, manufacturers, and all the other activities of magic.

In recent years there has been a great public rediscovery of magic's delightful age-old fun of theatrical make-believe. This has not been a rebirth of magic, because magic was never dead. As one of the oldest of all performing arts it has steadily enchanted audiences for hundreds of years. But magic has been caught up in an explosive boom of new popularity, both as an entertainment and as a hobby, with thousands of newcomers eager to discover the pleasures and satisfactions of being part of it.

Magic is not a single hobby, but a great variety of related hobbies, each with specialized fields that have multiplied as hobbies within hobbies. Performing is of course magic's main hobby, but in that area alone there are dozens of choices for each hobbyist to make, and performing is only the most visible of magic's many hobbies.

The purpose of this book is to explore America's magic hobbies and activities, the who, what, where, why, and how of them, to give the magic enthusiast some greater knowledge of what they are all about, and to provide a guide to sources of further information.

It includes a brief history of magic as a hobby, much about performing and presentation, about the selection and creation of tricks, about teaching, lecturing, books and magazines, about collecting, clubs, and conventions, the showplaces of magic and the dealers. It is not a how-to book of magic tricks and is not intended to be an instruction manual or an encyclopedia, but rather an informal "travel guide" for an exploratory trip through the present-day world of magic in the United States.

Mainly it is a book that tells of magic through the stories and experiences of the men and women involved. Obviously it could not have been written without the help of many friends who generously supplied material about their activities and special interests. Since I cannot thank them individually here, I hope they will collectively accept my gratitude.

I have enjoyed magic for more than fifty years, as a professional in my youth, semi-professionally at other times, and for all those years as a hobby. One of its constant fascinations is in the fact that there is always more to learn. Nobody can ever know all there is to know about magic, and the longer one is in it the more he learns how much there still is to discover.

In the end each person must make those discoveries for himself, and find his answers according to his own hobby goals. Certainly no book can promise to guide him to that destination. But I hope that this book, by pointing out some of the paths others have taken, and by offering some advice and suggestions along the way, will help to shorten the search for the real fun that I know magic can be.

1

THE MANY HOBBIES OF MAGIC

The father of modern magic, Jean Eugène Robert-Houdin, first took up magic as a hobby because of a book he had never intended to read. He was to become the greatest of French magicians, whose creative originality revolutionized the presentation of magic, but he had no thought of such things when he strolled into a bookstore in his native town of Blois one evening in the early 1800s. He was a young apprentice watchmaker and he wanted to buy a book on watches and clocks.

Busy with other customers, the bookseller made a mistake and wrapped up the wrong book. When Robert-Houdin got it home, he discovered that instead of a text on clockmaking he had a book that revealed some of the secrets of conjuring. It was a discovery, he afterwards wrote, "that caused me the greatest joy I have ever experienced."

Fascinated by it, he found himself "eagerly devouring every line," and the "excitement produced by the book prevented either sleep or rest." He read it through the night, until his only candle had burned itself out. Even then he couldn't put it down, and went out to the street in front of his house to try to finish reading it by the light of a street lamp.

"How often since have I blessed this providential error, without which I should have probably vegetated as a country watchmaker," he wrote. "My life would have been spent in gentle monotony; I should have been spared many sufferings, emotions and shocks; but on the

Commemorative postage stamp issued by the French government to honor Robert-Houdin, father of modern magic. The great 19th-century conjurer (1805–1871) was an amateur hobbyist for twenty years before he turned professional and revolutionized the presentation of magic.

other hand, what lively sensations, what profound delight would have been sacrificed."

He set about learning all the secrets in the book "with great ardor" and within a week "knew them all by heart." But he also quickly discovered that merely knowing the secrets of tricks wasn't at all the same as knowing how to do them. The book gave no instructions in the methods of performing and presenting the tricks. Practical books of magic, which really taught the doing of it and not just the bare secrets, had not yet been written.

Still the book inspired him and he learned from it what he could. He also took a few lessons in basic sleight of hand from a chiropodist in Blois who had a reputation not only for painlessly removing corns from people's feet but for entertaining them as an amateur conjuror.

Robert-Houdin practiced inces-santly, even manipulating cards and coins in his fingers as he walked along the streets. At the dinner table, he often ate his food with one hand while practicing with the other, and "the slightest moment of relaxation was devoted to my favorite pursuit." He began showing tricks to his friends, giving little parlor magic shows on Sunday afternoons, but he hadn't the slightest thought of staging a public performance or of abandoning his clockmaking trade to make a profession of his hobby of magic.

His work eventually moved him to Paris, and there he found a magic shop operated by Père Roujol, a place where he could meet and make friends with other amateur and professional magicians, buy equipment, and broaden his knowledge and pleasure in his hobby. He went to every magic show he heard about, saw all sorts of Parisian and visiting foreign magicians perform, and gradually formed his own concepts as to how magic should be presented.

Life as a professional magician began for him nearly at the age of forty, after twenty years as an amateur. He started his own small theater of magic in the old Palais Royal and on July 3, 1845, the billboards of Paris announced the first performance of the "Soirées Fantastiques de Robert-Houdin." Opening night he suffered such an acute attack of stage fright that the first show was a fumbling disaster, but his performances soon ran more smoothly, winning him high critical acclaim and much publicity.

2

He had done away with many of the cumbersome trappings of old-fashioned wizardry, its eccentric costumes, pretentious bombast, gaudy settings, heavy-handed mysticism, and tin-can trickery. His stage equipment was designed to look like the furnishings of a fashionable drawing room of the period. He played to perfection the role of a smartly attired Parisian gentleman, with charming wit and pleasant good humor, offering a refreshingly different evening of entertainment.

Every trick he performed, whether his own invention or borrowed from the past, was clothed with his originality, presented in a way that then seemed startlingly new and modern. He understood that magic had its basic appeal in what theater itself was all about, the creation of illusion, and he saw himself as an actor playing the part of a magician. He became an excellent actor, able to sway an entire audience to follow his shifting mood from the comic to the serious.

The "Fantastic Evenings of Robert-Houdin" gained popularity and prestige that had seldom been given to magic shows. Attending a performance became one of the smart things to do in Paris, with tickets so difficult to obtain that the box office sometimes turned away four times as many people as could be accommodated.

After a good part of his lifetime as an amateur, his professional career had spanned only a decade, in Paris and touring London and other cities, before he retired in comfort-

Robert-Houdin poster, used during his performances in London in 1848. Pictured at bottom is his "Suspension Ethereenne" in which he dramatically floated his son Adolphe in midair. Public controversy was then raging over the early use of ether for anesthesia. Robert-Houdin pretended to have his son breathe it in, pattering that as a result the young man's body "becomes in a few moments as light as a balloon."

After several royal command performances for Queen Victoria at Buckingham Palace, Robert-Houdin used this poster during London appearances in 1853, advertising the fact that he had just entertained Princess Louisa during her birthday party at the palace. He went on to tour the biggest theaters in England's other cities, earning enough to buy himself a country estate near his French hometown of Blois, where he had first taken up magic as a hobby years before.

able wealth to a country estate near Blois. But in that time, Robert-Houdin achieved international renown and lasting fame.

For amateurs or professionals who might hope to follow in his footsteps he wrote the first really thorough textbook on the methods, sleight of hand, presentation, and psychology of magic, *Les Secrets de la Prestidigitation et de la Magie.* He also wrote his autobiography, highly praised by critics for its literary merits as well as for its entertaining if sometimes fanciful account of his life and adventures. First published in France in 1858, *Confidences d'un Prestidigitateur* was republished in numerous editions, including those in English variously titled *Memoirs of Robert-Houdin* or *King of the Conjurors.* It inspired many of its readers to take up magic as a hobby, and some to make it a career.

Among Robert-Houdin's devotees was Ehrich Weiss, born in Budapest in 1874 and brought to Appleton, Wisconsin, as a child in his immigrant mother's arms. His father served for a time as Appleton's first rabbi, but the family soon moved to Milwaukee, and after many financial hardships and struggles finally settled in a flat on New York's upper East Side.

As a teenager, Ehrich had the first steady job of his life, cutting linings for neckties in a factory on lower Broadway. Magic was only one of his hobbies, but he had read every book on it he could find and had become a quite good amateur performer, especially of card tricks.

He was sixteen when he bought a

second-hand copy of the *Memoirs of Robert-Houdin* and was so entranced by the romantic autobiography of the great French conjuror that it changed the course of his life. "At once, Robert-Houdin became my guide and my hero," he later wrote. "I accepted his writings as my textbook and my gospel." Fired by his new ambition, he soon quit the necktie factory and set out to be a professional magician.

For a stage name, he added the latter "i" to the name of his idol, to mean "I am like Robert-Houdin," and from then on he stopped being Ehrich Weiss and was Harry Houdini. The rest, of course, became legend: the most publicized showman magic ever produced, whose very name was synonymous with the word "magic," and who, more than a half-century after his death, was still regarded by the public as the greatest magician who ever lived.

After he had become a success, Houdini regretted having put himself in the shadow of Robert-Houdin's prior fame by taking his name. Perhaps to boost his own ego, although he claimed it was done in a desire to set the record straight, Houdini devoted a lot of time to research for a series of articles and a book called *The Unmasking of Robert-Houdin*. It was a bitter attack, which attempted to prove that his boyhood hero had been a copyist who had stolen his tricks from others, and that the *Memoirs* that had once so inspired Houdini himself were more fiction than fact. But Robert-Houdin's greatness, like Houdini's,

has remained well established in magic's halls of fame.

Houdini never became famed, as Robert-Houdin was, for his adroit and artistic presentations of a dazzling variety of tricks and illusions. He started out with such tricks, and for a time in his early performing years billed himself as the "King of Cards." But he dropped them from his act to capitalize on the specialty that brought a different fame: the sensational escapes from handcuffs, ropes and chains, from jail cells, underwater packing boxes, and all other restraints that anybody could devise in a vain attempt to confine him.

He challenged death with his magic and kept his vast audiences in the suspense of wondering not only *how* he did it but whether he *could* do it and come out alive. He often included two or three magic tricks of other kinds in his performances, ranging from the swallowing and reproduction of a long string of threaded needles from his mouth to the mammoth illusion of vanishing an elephant. But Houdini was mainly a vaudeville headliner, not a magician touring with his own full-evening show, and it wasn't until near the end of his life that he successfully produced such a show.

Although escape tricks were his specialty, Houdini was interested in magic of every kind and in magicians everywhere, of whatever standing, who had ideas and information to share. Along with the professionals who shared his friendship and confidences, many skilled amateurs were among his close

Houdini poured his energy into dozens of magic activities that were his hobbies as well as part of his professional life. He was part-owner of a New York magic shop, was editor and publisher of a magazine for magicians, wrote several books on magic, and gave his time and financial support to the publication of other books for magicians.

Houdini showing "how and where I hit the cuff to open it" as part of his exposure of handcuff secrets. He first published the explanations in 1906 issues of The Conjurers' Magazine, *which he edited for magicians.*

Houdini publicly exposed some of the handcuff secrets of his would-be imitators, but not the secrets of his own sensational escapes, in magazine articles and in a booklet sold to his theater audiences. Here he demonstrates how any magician might use a handcuff that was tricked "by removing the strong spiral spring and inserting a weak one." But he himself escaped from genuine examined handcuffs, challenging the world to produce any restraint that could hold him.

friends. He was fully aware that as far as magic was concerned, he was making history, and the respect and recognition of his fellow magicians meant as much to him as public acclaim.

Wherever he performed he welcomed local magicians to his dressing rooms, attended meetings of magic clubs, was a founding officer of some of them. Largely through Houdini's efforts, many affiliate assemblies of the Society of American Magicians were formed across the United States. In 1917 he had the dual honor held by no other magician before or since, of being elected president of both the Society of American Magicians and the Magicians Club of London.

As a collector, he was voracious, searching out the bookstores and back corners of the world for almost anything related to magic: books, magazines, playbills, posters, memorabilia, and equipment. His desks, shelves, and closets spilled over with a helter-skelter of collected treasures. He squirreled away notes, papers, scrapbooks, diagrams. After his death, the books and periodicals formed the Houdini Collection at the Library of Congress, and the programs, playbills, and theatrical materials eventually went to the Theater Library of the University of Texas.

Magic grew enormously as a hobby during Houdini's lifetime, and a man who had much to do with influencing hundreds of people to become magicians was Angelo John Lewis. Under the pen name of Professor Louis Hoffmann, he wrote the first thoroughly practical and comprehensive book in the English language on modern magic, called just that, *Modern Magic*. Clearly and simply, in language anyone could understand, it explained most of the

Angelo Lewis, who wrote under the pen name of Professor Louis Hoffmann. He greatly inspired magic's first big growth as a hobby in the years just before and around the start of the 20th century by writing the first thoroughly practical English-language magic book for the general public, Modern Magic *(1876). A London lawyer turned author and literary critic, Lewis was an amateur magician himself, not an outstanding performer, but had the writing talent to really teach magic instead of merely exposing its secrets.*

then standard tricks, and more than that, it explicitly taught how to do them and how to present them entertainingly.

Written for the general public and first published in England in 1876, it quickly became a best-seller of its kind and was republished in nearly a score of other editions in England and the United States that kept it in print well into the twentieth century. It became the standard guidebook for a generation of amateur mystifiers, converted many who otherwise might have had only a passing interest in magic into becoming performers and dedicated magic hobbyists, started some toward part-time or full-time careers, and probably had more effect in generally revitalizing the world of magic than any other single book ever written.

For today's readers much of it has become outdated, but *Modern Magic* was a revelation of all that was the best and most up-to-date in magic in its time. Lewis, an Oxford-educated London barrister who had turned to a writing career, was an author of books on other subjects, an editor and critic, and for many years was on the staff of the London *Saturday Review*.

At the age of ten, he had been taken to see a magic show, which sparked the interest that made him an ardent amateur magician the rest of his life. Passionately devoted to magic, he was not an outstanding performer himself and never a professional. But he was the friend and confidant of many of the leading magicians and had a broad knowledge of magic, as well as the rare ability to teach his readers what he knew. As Professor Hoffmann, he wrote *More Magic, Later Magic,* and a number of other magic books, all of them popular but none as sensationally successful as *Modern Magic*.

Howard Thurston, who was to become among the world's greatest magicians during the first three decades of the twentieth century, was given a copy of *Modern Magic* as a boy and learned some of his first tricks from it. He also used it as a source book later in his youth when he gave his first small amateur magic shows to entertain at a farm home for juvenile delinquents where he was working while preparing to study for the ministry.

But what diverted Thurston from the ministry and from amateur to professional magic was the ambition inspired by watching performances of Alexander Herrmann, the greatest of the late nineteenth century magicians and the first to become a millionaire from the earnings of his big touring magic shows. In his own time of fame, Thurston also would earn more than a million dollars from magic, though he lost most of it through speculative investments and stock failures.

It was Boston physician James W. Elliott, another magic amateur soon to turn professional and an expert card manipulator, who showed Thurston the then-novel back-and-front palming of cards. Thurston built a presentation around it that became one of the features of his vaudeville card magic act, which he expanded over the years into the biggest and most elaborate magic shows ever regularly presented in American theaters. The Thurston shows grew from tricks with cards into touring full-evening extravaganzas of illusions and magical wonders that required a staff of forty

8

It wasn't only the famed stage performers who spread the popularity of magic as both entertainment and hobby. Shown here, as sketched by an artist for the Illustrated London News *in 1877, is a typical late 19th-century "parlor magician," performing for an English family at a home Christmas party.* PICTURE COLLECTION, NEW YORK PUBLIC LIBRARY

people, plus three railroad freight cars to carry the equipment.

The shows of all the great magicians and their lesser contemporaries influenced the swelling growth of magic as a hobby. Vaudeville brought magicians into cities big and small. Chautauquas and tent shows featured them. They wagon-toured the hinterlands of village halls and church basements. Everywhere the touring professionals went, interest in magic quickened and more amateurs took up the hobby.

Amateurs awakened the desire to perform in others who became amateurs. Often the inspiration came from close at home—relatives or friends who could do a few simple tricks that led others to try and started someone toward a lifetime hobby. The Christmas or birthday gift of a magic set was the open sesame for many youngsters who kept their interest as they grew up from the child's play of magic sets into the largely adult world of magic hobbyists.

Good magic books led to the increasing demand by hobbyists for more magic books, and to a proliferation of the whole literature of magic. It was also the enlarging readership of amateurs that brought into print and supported the magazines for magicians, the booklets and pamphlets of tricks and routines, the more widely cir-

9

culated dealers' catalogues of wondrous effects and equipment. The catalogues themselves were books of inspiration as well as dream books for beginners convinced that but for the lack of a trick deck of cards or a handkerchief-vanisher instant success as magicians awaited them.

The business of the magic dealers grew mainly on the purchases of amateurs, who were the buyers of whatever was new, different, or seemed the better to conjure with. It was the hobbyists who spurred much of the creation and marketing of new effects and improvement of older ones.

Groups of amateurs organized the first magic clubs to bring themselves and professionals together in regular meetings to share their common interests. They founded the national and later international magic societies, expanded them, ran them and sustained them through memberships largely amateur. The first annual magicians' conventions, which gradually were to grow into a world-circling circuit of such conclaves, were begun by amateurs.

The hobbyists were of all trades and occupations, and they brought much of their practical skill, specialized knowledge, or scholarship in various fields to the advancement of magic. They became the active collectors of all things related to magic and magicians, researchers and writers of magic history, theory and practice, the creators of effects and of techniques and methods, and explorers and discoverers.

As performers, they were of every sort: part-time professionals; spare-time entertainers at clubs, parties, and local affairs; those who gave mostly private or charity shows; performers of stage, small-platform, parlor, or close-up magic; some who confined their magic to tricks carried in their pockets and shown to friends and business acquaintances; and some who seldom performed at all but who had strong hobby interest in other areas of magic. They did magic to earn extra income, or to help pay the costs of their hobby, or they did it for nothing but fun.

And so the hobbyists grew, drawn into magic in much the same ways and for the same reasons amateurs were attracted to it in Robert-Houdin's time, or in Houdini's or Thurston's. They multiplied by the hundreds before World War II, and by the thousands after it. By the late 1970s, after magic had boomed into the greatest popularity it had known in years, amateurs outnumbered professionals by at least ten to one.

But professionals, semiprofessionals, and amateurs share in all of magic's activities. The word *amateur* doesn't define skill or ability, but simply means someone who doesn't earn a full-time living solely from magic. Throughout the world, magicians of every kind share an international friendship that has swept aside rank, wealth, race, creed, and political differences, in a fellowship of magic that embraces anyone who has a serious interest in it.

The top professionals bring to reality the amateur's dream of magic presented at its best—dazzlingly and entertainingly in the big theaters, the talked-about night clubs, for network television's millions of viewers. They give magic its public stature and spectacle-appeal, its showcasing and star-quality glamor, and generate enormous publicity that centers public attention on magic and magicians generally. Directly and indirectly, the professionals give vitality and meaning to all the hobbies of magic.

From the hobbyists, the professionals get not only the admiration, praise, and respect of those who know magic best and know what it takes in hard work and talent to win and sustain success, but also the ideas, tricks, and methods developed by thousands of constantly experimenting amateurs all over the world. Uniquely in magic, unlike other performing arts such as acting, music, or dancing, in which amateurs and leading professionals are far apart, there has always been a two-way street of sharing and friendship between professional and amateur magicians.

For the nonprofessional, magic offers rewards and satisfactions as individual as each person who takes up the hobby. In a world where so many working-day occupations stifle individuality, magic provides an escape from the humdrum, opportunity for creative self-expression, and a wide range of hobby interests adaptable to each in his own way. For most amateurs the goal is seldom entirely to earn extra money, although there are good chances for that, not only in performing but in some of the other hobbies of magic.

There are those who bring their whole families into the hobby, whether to take part in performing or simply to enjoy its social activities. Families spend vacation time together attending magic conventions, mixing with the greats and near-greats, being part of an "in" group that shares a somewhat secret knowledge that is not known to the general public.

Hobbyists include the collectors of all the things of magic, the creators and inventors, home-workshop builders of equipment, writers and researchers and scholarly students of its history, and some mainly "armchair magicians" whose chief pleasure is in reading the literature of magic and imagining themselves as the skilled performers they read about.

Others delight in devising and performing magic not for the public but for fellow magicians. They find satisfaction in the accomplished skills of intricate sleight of hand or subtleties of method that win them the admiration of their peers. They enjoy the fellowship of showing each other endless tricks in close-up sessions, of puzzling out ways to perform seemingly impossible effects, exchanging letters about some particular move or solution to a problem. Mostly they do it for their own amusement, but such magic for magicians frequently is the source of new principles, methods, and tricks that are put to more practical uses for public entertaining.

Some adapt magic to their interest in other hobbies, such as designing and making costumes, tie-dying colorful silks, photographing magicians, making films and sound recordings. Some are amateur artists who illustrate tricks in magic books and magazines. Magic is used by its hobbyists in lectures on all sorts of subjects, in teaching, in public talks, in community historical pageants, in school and recreational programs, for mental and physical therapy, remedial reading, for the bedside entertainment of those confined to hospitals and other institutions.

Advertising and marketing executives, who are numerous among amateur magicians, have been alert to use the attention-catching values of magic in their work, as have salesmen, store-window display decorators, and the manufacturers and promoters of every type of product from soft drinks and candy to automobiles and farm machinery.

Among the professions, lawyers, doctors, and educators seem to outnumber others in their devotion to magic hobbies. But many scientists, musicians, and authors have been attracted to magic, and it also seems to have a special appeal for actors and other show business personalities.

Magic was the stepping-stone into show business for Johnny Carson, an active club-date magician in Nebraska in his youth, before he became a comedian, television star, and late-night talk-show host. When celebrities who have an interest in magic appear on his show, Carson is likely to do a quick trick or two himself, and on occasion has pulled his old magic equipment out of the closet to perform a full act and demonstrate the skill which as an amateur magician led him into a theatrical career.

Dick Cavett also owes much of his show-business start to magic, in which he has never lost his interest. Prominent magicians have frequently appeared on his programs and Cavett himself has performed on magic specials he has hosted. Orson Welles, long associated with magic, has used his expert knowledge of it and his theatrical genius for dramatic presentations of large-scale illusions, and has also baffled television audiences with his card tricks and mental magic. Film star Cary Grant's fascination with magic has led to his becoming a member of the governing board of directors of the Academy of Magical Arts, whose clubhouse is Hollywood's famed Magic Castle.

Some amateurs are drawn into magic for much the same reason people might join in a little-theater group, to enjoy play-acting and make-believe. But magic allows them as individuals to create their own entertainments and to star themselves in them. They don't even need a stage; magic can be done almost anywhere, in the living room or at a dinner table with a few friends as audience.

Consciously or unconsciously, some seek to advance themselves socially or in business relationships by using magic to interest others in them and to help make friends more easily. There also may be indirect rewards from doing magic, such as gaining self-confidence, learning to speak better in public, to present ideas clearly and logically, and to communicate better with people. A good part of the successful performing of magic rests upon "making friends and influencing people."

Whatever the individual desire for personal pleasure or self-fulfillment may be, most magic hobbyists are in it for the simple and obvious reason that it is good fun. In the true sense of the word *amateur,* they are lovers of magic.

For Further Reading

Most of us are first attracted to magic by its tricks, by curiosity to know how they are done, and then by a desire to learn to do some of them. But before a person can decide intelligently where he wants to go in magic and what he wants to do, he needs to know something about where magic has been and what others already have done.

For his own greater pleasure in whatever magic hobbies he decides to explore, and simply to be better informed and to share the knowledge most magicians take for granted when they talk about or write about magic, he should read some of its history. Even if that means temporarily putting aside the books of tricks, the reader will go back to those tricks with a much clearer understanding of what they are.

The books suggested in this list are all fairly recent, were printed for the general public, and most should be available on order through any bookstore if they are not in stock. But don't overlook your public library, which may have some of them on its shelves, and which can get others for you to borrow through state or interstate library loan systems. This first list does *not* include books of tricks. For those, see Chapter 2, "Performing Magic."

Magic History and the Magic Scene

Christopher, Milbourne. *The Illustrated History of Magic.* New York: Thomas Y. Crowell, 1973. Acknowledged to be the best history of magic. Written with the special insight of a world-famous modern magician, it is comprehensive, informative, and scholarly in its research, but entertainingly readable and in no way a dust-dry academic tome. Illustrated with many fascinating prints, photographs, playbills, and engravings from Christopher's own collections.

Claflin, Howard, and Sheridan, Jeff. *Street Magic.* New York: Doubleday, 1977. Paperback. An illustrated, interestingly written and unusual view of the history of magic, mainly centered around its wandering outdoor performers, from conjurors of the old marketplaces and fairgrounds to modern big-city street magicians.

Clark, Hyla M., and Levin, Paul. *The World's Greatest Magic.* New York: Crown Publishers, 1976. A photographic look, with an interesting text, at some top magicians, past and present. This ranges over the history of magic and various types of performing, but concentrates on popular modern magicians (color-photographed in action by Paul Levin), their personalities, and their audience appeal.

Doerflinger, William. *The Magic Catalogue*. New York: E. P. Dutton, 1977. A magic sampler that includes a little of everything to give a broad introduction to the world of magic. Brief history; types of tricks and performing; personality sketches; selected pages from dealer catalogues; prints, photographs, collections, museums; listings of some dealers, magazines, clubs.

Hay, Henry. *Cyclopedia of Magic*. New York: Dover Publications, 1973. Paperback. This is a reprint of the original published in 1949, outdated in some respects but still a valuable reference to all things magical as they were then—and some things have not greatly changed. There are thumbnail biographies, concise explanations of then-standard and classic tricks, specially written articles, excerpts from older magic books, and other information from magic's past that is not elsewhere currently in print.

Reynolds, Charles and Regina. *100 Years of Magic Posters*. New York: Grosset & Dunlap, 1976. Paperback. Large-size reproductions, many in color, of the posters of famous magicians, with historical notes and brief biographies. Good reading and a visual delight.

Rydell, Wendy, and Gilbert, George. *The Great Book of Magic*. New York: Harry S. Abrams, 1976. An entertainingly presented big book of magic history with more than seven hundred illustrations and many full-color prints. Covers magic from prehistoric to modern times, with full biographies of some great magicians, and includes a section of easy-to-do tricks.

Biographies

Christopher, Milbourne. *Houdini: The Untold Story*. New York: Thomas Y. Crowell, 1969. This has become the definitive biography among the flood of books, plays, films, television fables, essays, and psychological studies about Houdini. It deals with the man as well as with the legend and blows away many of the myths without diminishing his greatness as a showman, self-publicist, and one-of-a-kind magician.

Robert-Houdin, Jean Eugène. *Memoirs of Robert-Houdin*. New York: Dover Publications, 1964. Paperback. A reprint of the autobiography that originally inspired Houdini, among others. It reads like an exciting novel, and in places may be more fiction than fact. But it clearly shows the originality and the detailed hows and whys of planning and presenting effects that revolutionized the performance of magic and won the French conjuror lasting fame as the father of modern magic.

2

PERFORMING MAGIC

Performing magic is not something that can be learned in a hurry. If it were, there wouldn't be much fun in it as a hobby. The pleasure, both for those who do it and those who watch, comes from doing it well, not from just showing tricks, but from using them to create entertainment.

Learning to do magic well grows out of experience and self-discovery, from trying this and that and gradually finding out what works best for each person in terms of his personality and the kind of performing he hopes to do. It involves the accumulation of knowledge that goes into the selection of tricks, the testing of them by repeated performance.

Probably most of all it requires thinking of magic *from the viewpoint of those who will watch it*. The ability to do that and to present it in a way that will please people doesn't come in a week or a year.

But the learning is in the doing, and so is the fun. It doesn't take long to learn to do a few simple tricks passably well. Starting from there, frequent performing will make almost anybody a better magician.

Magic is performed in many ways and in many places, and perhaps the best view can be had of its broad range of performing activities by looking at what some of the top professionals have done. They all began as amateurs, and while magic is no longer only a hobby for them but a business and a way of life, the basic types and areas of performing are much the same for both professionals and amateurs, if on a different scale.

Milbourne Christopher

For famed magician Milbourne Christopher, the performing of magic began at the age of twelve with a show he gave in a church hall near his Baltimore home. His father, a salesman who knew a few magic tricks, had started him on the hobby by teaching him one of them—how to cut and restore a string.

There's no restraining the magic of Milbourne Christopher's hands, even when his thumbs have been tightly fastened together by the audience in these thumb-cuffs, which bind them by the tight turning of the screw. In this picture, he is about to pass his locked hands through various solid objects. A recognized authority on Houdini, author, historian, and top performer in all fields of magic, Christopher did much to start magic on its new boom of popularity by bringing his magic shows to Broadway and creating the first network television magic spectaculars.

That string trick and an interest in ropes and knots that began when he was a boy scout led to Christopher's first specialty in magic. He built an act around a highly entertaining presentation of rope tricks. While still in his teens, he captured a prize for originality at a magicians' convention with his effect of stretching a rope to twenty times its original length.

He had already decided to become a professional magician. Although he did all kinds of magic, his rope routines were then a novelty, something off magic's beaten path, and they helped to gain him vaudeville and nightclub bookings.

At the age of twenty-one, he was appearing at a Washington nightclub in 1935 when his first big break came. The Roosevelts invited him to entertain that Easter at the traditional egg-rolling party on the White House lawn, an event widely publicized by reporters and photographers. Within a year, Christopher was on his way to Europe for the first time, to present his novel rope magic in theaters in London, Paris, and Berlin on a tour with the noted pantomimic comedian Fred Sanborn. That was followed by the first of his nine trips to perform in South America. Through the years his magic would take him to more than seventy countries.

There were fewer than a million American homes equipped with television sets in 1947 when Christopher appeared on one of the early sponsored programs televised in New York. Ten years later television had grown phenomenally toward the showcase it was to become for every form of magic, from close-up to sensational illusions. In 1957, when he conceived and starred in network television's first big magic spectacular, "The Festival of Magic," a ninety-minute program transmitted live in the then new color as well as black and white, Christopher had an audience of thirty-three million viewers, plus additional millions who saw it on kinescope in Europe.

In the show, he featured his version of the dangerous trick of magically stopping a bullet fired at him by a trained marksman, a death-defying feat that has accidentally cost the lives of quite a few magicians. Later, in another of the television specials he produced, Christopher recreated Houdini's effect, by a different method, of vanishing a live elephant. Television had never before seen such things.

New York theatergoers meanwhile first saw him in 1954 in *Now You See It,* a one-man show at the Longacre Theater; this marked the first presentation in years of an all-magic show on Broadway. After the New York production in 1961 of another, more elaborate illusion show, *Christopher's Wonders,* he took that, a score of dancers and assistants, and ten tons of equipment on a tour of the British Isles. Big illusions also were featured in his "Magic World" show at Madison Square Garden in 1968.

But by contrast, when Christopher performs at concert halls and in his lecture appearances, he carries all the magic props he needs in a single briefcase. When he is co-

Christopher's Wonders, *the elaborate illusion show that Christopher produced in New York in 1961 and then took on a tour of the British Isles with a score of dancers and assistants and ten tons of equipment, included this charming presentation of what magicians know as the Doll's House illusion. Christopher formed a paper dove in his hands, placed it into the dovecote shown at the right, and transformed it into a live dove—held by a girl who suddenly appeared by bursting open the roof of the empty dovecote.*

hosting a television variety show, or when a guest on talk shows, there may not even be a briefcase in evidence. Everything is in his pockets, arranged so they don't noticeably bulge.

Magic has remained his lifelong hobby as well as his profession, and

18

his life in magic has many sides. Past president of the Society of American Magicians, which elected him to magic's Hall of Fame, he was for nine years editor of the society's magazine *M-U-M,* and has been an editor, writer, and columnist for other magazines. Interested in psychic phenomena since his early teens, he heads the society's Occult Investigation Committee, is a scholarly historian of magic, an authority on Houdini, and has written many books for the general public in addition to a score of books for magicians.

Facing Central Park, the seven rooms of his Manhattan apartment, shared with his wife, a busy advertising trade magazine editor, are filled with tricks and equipment of every sort, and the overflow is stored in a nearby warehouse. The apartment amounts to a museum of magic, shelved with rare and historic apparatus, the corridors hung with paintings, woodcuts and lithographs; it houses his collection of seven thousand books and fifty thousand pieces of memorabilia.

His public shows are varied: television, nightclubs, theaters, concerts, lectures, business, trade, and commercial. An average of eighty performances a year have earned him an annual income that, according to the *Wall Street Journal,* "bulges well into six figures."

When he presented his evenings of "Magic & Music" in 1978 at the Rainbow Grill, high atop New York's Rockefeller Center, the critic for *Variety,* the theatrical trade paper, took particular notice of the kind of magic Christopher selected. His presentation, said the reviewer, was exactly suitable for that type of performance, which gave the show the "solid values" of "excellent entertainment."

Variety reported that "in keeping with the intimacy of this room, Christopher has chosen small tricks," rather than more elaborate illusions. "He reaches out for entertainment with a series of tricks charmingly done and with the aid of members of the audience."

Christopher recreated some of Houdini's magic and exposures of fraudulent spirit mediums for his "Magic vs. The Occult" concert presentations, as in this appearance at New York's Lincoln Center. The performance drew a full-capacity audience to Alice Tully Hall.

Christopher believes, as Robert-Houdin did, that a magician is an actor playing the role of a magician. "He does the impossible, makes dreams come true, and that can be very appealing," he says. "But even while he is fooling people, he lets them know that they are being fooled. Magic is largely psychology and the understanding of people. The effect on the onlooker should be the principal concern."

He feels that individual tricks, no matter how good, are only the tools of magic, and that what each magician brings to them of his personality and ability as an entertainer is what counts. "The most adept conjurers delight as much with their talk or their pantomime as with their tricks," he says, "and as much with their manner as with their manipulations."

His advice to the amateur who is still learning to program and present magic is to see as many other magicians perform as possible. "Study how they walk out on the stage or begin a close-up routine," he suggests. "Take note of how they work with volunteers and what they say as well as what they do. Analyze how they build suspense, how they manipulate the audience's interest, and how they stage their concluding feat."

Mark Wilson

Mark Wilson transformed himself from a small-time club-date performer into one of America's best-known and most successful magicians by combining magic with big-business salesmanship, and by creating, staging, and presenting magic that could compete for audience attention with any other kind of contemporary top-level entertainment.

For five years he presented the first nationally televised weekly magic show and continued to star in other series and syndicated shows, in hour-long specials, and in nightclubs. But his own performing, as important as it is to him in keeping his name before the public, is only part of the work that has involved him in the presentation and selling of magic every day of his life since he was in high school.

For his first paid performance, a show he gave as a boy for a Rotary Club party, he collected five dollars. As head of a corporate Hollywood enterprise that produces packaged magic shows for fairs and amusement parks and provides many kinds of magic for television, films, and advertising and marketing campaigns, his gross income has averaged over a million dollars a year.

Wilson's interest in magic began at the age of eight, when his salesman father took him to see a vaudeville show in which a magician produced cards from the air. Mark discovered the secret in a book of card tricks, tried the trick himself,

Mark Wilson, who linked magic to television and to big business and achieved both his boyhood ambitions of becoming a famous magician and attaining financial success.

and decided he wanted to become a magician.

As a boy growing up in Dallas he soon was spending most of his allowance buying other magic books and tricks, and spending most of his free time at a local magic shop. He was thirteen when the magic-shop owner gave him a part-time job, afternoons and Saturdays, working behind the counter, demonstrating and selling magic. It was a job that rapidly increased his performing skill and magical knowledge. During his high school years he also was giving shows for clubs, church groups, and children's birthday parties.

For a schoolboy, he was doing well. Magic was a wonderful hobby and a source of spare-time earnings. But as a future full-time career that kind of performing hardly seemed to promise much of a living. "I wanted to be a professional magician, but I also wanted to be a financial success," he recalls. From a practical point of view, he had been considering a career in advertising and he convinced himself he could combine the two, by using magic to sell products and services as well as entertainment. "I could be successful and still be doing what I wanted to do."

With that plan in mind he went to college at Southern Methodist University's school of business administration and majored in advertising. Magic shows helped pay for his business education, and while still in college he sold a potato chip manufacturer the idea of promoting sales with magic.

Wilson with his wife and co-star Nani Darnell and their youngest son Greg. Greg has followed rapidly in his father's footsteps to become an accomplished young magician himself.

The potato chip company would send him out to perform for any group of thirty-five or more people who asked to have him give a magic show. The group got free entertainment, the company got good advertising, and Wilson was paid by the company for each performance. Some months he did as many as eighty half-hour shows.

It was not only a profitable arrangement but the best kind of experience for a magician: constant public performing before all sorts of audiences. "It gave me the background I needed," he says, "to work full time as a professional magician."

Wilson began his professional career as a club-date performer when he finished college and soon expanded the act to co-star dancer Nani Darnell, who became his wife

in 1952. But his earnings were small at first. He saw television as his best opportunity to link merchandising with magic, but he had never been on television, had no agent, and no station was interested in putting him on the air. So he tried a different approach.

He went to station WFAT in Dallas, found out what time periods were available to sell to a sponsor, and their cost, and then used his business school training to put together a complete package for the Dr. Pepper soft drink bottling company. The company bought the whole package and sponsored Wilson's first local television series. "Presenting the complete package," he says, "is the key to the success that we have achieved over the years."

Starting in 1953, he performed two fifteen-minute shows a week, called "Time for Magic," on the Dallas station. As a direct sales-promotion tie-in, he appeared on commercials between the two shows, demonstrating one trick each week, which viewers could obtain as a premium by mailing in twelve bottle caps. He also made personal appearances at supermarkets where the company had point-of-purchase displays of its soft drink products.

The show became the station's most popular afternoon program, even outranking network competition, and ran for seven years. Meanwhile Wilson had managed to sell it for local programming in other Texas cities. At one point, he was on the air in Dallas, San Antonio, and Houston. All the shows were live,

that being before the use of videotape, which meant he and his co-
star wife had to spend much of their
time hurriedly driving from city to
city. In addition, they packaged a
line of children's magic sets, which
they demonstrated and sold in department stores in the cities where
their shows were on the air.

The success of the local programs
convinced Wilson it was time to
move up into national television
with a regular weekly series network
show. Still without an agent and
entirely on his own, he started out
in 1958 to sell what had never before been sold.

"I didn't know how difficult it
would be for an individual to sell a
network series show," he says. So he
just drew up a prospectus and began making calls. Whenever he had
a little money saved up, he would
make a trip to some city to talk to a
possible sponsor. "I called on practically every major advertising
agency and prospective client in the
country, anybody I could think of
who might be interested."

It took two years of salesmanship
before an advertising agency
bought the show for the Kellogg
cereal company. But in 1960, Wilson and Nani Darnell, with the talented Bev Bergeron as Rebo the
Magic Clown, began appearing
every Saturday morning over the
CBS network in their "Magic Land
of Allakazam." Two years later the
program switched networks without
a break, going off CBS one Saturday and reappearing on ABC the
next Saturday to start a new three-
year run. It became the longest-

running—as well as the first—network television magic series.

Many magicians are able to present the same shows for a full season, or even for years, without
changing their routines. Wilson and
the expert creative staff of seventeen people he recruited were faced
with having to devise, build, rehearse, and stage an entirely new
show each week. The shows were
elaborate, with special music, dancing, scenic and lighting effects, and
with the magic specially designed to
fit the themes of acted-out comic
skits and storybook scenes.

The staff included five or more
knowledgeable magicians who took
part in the brainstorming and planning sessions. Among them was
John Gaughan, who as a fourteen-
year-old boy had first worked for
Wilson in Dallas, assembling and
packaging magic sets. Gaughan was
to become a master builder of illusions, with workshops that would
produce custom-built equipment
for many of the nation's prominent
professional magicians and big
magic shows.

After "Allakazam" finally ended
its long run in 1965, Wilson turned
from television to the development
of other magic projects. He concentrated mainly on trade and industrial shows, incorporating magic
themes into the marketing of a variety of products. His staff expanded
to fifty people and he had offices in
New York, Chicago, and Los Angeles.

What was to grow over the years
into one of Wilson's busiest activities
began at the New York World's Fair

of 1964-65 with his "Hall of Magic" pavilion for the General Cigar Company, which presented magic shows seen in person by more than two million people. That was the forerunner of his concept of "package shows in a music box," which he and his staff would produce for many fairs, amusement parks and theme parks.

Wilson doesn't perform in such shows himself, since there may be a dozen or more playing different places at the same time. He creates them and the magic for them, supplies all the props, scenery, costumes, and scripted routines, and supervises the training and rehearsal of professional actors and dancers to present them. Some of the actors who do the magic have never done magic before, but it is stage magic that requires no intricate sleight of hand and they are taught to give polished performances. The music is recorded, as are the voice-over commentaries.

"We cycle the shows four to six a day, but can lengthen or shorten the performances depending on what the park wants," Wilson says. "Each show must be created to fit the individual park and its facilities. We can play small theaters or four-thousand-seat amphitheaters, with material specially written to suit the theme and audiences of that park. We maintain all the props during the run of the show."

With the new business ventures established, he resumed producing and personally performing in a succession of television and nightclub shows, which merged magic with

Wilson's television and night-club shows merged magic with contemporary music and dance, modern-looking props and costuming, and the up-to-date staging and production that today's audiences are accustomed to in other forms of popular entertainment.

contemporary music and dance, modern-looking sets, props, and costuming. Modern magic, Wilson is convinced, must be as up-to-date in the excellence of its production values as those other forms of entertainment that audiences are accustomed to from television, films, and the recording industry.

"What the successful magicians of the past did and the way that they did it was right for their time," he

24

says, "but today's magician has to take a modern approach that is right for our time."

His 1974 Las Vegas Hilton show with singing star Glenn Campbell was staged and directed by Walter Painter—who had choreographed the successful Ann-Margaret shows —with an original musical score, specially written script, and additionally written comic material, and with the glittering sets and costumes done by prominent Las Vegas show designers.

Wilson's television work meanwhile has included the production of six one-hour specials, "The Magic Circus." He has created, performed in, and provided the magic for many other specials, and has made sixty-five different five-minute shows for syndicated use in various children's television programs.

As an advisor and consultant for television and films, he has also furnished the know-how and the magical effects for dozens of episodes in various dramatic and comedy shows, and has taught the stars how to do tricks and illusions that are worked into the scenes. "The Magician" series, starring Bill Bixby

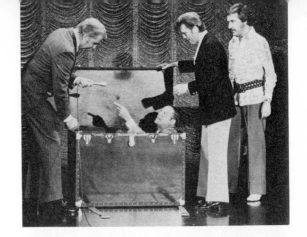

Scenes from one of Wilson's "Tonight Show" appearances, in which Ed McMahon and Doc Severinson assist him in locking comedian Don Rickles in a trunk. But a moment later Rickles escapes and singer Glen Campbell magically appears from the locked trunk.

in the early 1970s, rested heavily on Wilson's magic-planning and coaching. In other later shows he taught Wayne Rogers to float Karen Black in midair, Peter Fonda how to divide Claudia Cardinale into three beautiful parts, and Ed Asner how to cut and restore John Travolta's handkerchief and burn Jack Klugman's twenty-dollar bill without destroying it.

Wilson maintains a full-time staff of some thirty people on a year-round basis for his various magical

---

What looks like the world's largest card trick (upper left) really involves the young woman Wilson has inside the box, who is being "shuffled" into four sections as the giant cards magically penetrate her body, so that the divided sections can be shown separately before she finally is put back together. The suspension on the point of a sword (upper right) and the topsy-turvy girl (lower right) were among other illusions Wilson performed on his series of hour-long "Magic Circus" television specials.

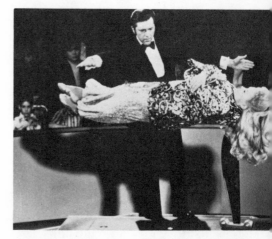

Doug Henning

On the night of Tuesday, May 28, 1974, a new Broadway star was born. Doug Henning magically seemed to have appeared out of nowhere, as a professional magician playing the role of a magician in a musical comedy, *The Magic Show.* He was no singer or dancer, was unknown to the New York theatergoing public, and the show's tricks and illusions were all based on effects other magicians had done before.

But nobody had done them quite the way Henning did them. He *was* magic, theatrically and with a charm of personality that conjured up in the minds of that sophisticated first-night audience a sense of wonder and delight. His magic seemed all

enterprises, doubling to twice that many during peak rush periods. His North Hollywood warehouse holds what is probably the largest collection of magic equipment housed under one roof anywhere in the world. Like any business executive faced with dozens of problems demanding immediate attention, he works in an office that is a place of busy conferences, ringing telephones, intercoms, and clattering typewriters.

But in the midst of it all he is likely to be found manipulating a coin or trying some new move with a pack of cards, mostly for his own amusement, still fascinated by what he calls "the most satisfying of all hobbies." He believes that almost anybody can learn magic. "But it's like learning to play the piano," he says. "Some learn to play well and some play 'Chopsticks.'"

Doug Henning, the "kid in tennis shoes," who—by creating a real sense of magic instead of just showing tricks—rose from obscurity to stardom, but not overnight. IRVING DESFOR.

the more real because he was the least likely-looking of magicians, a short, lean, long-haired, curly-mustached kid in blue jeans and tennis shoes who appeared to be one of the last cheerful survivors of the age of Aquarius.

He was as modern as the rock musical that had been skillfully constructed to make him its centerpiece. When the curtain went down, the audience gave him a rare opening-night standing ovation, and people walked from the theater not humming the tunes but remembering his magic.

Clive Barnes, then drama critic for the *The New York Times*, whose verdict reputedly could make or break a show, wrote: "Doug Henning is terrific. He is the greatest magician I have ever seen." Most other critics agreed that Henning's performance was brilliant, and *The Magic Show* was on its way to becoming Broadway's "hottest ticket," starting one of the longest runs of any recent musical comedy. Henning had become almost instantly famous.

But Broadway stars and famed magicians are not really made overnight. Henning was twenty-seven when he opened in *The Magic Show* and by then he had been performing magic and developing his ideas about the presentation of it for half his young life.

He was fourteen when he gave his first paid performance, at a birthday party for a friend of his sister's, for which he pocketed a fee of five dollars. But his interest in magic had started when he was six, watching a program, on his home television set, in which a magician made a young woman float through the air. His family soon bought him a toy magic set and when he was a little older he discovered the magic books in the public library, from which he learned to put together his first shows with home-made props.

Born in Winnipeg, Manitoba, in 1947, Douglas James Henning later moved with his family to Oakville, Ontario, a suburb of Toronto, where he grew into his teens as a proficient amateur magician. As a member of a Toronto magic club, he shared the knowledge of a well-informed magic fraternity. By the time he was in high school, he was performing at clubs and parties, being paid for it, and had made his first appearances on local television. He advertised his services in the newspapers: "Magician. Have rabbit. Will travel."

When he went to McMaster University, where he majored in psychology, his ambition was for a career in medicine, not magic. But he used magic to help pay his way through college, giving shows at children's birthday parties, and with a young woman partner in a nightclub act. After he graduated from the university, he decided to take some time out before entering medical school, and he never went back.

Henning applied to the Canadian Arts Council for a grant to study magic as a performing art. That body usually supported projects in music, dance, experimental theater, and the more recognized arts, and had never allocated funds to a magician. But he convinced the Council that magic plus theater could equal art, and was awarded a grant of $4,000.

He traveled to wherever there was good magic to see, talked to scores of magicians, sought their advice and knowledge about the best tricks and best methods of doing them, took lessons in expert sleight of hand from such masters as Dai Vernon and Tony Slydini. But more than the learning of tricks and techniques, Henning's fund-grant for travel and study among magicians gave him a clearer concept of the magician he wanted to be. He saw magic's basic appeal as akin to poetry, fantasy, fable; he wanted to present magic not merely to mystify audiences, but to create in them a sense of wonder.

He performed in coffee houses, discotheques and other gathering places of his own young generation, and then toured with Canadian rock groups, combining routines of magic with music. That went so well he decided to try to create a musical comedy for the stage, with a plot built around magical happenings.

Canadian film and television producer Ivan Reitman became interested in producing it and funds were raised for Henning to have illusions built. With only a still-sketchy outline of the show they hoped to present, they staged an audition for prospective backers, who invested enough to put it on.

They booked the Royal Alexandra Theatre in Toronto for what was to be called *Spellbound*. The plot and musical score still had to be worked out and everything took so long to pull together that there was time for only two dress rehearsals before the opening.

But *Spellbound* gradually caught on, audiences liked it both as magic and theater, and it went on to break all box-office records at the Royal Alexandra. Word of the Canadian success reached New York and Edgar Lansbury and Joseph Beruh, the producers of *Godspell* and other shows, went to Toronto to see Henning. They became convinced that he had the makings of a potential Broadway hit.

Henning was less easily convinced. He was doing well in Toronto, and as he later told interviewers, "I was not sure how New York audiences might take to it. I thought they might be too sophisticated." But an agreement was reached and the transformation of *Spellbound* into *The Magic Show* began.

He kept most of the same magic and illusions, but the rest of the play was remade, with songs and music written by Stephen Schwartz, composer of *Pippin* and *Godspell,* and a new book by Bob Randall, author of the long-running *6 Rms Riv Vu.* The award-winning choreographer Grover Dale became the director.

Playing opposite Henning as his girl friend in the show was actress-singer Dale Soules, previously featured in *Hair,* and Anita Morris had the role of a beautiful if somewhat unwilling magician's assistant. She was the one who, during a brilliant presentation of the sawing-a-woman illusion, was left with only the boxed top half of her body on stage to carry on the dialogue while villains ran away with her lower half.

The Magic Show's action took place in a third-rate New Jersey nightclub, with Henning as "Doug," a young today's-generation magician trying to make it into big-time show business. Plotting against him with comic melodramatic villainy was his rival "Feldman," a broken-down has-been of a traditional old-fashioned magician. Most of the big illusions were woven in as background sequences in the plot, but before the boy-gets-girl ending, Henning also presented "Doug's" nightclub act of superbly done smaller magic.

Henning brought to *The Magic Show* more than just tricks. As an actor using those tricks to create theatrical illusion, he was a personification of magic. Thinking of magic as just tricks, he felt, was like thinking of ballet as just a form of exercise. "My whole personality and energy come out through my magic," he said. "I *feel* the amazement and magic within my effects. These feelings are carried over to my audience."

When a major oil company decided to present him on network television in a big hour-long special show planned for the 1975 Christmas season, Henning convinced the sponsors that it should be presented live, not taped, to give it the same immediacy and impact his magic had with live theater audiences. He felt strongly that the millions of home television viewers had to be convinced they were seeing it ex-actly as it happened, with no suspicion of doctored tapes or electronic trickery.

By the time the 1975 show finally took to the air more than a hundred people were involved and costs ran into hundreds of thousands of dollars. David Susskind became the producer, NBC put its expert television resources and know-how behind it, and the sponsoring oil company's money flowed into the production and into a big promotion campaign, with billboarded posters and full-page advertisements in leading newspapers and national magazines.

Henning's good friend Charles Reynolds, picture editor of a popular photography magazine—and also a magician with an unusually broad knowledge of the methods, principles, and effects of magic—became his magic consultant, as he would be in later television shows. Together, in many long sessions of talking out ideas, they came up with an unusual array of tricks and illusions, some of them recreated from magic's historic past.

Rehearsals started in New York a month before air time and then were moved to the West Coast, into a former Culver City motion picture studio where scenes for films such as *Gone With The Wind* once were made. A completely equipped theater was built for the magic special on one of the big sound stages. Henning meanwhile had taken a leave from Broadway, after coaching a professional actor, Joseph Abaldo, to perform the magic and replace him in *The Magic Show*, which continued what was to be an unbroken five-year run.

Introduced by Gene Kelly and hosted by Bill Cosby, the 1975 Christmas special, "Doug Henning's World of Magic," was a fast-moving hour of novel illusion spectacles and smaller magic. The illusions included a long-neglected classic, the "vanishing lady"—as first presented in the 1880s by Buatier De Kolta, in which singer Lori Lieberman, seated in a plain chair at the front of a bare stage and covered with a thin silken sheet that outlined her form, instantly vanished when the cloth was whipped away.

The much-advertised climax of the show was Henning's attempt to duplicate Houdini's water-torture-cell escape. With his hands shackled and feet locked into wooden stocks, he was lowered head down into a narrow glass-walled tank filled with two hundred gallons of water, where he was securely imprisoned. As a time clock ticked off the seconds, an assistant ran out with an axe, in case it became necessary to break the glass to save Henning from drowning. Henning not only escaped, but vanished from the water tank, and revealed a moment later that he had magically changed places with the stage assistant who had been holding the axe.

The show attracted a large viewing audience, the ratings were high, and it became the first of what were to be a series of Christmas season Henning television specials. Work on the second one, for 1976, began with planning sessions ten months before it took to the air. It featured

the vanish of an elephant at the show's beginning and the magical reproduction of the elephant at the end.

There was also a beautiful and original water fountain illusion that started with a Thurston-like production of a single jet of spraying water, which was transferred from person to person and place to place until Henning had multiplied it into many streams fountaining upward from a platform. A girl appeared in the middle of the fountain and then was floated upon the dancing waters.

It was an illusion Henning had wanted to present since his teenage years in magic, when he and another young magician friend had first dreamed up the basic idea, without any way then to accomplish it. During the planning for the 1976 show, it came to his mind again and inspired the fountain levitation that he and his staff worked for weeks to make practical.

Henning's third "World of Magic" show, televised live over NBC for an estimated 60 million viewers on December 15, 1977, was packed with startling surprises. He roared on stage astride a motorcycle; then he and the cycle visibly vanished from a hanging net, and both quickly reappeared in a box high above the stage.

In a charming children's toyland sketch, a toy deer was changed into a live one and giant-sized toy blocks stacked together produced his co-star, Sandy Duncan. She slid down a slide through a big empty tube and popped out the bottom transformed into a little girl. Henning also was made small, other magical things happened to the little boy and girl, and at the end of the scene they grew back to their full-sized selves. In the show's final illusion, patterned on the Houdini legend but done by an entirely different method, Henning apparently walked through a solid brick wall.

"There is real magic," he told his audience. "It is all around us all the time. Magic is always and everywhere. And all you must do to experience it is to open your mind and your heart. Then you can see the magic that life truly is."

The Henning specials became yearly features of the Christmas television season. He also found time to tour the lecture circuits with an "Illusion and Reality" presentation. In the spring of 1978 he took a condensed forty-minute version of his "World of Magic" to Las Vegas for his first big-time nightclub appearances at the Hilton. Between two appearances there, he took to the road with his full magic show, for a whirlwind tour of theaters and auditoriums, before starting work on the next television special.

"Instead of being merely a demonstrator of tricks," Henning believes, "the magician should be more a giver of wonder." And in summing up his feelings about learning to do magic, he has said, "The difficult must become habit, the habit easy, and then the easy becomes beautiful."

David Copperfield

David Copperfield dreamed as a very young boy of becoming an actor, a dancer, or a magician, and grew up to be all three. He combined his other theatrical talents with magic in a way that won him recognition by the time he was barely out of high school.

He jokingly says that perhaps his parents hoped to pull a rabbit out of a hat and got a magician instead when he was born in Metuchen,

David Copperfield, who borrowed his stage name from a character of novelist Charles Dickens, filled his boyhood with the hobby of magic and with dreams of becoming an actor and dancer. By the time he was hardly out of high school, he had combined his theatrical talents and launched a successful career.

New Jersey, in 1956. They named him David Kotkin, but through his early years in magic he called himself "Davino," until Charles Dickens's novel finally inspired him to adopt the stage name of David Copperfield.

His boyhood was filled not only with the hobby of magic but with a passionate interest in all things theatrical—school plays, mime, and even a brief attempt to become a ventriloquist. From films he saw he tried early imitations of Gene Kelly and Fred Astaire, who became childhood idols, and he hoped to put something of their "polished cool" into his magic. To present magic with that sort of grace and style became a lasting ambition.

When he was twelve he put together an act combining music and acting with magic, using home phonograph records for the music. Living close to New York, he became acquainted with its magic shops, and while visiting one he saw a demonstration of the "dancing cane" trick. It fascinated him, not just as a trick but with the image in mind of what a Fred Astaire might do with it, and he developed a cane routine that became his first big featured effect.

He added to his already acquired knowledge by taking lessons in magic, developed a skill that began to attract the notice of older magicians, and became one of the younger members of the Society of American Magicians.

His first real encounter with professional theater came when he was asked to teach some magic to singer-dancer Ben Vereen, preparing for his role in what was about to become the hit musical *Pippin*. Working with Vereen gave him an inside view of a top Broadway show in the making, under the talented direction of famed choreographer Bob Fosse.

Pippin was an inspiring experience for Copperfield and it turned him to seek more professional training in the theatrical arts. He studied modern dance with dancer-choreographer Peter Gennaro, and also acting and voice. Soon he was doing some teaching himself, giving a course in the art of magic for the drama department of New York University.

His unique style of performing and his theatrical approach to magic interested the producers of the musical *Grease*, Philip M. Getter and Anthony D'Amato, who were collaborating on a new show to be presented in Chicago, *The Magic Man*. They chose Copperfield to create and perform the illusions, and to play the starring role in it, and the show was built around him.

Billed as "a new 1913 magical musical comedy," it began a successful run in 1974 at the First Chicago Center. As "Omar, the Magnificent," eighteen-year-old Copperfield was the tall, dark and handsome young hero, struggling to gain fame as a legitimate magician who exposes a fraudulent mentalist's claims to psychic powers, thwarts a scheme to bilk a wealthy family of its money, and wins the beautiful heroine.

The show had catchy tunes, pleasant singing and dancing, colorful sets and costumes of the period

Copperfield's unique style and theatrical approach to magic started him toward stardom at the age of seventeen when the producers of a new musical comedy that was to be staged in Chicago, The Magic Man, *chose him to create and perform the illusions and to sing, dance, and play the lead role. The show was built around him.*

---

before the First World War. But as far as Chicago's critics were concerned, the rest of the show was a framework for Copperfield's magic, and he drew rave notices.

Pointing out that "the art and science of make-believe have always been at the core of theater," the *Sun-Times* reviewer said that thanks to Copperfield's "uncommon skill" he had created a sense of both theatrical and magical illusion. "A tall, slender, almost shy magician, he does more than just pull bouquets, birds and umbrellas out of

silk handkerchiefs . . . he's just a marvel."

He had not only "unbelievable sleight-of-hand movements," the *Herald* said, "but a remarkable stage presence that mesmerizes as well as awes his audience." In the view of the *Tribune,* he was "a magician of extraordinary skill combined with a rare grace that enhances every illusion he performs."

Copperfield afterwards told interviewers that he had planned the illusions, not as magic acts, but to fit into the show. He had tried to integrate them so completely into the show's story line that even if the magic were removed each scene would still stand on its own as good entertainment. That became the foundation of his own later shows, in which each illusion was part of an acted-out scene, surrounded with music and dance to create a total theatrical effect that did not rest upon the magic alone.

He believes that magic, simply presented as a series of tricks, more often bores than entertains. "Where music pleases the ear and dance the eye, magic pleases the mind. But it's not enough alone," he says. "I don't believe in showing a few effects to pull you through. But if you combine music, dance and magic, then you've elevated the art of illusion to the theatrical level at which it belongs."

The magic must be good and the illusion strong, but beyond that he believes it must have setting, style, the personal charisma of the performer—so that what the audience applauds is not the trick but the magician. "A good magician," he says, "is a performer you are glad to see on stage even when he isn't doing magic."

After his success with *The Magic Man* in Chicago, Copperfield took his magic into nightclubs. During one of his appearances in Hawaii, a critic there summed up his appeal by saying: "He is what all too few magicians are, a theatrical person, with a vital stage presence."

He was just turning twenty in the fall of 1976 when his fellow magicians, as a group, had a chance to see him in a forty-five-minute performance before some twelve hundred of them assembled for a magic convention at Brown's Hotel at Loch Sheldrake, New York. They had spent most of three days and nights watching every kind of magic before he took to the stage and brought them to their feet applauding.

Acting out the illusions with his assistants in comic and dramatic skits with music and dance, he charmed the magicians with his personality, surety, and grace. As one reporter put it, Copperfield made it all seem "like beautiful poetry . . . the ultimate in magical entertainment."

He had been doing promotional magic and starring in industrial shows for such corporations as Bell & Howell, RCA, Bell Telephone, and IBM, and that lucrative branch of magic was to become an even busier part of his career. But meanwhile ABC television executives saw one of his corporate shows and decided that millions of Americans who had never seen his magic should watch it on network television.

Copperfield made his network debut on September 7, 1977, in an hour of magic, music, comedy, and dancing, surrounded by a dozen of ABC's top stars as a special preview of the coming season's programs, "The Magic of ABC Starring David Copperfield." He used his illusions to introduce the various television personalities.

"Laverne and Shirley" stars, Penny Marshall and Cindy Williams, joined him in a magical spoof of the film thriller *Psycho.* In another illusion, his assistants were "Charlie's Angels." Donny and Marie Osmond helped him give a new twist to the classic sawing a lady in half. There was a comedy-magic skit based on *The Maltese Falcon,* and a series of unusual levitations staged in the tradition of early Hollywood musicals.

Aside from planning and rehearsing the magic for the first of his television specials, Copperfield had to put in two solid weeks of six-hour sessions rehearsing the dances, "until I felt like it was my legs that were going to disappear."

The show drew good ratings and praise. But what most impressed the television people who worked with him on it was his creative flexibility in adapting his magic to the musical and comedy sequences. Copperfield thoroughly enjoys that creative side of magic, the search for interesting presentations that will give new dimensions to the old effects.

Basically it is a matter of "taking old principles and making them modern," he said. "For instance, the levitation is not new, but there are things you can do to make it *seem* new. There is nothing new about sawing a lady in half, but again you can devise ways to make it different and original."

During his 1978 Halloween season special for the CBS network, Copperfield, instead of sawing a young woman assistant in half, was himself sawed in half by her. The sawing was done lengthwise rather than in the standard crosscut manner, and at the end his apparently severed body vanished from the box and he magically reappeared elsewhere, wholly himself again.

In that 1978 special he recreated a scene from the films of the 1920s, a sequence in which he escaped from handcuffs while being chased

Copperfield's network television specials, like all his shows, have been based on making the tricks and illusions part of acted-out comic or dramatic scenes, surrounded with music and dance to create a total theatrical effect that does not rest upon the magic alone.

"He is what all too few magicians are," one critic said of Copperfield, *"a theatrical person, with a vital stage presence."*

by dancing girls dressed as Keystone Cops, and then also escaped after being shackled with chains in an upright frame—with the entire action a part of the comic dance routine. In another scene, he turned the old dancing handkerchief trick into a charming ballet in which a pair of handkerchiefs flirted about in midair, the handkerchiefs acting out a romantic story like a pair of human dancers.

Each new show has presented a challenge in the need to create plots, themes, and staging that will theatrically fit the magic into that particular production, and Copperfield wouldn't have it any other way. "If I had to go out and do the same act night after night," he jokes, "I'd rather be a lawyer."

Abb Dickson

The first big magic show Abb Dickson created became one of the biggest touring magic extravaganzas the country had seen in years. Called *Presto*, it was begun as a children's theater production and built into a traveling road show with a cast and crew of thirty people and two hours of acted-out magical scenes that included twenty-nine major illusions.

Presto opened in October, 1975, and toured the United States and Canada for a full year, booked out of New York as a legitimate theater production and playing theaters and auditoriums along the same circuits as touring companies of some top Broadway shows. Moving it around, with its caravan of cars, vans, a thirty-foot semi, and a Greyhound bus, was somewhat like moving a traveling circus.

For Dickson, there was much that he learned from putting together and touring his first big road show that could be applied to any kind of magic, big or small. After its tour, he brought it back to his home in Morrow, Georgia, near Atlanta, for rebuilding into a planned new version.

In Morrow, with two big warehouses filled with magic, illusions, props, and stage equipment, Dickson established an East Coast magic supply and production center for trade, industrial, and television shows, with a permanent staff of five people. Also kept busy with

Abb Dickson, who created one of the biggest touring magic shows the country had seen in years, is shown here doing what audiences expect a magician to do, producing a rabbit from a top hat with a wave of the magic wand. Despite tradition that has made the rabbit and top hat symbolic of magic, the old trick is not often performed by modern magicians, who prefer to use production boxes or other apparatus, or to conjure up doves instead. Dickson decided to do it in the simple traditional way because it was what audiences wanted to see. MARTHA SWOPE other consultant and performing projects that frequently draw him away from Morrow on trips to Hollywood and elsewhere, he insists he is only a man who is following his hobby. "If it ever gets to be work," he jokes, "I'll quit."

Born in Atlanta in 1948, Dickson turned professional magician his senior year in high school, working in an amusement park where he performed ten times a day, six days a week. He moved from that into the large Six Flags theme park organization during his college years, planning and writing productions for them and starring in his own magic show. He staged shopping center shows, became involved with several small road shows, did club date performing, and later ran a magic shop.

He believes his early amusement park shows were about the best experience any young magician could have had. "Amusement parks are among the few places left that are something like the old-time vaudeville theaters in the chance they give a performer to put together an act and then work it for audiences day after day," he says. "School assembly shows are also good for that, and shopping centers where you can do three or four shows a day. I think more magicians should get into something of that kind, where they can really work an act until it's right, and *then* go out and sell it."

Dickson started planning the *Presto* show on paper in the fall of 1973. It was originally designed as a project financed by a federal grant

Poster for Abb Dickson's Presto!, *which opened in October, 1975, and toured the United States and Canada for a year, with a cast and crew of thirty and two hours of magic that included twenty-nine major illusions. It was Dickson's first big traveling show, and moving it around was somewhat like touring a circus. To set it up for a performance required five hours, and to tear it down again required four hours.*

to him and to the Atlanta Children's Theater, one of the largest in the country, to create it and present it to the children of Georgia.

With a somewhat smaller company than it eventually would have, *Presto* played for six months in Atlanta and then traveled for six months more on a tour arranged by the Children's Theater to auditoriums in the state and nearby Florida and Alabama, and was seen by more than 100,000 people. When his association with the the-

38

ater group ended, Dickson took some time out to expand the show and plan his own national tour.

He had spent a year and a half traveling around the country, gathering information from people who operated theatrical road shows, ice shows and other productions, learning what they did and how they did it. He filled notebooks with detailed advice on nuts-and-bolts problems: packing, loading and unloading, assembling a show, taking it apart. He also had the help of magicians with show-business experience, including some who as younger men had been assistants in the traveling big magic shows of the past.

"With any magic show, whatever its size, you've got to put in at least as much time on the preparation of it as on selling it or doing it," he says. "I did a lot of homework, but it was worth it."

One thing he did to help him plan the magic he would include in *Presto* was to make a survey of the tricks the great magicians of the past had most often used. "I didn't want to choose tricks just to please myself, but magic that had real audience appeal."

He went through his magic books and magazines and made out a separate file card for each trick that Thurston, Blackstone, and other successful magicians had in their programs, and from those he made a listing of the all-time most popular tricks. Dickson found that a lot of the tricks the greatest magicians did were the sort every magician does. There were classic card tricks, the "cut and restored rope," such effects as the "sympathetic silks," "twentieth century silks," "vanishing birdcage."

The famous magicians had warehouses filled with magic of every kind, and had men working for them who could provide almost any trick they wanted to do. Why then did they keep such old tricks in their shows? "They chose those tricks because they were entertaining and audiences enjoyed seeing them," Dickson says. "You don't do tricks for magicians. That's important for any performer to learn. You have to go through all the tricks you do and carefully pick out the things audiences like best."

When he began organizing *Presto*'s national road tour, Dickson first chose the staff. The show carried its own spotlight men, former ice show people experienced in spotlighting swift motion. The truck drivers were professionals who knew the roads, and the crew were all regular theater men. There was a company manager, a production stage manager and his assistant, an electrician and assistant, a costumer, and also a dresser to handle quick offstage costume changes.

Aside from Dickson himself, probably the most important of the thirty people on the show was Bill Smith, brought in from California as the illusion mechanic; his constant labor and repairs kept all the magic in working condition.

"Most people don't realize the tremendous wear and tear magic props take on the road," Dickson points out. "The average magician may touch up his props once in six months or so, give something a needed coat of paint or tighten a screw here or there. But when you have a traveling illusion show, everything has to work right all the time and has to be taken care of completely."

Presto had a story line that provided a framework for a brief history of magic, portraying the ways magic had been used in different times and places through the ages. Unusual ways of presenting and performing the magic had to be worked out to fit each trick and illusion into the story. Dickson played the part of a magician in Egypt, in China, a performer in the circus, and other roles.

It was cast as a theatrical production, not as a straight magic show, since the need was not only for illusion assistants but for actors and actresses to play a leading lady, a handsome young man, a character man, a "funny girl" type, and other parts. Auditions were held and eighty-five people tried out for the eight main parts before the casting was completed.

They rehearsed eight hours a day for three weeks before the initial opening in Atlanta, and held additional rehearsals while it was being shaped for its road tour. There was also a full-cast rehearsal at least once a week after it took to the road.

"We also rehearsed our mistakes," Dickson says. "We rehearsed ways to cover every problem we *thought* might come up, tried to figure out everything that possibly could go wrong and to find a solution for it.

During performances things occasionally happened that we weren't prepared for, but many times we were. Thanks to rehearsing what might go wrong, we could catch something before it became a problem and set it right."

One night during the levitation illusion, part of the cloth covering the floating lady became caught in the apparatus so that she couldn't soar into the air and disappear. A well-rehearsed assistant saw the trouble, stepped off into the wings, got a mat knife, and cut free the bit of trapped cloth so the lady could properly float and vanish, and the audience never knew anything had gone wrong.

Another time, a rough stage floor broke one of the casters off the bottom of an illusion cabinet as it was being wheeled out in front of the audience, leaving it tottering on three wheels so the scene couldn't be performed in the usual way. The assistants caught it, signaled Dickson, and changed their stage positions. He didn't know exactly what had happened, but he went ahead and finished the illusion without a hitch, and they got the crippled cabinet off the stage so the show could continue.

"Thank goodness, we were ready for that," Dickson recalls. They hadn't expected a wheel to break, but they had rehearsed shifting their patterns of stage movement to cover various emergencies. "Very often, the audience doesn't even notice such mistakes. The magician is more aware of them than the people out front. If he just goes ahead and makes the best of it, carries on with the trick as though he knows what he is doing and doesn't let the audience guess from his manner that there's anything wrong, they may never know the difference. I guess that's part of what Robert-Houdin meant when he said a magician should be a good actor."

All the problems of a small show were multiplied many times by a big road show like *Presto*. While the average club-date performer might carry his props in a station wagon on a short drive from home and spend half an hour setting up for a performance, there were miles of travel for *Presto* and hours spent just putting together its tricks and twenty-nine illusions, hanging scenery, setting up lighting and sound equipment, sorting out costumes, shoes, and a thousand other things. Even with its traveling company of thirty and ten local workers, it took five hours to set it up, and four hours to tear it down again.

For Dickson, in addition to the full stage performances, each city meant personal appearances to promote the show, doing magic at luncheon clubs, on television programs, showing close-up tricks to interviewing reporters, entertaining children in hospital wards. He also met local magicians everywhere, attending their club meetings when he could.

The show played in theaters of every size, from the smallest with only eight hundred seats to a twenty-six-hundred-seat auditorium. It toured up the East Coast, across Canada, back down to the Midwest, and played its closing date in Omaha, Nebraska.

"It was quite a learning experience for me," Dickson says. "Putting it all together, organizing it, moving it around for weeks on the road. I learned a lot about doing magic for all kinds of people. I enjoyed it, had a lot of fun, and people had fun watching it."

He has long made it a habit to put in an hour and a half each day practicing magic—not just moves and manipulations, but taking some specific trick he wants to develop and working on that.

"A famed pianist once said that if he doesn't practice for one day, he knows it; if he doesn't practice for two days, his audience knows it," Dickson says. "But *what* you practice is important. You have to take each trick and work on it until you make it really your own. Work out a way of presenting it and a line of patter that goes with your personality and style of performing."

Dickson feels that beginning magicians too often try to copy other performers instead of taking a few good tricks and working to make them theirs. "You may be able to copy somebody else's trick, his routine, his patter. But you'll never get away with doing what he does the way that he does it, his misdirection, his actions, his manner of speaking, smiling, making contact with the audience with his eyes, his gestures. That's him and it's not you, and it's impossible to copy his style and personality."

As Dickson discovered again

while on the road with *Presto,* a simple and inexpensive trick may entertain an audience as much as a costly and elaborate illusion. "We had one illusion in the show that cost ten thousand dollars to build and took a minute and a half to perform," he explains. "Just to fill in while they were setting it up backstage, I was doing a comedy card trick that is familiar to most magicians, one that involves some fun with a big card and a kitchen eggbeater. I found I got more audience reaction from that than I did from the ten-thousand-dollar illusion. It taught me again to go back and dig out the things people like and to do those."

Rehearsals, he believes, are important for any kind of a magic show, whether it is to be performed close-up, in a club hall, or on a stage. "You can set things up in your home basement, your room, anywhere you have some privacy," he says. "Run through the whole show, word for word, trick for trick, the way you are going to perform it, from beginning to end. Work on the staging of it, the arrangement and handling of things. Unless you plan the setup carefully and rehearse the whole show as a unit, you'll look fumbling and amateurish no matter how good each individual trick may be."

Dickson suggests not only acting out the entire show just as though an imaginary audience were watching, but also running through the unpacking, the setting up, the repacking afterwards. "Plan your packing so everything in your carrying case has its place. You may want to use cardboard partitions, or capped containers for certain things, boxes or cloth bags to protect them. Figure out how you are going to repack things after they have been used in the show—a pile of silks, a scatter of cards and coins, an expanded bunch of flowers, rice or confetti, or a newspaper into which you have poured a broken egg."

He has found that a simple portable background screen, a folding metal stand-up frame with a curtain that hangs on it, is very useful for club-date performers. "You can use it to curtain off an area of a club hall or dining room and set up your things behind the curtain, out of sight of the audience," he says. "When you are ready to give the show, just move it around behind your things so it serves as a backdrop. After the show, stand the screen in front again to give you some privacy while packing up."

His answer to magicians who say they never know ahead of time what kind of a performing situation they may run into is that "they just haven't done enough advance preparation." He feels they should make it their business to find out whether the place where they are going to perform has an adequate stage, curtains, lighting, a sound system— exactly what the conditions are, by looking it over in person or at least asking enough specific questions.

"You should choose from among your tricks and plan your show for that particular place and that audience," he says. "Obviously you wouldn't want to present a big illusion in a little hall where there are only fifty people, or do a close-up trick like changing a copper coin into a silver one for an auditorium audience. But there's more than that to consider. What the committee has called a 'stage' may turn out to be a platform only six inches high, or if you plan to do a dancing cane and wait until you get there to discover there's not proper lighting for it, you're in trouble. You have to know those things in advance."

Much of Dickson's work, aside from his future road show and his television scripting and performing, has been in supplying illusions for industrial shows and in creating trade-show display booths in which some magical effect is used to promote the company's product. He applies various principles of magic to visual displays, such as using a mirror device so that whatever is being advertised suddenly seems to appear from nowhere and then vanish again. It is not a direct presentation of magic as such, but the use of visual illusion to capture attention.

More directly, he performs at sales meetings of various companies, doing magic to introduce a new product line or to inspire the gathered salesmen with some promotional message the magic gets across to them. "What I enjoy about doing those is the magical problem solving," he says. "For instance, a company may have a product that removes rust from the bottom of a ship without having to put the ship into drydock. I try to figure out how to show that with magic, to put it together for them so it will be interesting and entertaining. I have a lot of fun doing that."

MARTHA SWOPE

43

Bev Bergeron

"I am more a magician than I am a comedian," Bev Bergeron says. But audiences start laughing, at him and with him, from the moment he appears.

With his pixie-like grin, a toss of his head, the lines that he speaks, his stand-up comedy, and slapstick clowning, he is an actor-magician who plays many different characters to keep people laughing while the magic that goes off in his hands

Bev Bergeron and some of his many comedy magic props. As the busy man-of-all-magic at Disney World in Florida, Bergeron stars five times a day in a long-running comedy revue and stages all sorts of other magic shows, which involve everything from table-top close-up to spectacular illusions.

amazes them. He has successfully combined all forms of comedy with all kinds of magic, from close-up to stage illusions.

On the stage of the Diamond Horseshoe at Disney World in Florida, he began his eighth straight year in 1978 as the star of a show that has drawn capacity audiences five times a day since the resort opened. "I never get bored with the show," he says, "because what I like best is working with a live audience. Basically it's the same show every day, but it's a whole new show to each audience and I do it a little differently each time. It's the audience that counts."

Bergeron first became known to millions of television viewers who saw him every week for five years as Rebo the Magic Clown, the comic star of Mark Wilson's network television series, "The Magic Land of Allakazam." But by then he had already performed some four thousand magic shows, and had given up trying to count the number of different theatrical productions in which he had been involved.

His father was a former vaudeville entertainer, who when vaudeville all but died settled down to steadier employment in Baytown, Texas, where Bevely J. Bergeron was born in 1930. In those depression years, factory jobs drew several other ex-vaudevillians to the same area. "Two or three times a year they would get together and put on a show," Bergeron remembers. "It was exciting for a boy to watch and the shows were always funny. When I got interested in magic I began to see the way to go was to be a comic magician."

The first trick he learned was a card trick his grandfather taught him. When he was about ten he was inspired to take up magic as a more active hobby after he saw a performance by Willard the Wizard, a master magician who toured the Southwest for years with a big tent show of magic and illusions. Bergeron was fourteen, still in junior high school, when he began performing semiprofessionally, having already learned that paying audiences enjoy laughing while they are being mystified.

"Most of the young magicians I knew wanted to be mysterious, occultish or sophisticated, but they didn't want to be funny," he recalls. "I could see that they were missing a good thing. There was really room for a funny magician."

Willard the Wizard hired him as an assistant, at the age of sixteen, and Bergeron also became an advance man for Willard's big tent show. "He was a most amazing magician, one of the best," he says, "and he taught me a lot."

Bergeron spent four years in the Air Force as an entertainer and noncommissioned officer in charge of special services for his base, directing two service clubs, choosing and booking the talent for shows and special events, and staging them. During those years, he also produced versions of two big musicals, *Good News* and *Brigadoon*, in Wichita Falls, Texas, and staged an opera with the Wichita Falls Symphony.

He decided to get a solid business education at the University of Texas, which later helped him use his magic in hundreds of trade and industrial shows, promotional and advertising campaigns. While at the university, he also learned some of the basics of television as a student cameraman, floor manager, and then a director for the university's educational television station. He graduated in 1957 with a business administration degree in advertising and marketing.

Bergeron joined Mark Wilson and for the next thirteen years, with Wilson and on his own, created magic, performed in, and helped to write, direct, and produce television shows, commercials, films, stage shows, fairgrounds presentations. He put his magical skills to work on all sorts of advertising, sales meetings, conventions, displays, new products, grand openings, and special events.

From 1960 to 1965—during his five starring years of weekly network clowning as Rebo on "The Magic Land of Allakazam"— Bergeron also was production coordinator and major writer for the show. He devised many of its magic props and featured illusions, including the now widely performed "mismade girl." At the same time he was in "Allakazam," he was serving as a technical advisor, script writer, and assistant director on various other television shows.

He later appeared on television specials and on a syndicated show of his own, performed at state fairs, wrote comic skits for top television performers and material for night-club acts, was a co-author of plays and revues, and a comic actor in Los Angeles theaters. He made two tours of the Far East for the USO, twice toured Mexico, and appeared on Mexican network television. The U.S. Department of Labor sent him out in 1970 to tour its Job Corps centers.

In the many roles Bergeron has created for himself as an actor-magician, he has appeared as a tipsy drunk, a juggler, a fire eater, cowboy, quick-on-the-draw sharpshooter, stunt man, card shark, fast-talking confidence man, fencer, boxer, acrobat, mentalist, and escape artist, all mostly for laughs and with magic.

The Diamond Horseshoe show in which he stars in Florida was originally put together at Disneyland in California. Bergeron joined the show there, adapting his magic and his character part to fit into it, and moved with it to Florida for the opening of the new Disney World resort near Orlando in October, 1971. Every show, throughout its years of five performances a day, has played to standing room only.

With a cast that includes singers and a line of can-can dancers, Bergeron plays a traveling salesman who hilariously disrupts the show by firing a blank gun into the audience to get attention, and then presents his comedy magic as a spieling pitchman selling his wares. At the end of the magic pitchman act, he steps off into the wings for a ten-second quick change, and almost immediately reappears transformed

Every time Bergeron gives this boy his wand to hold, another wand magically appears, until the boy's hands are full of wands. The hilarious kid-show routine with the multiplying wands is among many tricks and illusions Bergeron has invented.

into a cowboy character, wearing an exaggerated Wild West costume, and does a "Pecos Bill" number with the singers.

That turns into a slapstick knock-about scene in which his "teeth" are knocked loose. He starts spitting out "teeth," really dried beans, and for a full two minutes they never cease to come flying out of his mouth, along with a few ping-pong balls that surprisingly pop from his lips as "giant teeth." He does some gun flinging, juggling, more funny magic, and his hairpiece gets dislocated as the show builds toward a climax of roaring laughter.

But his five-a-day performances at the Diamond Horseshoe are only part of his magical activities at Disney World. During one recent month he staged two performances a night of an "Evening of Magic" illusion show, presented a nightclub magic act for two weeks at a resort hotel, did three days of tabletop magic in a booth for a convention group, performed for half a dozen other groups, and on one particularly busy Saturday found himself booked to give ten half-hour shows in a single day.

When Disney World opened what was to become its swank dinner club show room, the Top of the World Dinner Club, a Bergeron magic show was the first entertainment staged for the new room's prestigious guests. With illusions, a pretty girl assistant, and several brought-to-life Disney characters, he also provided a lot of funny-gag magic that went all "wrong" when Goofy tried to do it.

He has produced three different Camp Grounds shows over the years at Disney World, using a western band, his magic act, and much audience participation. Each Halloween week there is an outdoor magic spectacle involving all the "big bad" Disney characters in the spooky fun. Witches float, monsters appear, and the shows end with the characters getting Bergeron to do a romping dance with them, the "Monster-Bash." During the annual Easter week events he plays the part of the bumbling Mayor of Main Street.

"I'm working on something all the time," he says, and usually he is working on half a dozen things at the same time. There are shows to be produced for trade and industrial clients, for all sorts of special events, and many shows for the conventions held at Disney World by business and professional groups.

He appears in a Bourbon Street production staged for convention groups, first performing close-up magic from table to table and then becoming magical master of ceremonies for a Dixieland show. For other conventions, he may perform a skilled sleight-of-hand routine with lighted cigarettes, or play the part of a comic magical golfer, or appear as a drunk who hilariously conjures with bottles and erupting fountains of liquid. Special kid shows, for the children of convention-goers, are also a frequent part of his daily magical work.

Bergeron probably performs as many magic shows in any given month as the average magician does in a year. He performs indoors, outdoors, on stage, close-up or surrounded, with or without music, with assistants or solo, spoken or silent, and with the comedy slant either broad or sophisticated as required by each particular show.

With his wife, two teenage daughters and a son, who is an eager magic hobbyist, Bergeron lives near Disney World in a home overlooking Lake Cane. Despite his heavy schedule and out-of-town perfor-

47

mances, he has organized his work so he is able to spend much time at home with his family, enjoying the sunny life in Florida that magic has given him.

His desk, surrounded by a library of magic books, is covered with sketches and plans for tricks and illusions, notes for new routines, scripts for shows in the making. "Magic is like mathematics," he says. "Once you have the basic principles, you can devise endless new equations." Generous about sharing his ideas with other magicians, he has often lectured at magic conventions, in the United States, England, France, and other countries.

"Simplicity is the highest form of magical knowledge," he says. "Keep the trick, the routine, the act simple." He also advises, "If you want to win an audience you must be an entertainer first. Magic is only a vehicle used to reach people, the same as singing, dancing and acting."

Bergeron thinks that what often makes the difference between the amateur and professional is timing, pointing up effects to lead to a clear climax, knowing when to pause. But beginners also frequently ignore simpler things, such as making sure the audience can see what the magician is trying to show them and can understand what he is doing with it. "Keep the props and magic up high," he urges. "People can't see tabletops."

Bergeron's advice for would-be comic magicians is to put some good magic into the act so it will amount

That's a "chicken sandwich" Bergeron has just produced. Stretched between the two slices of bread held apart in his hands is a scrawny rubber chicken.

to more than just a succession of funny gags. "If you do comedy magic," he says, "remember that you must still have some real foolers to gain the respect of the audience."

Walter Blaney

Walter Blaney's home state has officially commissioned him "Ambassador of Texas," and as a top entertainer on the convention and banquet circuit he has extended that fun-making ambassadorship from coast to coast.

48

Blaney presents his Texas style of magic and comedy to entertain convention-goers at national and regional gatherings of all sorts of clubs and organizations, wherever they may be held. As one of the busiest of professional magicians, he flies out from his home city of Houston to hopscotch the nation's convention centers in one-night appearances. He has logged more than three thousand such performances.

In his act, "Zaney Blaney" portrays the character of a genial, fun-loving Texan, which he is. Six and one-half feet tall, a dynamic personality with smooth Texas charm and polished talent, he gives the impression of a vacationing cattleman or oil millionaire, inviting his audience to join him in having a good time.

He comes on strong, with fast action all the way, telling his stories and jokes about Texas, combining the comedy with visually surprising and mystifying magic presented in a style entirely his own. With more than a quarter of a century of professional performing experience behind him, his showmanship turns every minute of the act into something for the audience to watch, and he draws the audience directly into what happens.

Everything is pointed toward that sharing of fun, with the aim of making the spectators feel "they haven't laughed so hard in years." During his "instant Texas" routine, small things instantly and magically grow "Texas big"; a small bunny becomes a monster twenty-pound

Six and a half feet tall, Walter "Zaney" Blaney humorously calls himself the "BIG one-man show." And big he is as a popular entertainer at banquets and conventions all over the country when he performs his unique style of audience-participation magic and tells magically illustrated jokes about his home state of Texas.

49

Everything grows big in Texas, as Blaney magically demonstrates by putting a little two-pound bunny into an empty paper shopping bag and instantly changing it into this giant live rabbit that weighs twenty pounds.

has invented for doing it, completely different from methods usually used, has fooled magicians for whom he has presented it at many magic conventions. (He also baffled space scientists and astronauts with it at a special showing at NASA headquarters in Houston.)

As he presents it, a five-foot board is laid across two small stepladders and a padded cloth is unrolled along the top of the board. A spectator is then invited to lie on the board, the stepladders are removed, and the person floats suspended in midair. Blaney walks completely around the floating spectator, and passes a steel ring over her in every direction to show there is nothing holding the board.

Born in Dallas, Blaney learned some of his first tricks from books in the public library after becoming intrigued at the age of nine when he saw the great magic showman Blackstone at a local theater. He wasn't long in discovering a magic shop, and soon afterwards joined a magic club. By the time he was in high school he was giving paid performances.

Club dates and birthday party shows helped Blaney earn his way through the University of Texas as a drama school major. When he graduated in 1950 with a dramatic arts degree, magic became his full-time profession.

During his early professional years he toured over half the country on the school-assembly circuits. He has also performed at times at fairs, in nightclubs and theaters. His network television appearances

live rabbit, "the biggest rabbit you ever saw."

Blaney relies heavily on audience participation, bringing up spectators to make them the center of nearly all the on-stage action. In a pickpocket routine, he makes their watches, wallets, and belts disappear while the crowd laughs, but he also carefully handles the audience volunteers "so they feel they are having more fun than anybody."

He sometimes even "borrows" a lady from the audience to float in midair for his original version of that classic illusion. The method he

Blaney about to perform his original version of the classic floating-lady illusion at a trade-show exhibit, with the spectators as close as in a home living room. When he removes the two little stepladders from under her, she will remain suspended in air while he walks completely around her floating body and passes a steel hoop over it. He has fooled other magicians with it and also NASA space scientists.

have included, among others, the Johnny Carson, Merv Griffin, Mike Douglas and Dinah Shore shows. But most of his performing has been primarily in the banquet and convention field, in which he is among the most popular entertainers of any kind.

The oldest of his three daughters, Becky, who sometimes acted as his assistant, has grown up to become a magician herself. Active in magic societies, Blaney frequently performs at major U.S. and European magic conventions. The Texas Association of Magicians dedicated its

1973 convention to him and the state's governor and senators joined in honoring him for his "outstanding contribution . . . to the conjuring art and for the national and international recognition he has brought to the state of Texas."

Blaney earns about half his annual income from banquet and convention shows. The other half comes from creatively putting magic to work for business, at which he has been equally successful. He has worked at creating trade show exhibits and magic-themed sales meetings for many of the same big corporations year after year, since the founding in 1965 of his Show Stoppers Company for "Magic in Sales Promotion."

"There are many ways to use magic in business and industry and there are many top-notch magicians doing a great job at it," he says. "Each has his own way of working and I have my way that has worked for me, but I am still learning. It's a lot harder to book such a show, a lot more work than a usual magic show, and it takes a lot of effort and thinking. But it keeps me from going stale, constantly provides a fresh approach to the presentation of magic, and keeps me on my toes as an entertainer."

At a big trade show where several hundred companies in that particular industry are competing to draw potential customers to their exhibit booths, the magic itself must be interesting enough to attract, hold, and entertain a crowd so they will actually enjoy watching the "commercial." But the magic and the product also must be tied together with a carefully tailored presentation to put across each specific appeal the company hopes to make with its sales message.

"I learn all I can about the company, the services and products, who the show is to be aimed at, and then I think up the best tricks to illustrate each of the sales points to be made," Blaney says. "Sometimes the various tie-ins seem a bit far-fetched, but even those get a laugh, make the point, and do the job."

Most magicians are familiar with the lota bowl, for instance; in its standard version it is a metal vase that repeatedly refills itself with water each time after it is shown empty. For a company that manufactures an additive for concrete, Blaney made a lota bowl out of the drum of a toy concrete truck. He used it as a running gag during the exhibit show, going back to it between his other tricks and each time pouring more from the concrete drum, to make the point that the company "always gives more value and better service than expected."

Blaney may magically link together the separate links of a steel chain to show how another product increases tensile strength and helps bond all ingredients together. To show contracting-company executives how a product can relieve them of the feeling that they have been *caged in* with all their problems, he may present a humorous sales message as he performs the vanishing birdcage trick. He may demonstrate for some other client how profits can be made to grow magically by doing his trick of changing a tiny bunny into a giant rabbit.

While he was doing the rabbit trick at one big Chicago trade show, Blaney was using a new giant rabbit that the breeder had sold him because the animal supposedly was past her breeding years. In the midst of the show's five-day run, the rabbit had six babies. Blaney alertly notified the newspapers, with the result that pictures and stories appeared in all the Chicago papers, under headlines such as "Rabbit Fools Magician." The company was pleased with the unexpected added promotion and the publicity more than doubled the crowds that came to the exhibit booth to see "the big mother."

For sales meetings and company conferences, Blaney often has to deal magically with concepts that challenge his creative ability, such as showing how a utility company's employees can make customers better aware of the service behind the invisible product of electricity, or how a chemical company's safety directors can reduce what may become disabling injuries by reducing the percentage of minor injuries.

He has had to demonstrate how a motor oil detergent suspends corrosive particles of sludge so that when the oil is drained out car engines are left clean, how a soft drink packaging company uses a special paper in its cartons to keep them dry and durable, and how the newly designed shelving of a display case for frozen foods keeps customers from mixing up products displayed in supermarkets. His magic presents such ideas clearly, directly and amusingly, and gives people visual images to remember.

Blaney sometimes livens up a sales meeting by making performers of the company's executives. To avoid the usually dull business of speech-making introductions, he may produce a company's president from an empty cabinet, and then also produce the president's wife and float her in air.

For one big oil company's sales meetings, he made magicians of the company's marketing executives and had them perform the tricks.

Walter Blaney, magical "Ambassador of Texas."

He devised a lot of easily performed tricks, bought all the props, wrote simplified instructions, wrote the scripts and sales tie-ins, and personally coached each of the executives of seven sales districts. They wore tophats and capes and their secretaries joined in the fun by acting as their pretty on-stage assistants. It was one of the most successful sales presentations the company ever had.

"I wouldn't want to do trade shows and sales meetings exclusively," Blaney says. "It's just one form of show business, and while it is satisfying and the pay is good if one works at it, I also need to work as a professional show performer and be a real entertainer without the commercialism. I think the fact that I am constantly in front of real show audiences keeps me alive and more exciting at my trade shows and sales meetings."

53

Karrell Fox

Karrell Fox, if you count him one at a time, is at least five or six of the world's best magical entertainers. He has created many different roles for himself, each for a specific type of audience, and has successfully performed as almost every kind of magician.

As the King of Korn he is a witty comedian who blends sly humor with nonsensical but mystifying magic. He is a brilliant master of ceremonies, a stage, television, and nightclub performer, and an expert close-up entertainer. Children love him in his costumed characterization of a storybook conjurer, Wow the Wizard, and in his guise as Milky the Clown. Other audiences laugh at him as the academically garbed and comically confused Professor Mix-Up. He is one of the best impersonators of the film comedian W. C. Fields, whom he somewhat resembles physically.

But he is also a serious mentalist, a hypnotist, a lecturer to college audiences, an inspirational speaker, a creator of top trade and industrial shows, a promotional consultant for major corporations. He is a show businessman who combines his creative talents, versatile skills, and personality with an ability to make whatever he does practical and commercial as well as entertaining.

"Performing is my love, getting out and doing shows, but I also like to do what I haven't done before," he says. "I guess that's why I've tried my hand at so many different kinds of performing."

Fox gave his first public performance at the age of eleven, on the stage of the Masonic Hall in his native city of Charlestown, West Virginia. His father had started him on the hobby a few years before that by giving him some magic tricks. By

Reflected in Karrell Fox's makeup mirror are faces of some of the characters he portrays in his many different roles as a magical entertainer. Clockwise are Milky the Clown, Professor Mix-Up, Wow the Wizard, Karrell himself in a comedy presentation, and Karrell's version of W.C. Fields.

Even when he plays "himself," Karrell Fox changes his performing personality for various audiences and according to the type of magic he is presenting.

In the shops he learned not only every possible way to do every sort of magic, but a lot about the business side of the profession and about combining magic with salesmanship. He met and exchanged ideas with dozens of famous and talented magicians. The shops became the first proving grounds of his creative originality, which was to lead to his invention of hundreds of tricks and routines over the years.

Meanwhile he had begun to develop his concepts of magical comedy, to polish his performing skills, had become a busy club-date magician, and was already winning national recognition among his fellow magicians. At the age of seventeen his picture had been on the covers of two leading magic magazines and he had written the first of his books of magic for magicians. He had been acclaimed with rave reviews for his performances at magic conventions, starting a tradition that was to make him a perennial favorite at magic conventions everywhere, as master of ceremonies, lecturer, chief fun-maker.

Fox was of military age when the Korean War came in 1950 and that put him into the army for a while, but even the war didn't remove him far from show business. He booked all the shows for his outfit, handled arrangements with top acts and name bands, and also wrote, staged, and performed in eight army musicals.

He had been among the first magicians to bring magic into trade shows back in the early 1940s, and after the war he became the first to

the time he was in his early teens, magic had become his profession and he got a thorough schooling in it by working for eight years in various magic shops, first in Toledo and then in Detroit, which became his permanent home.

He started work as a behind-the-counter demonstrator at Carlo's Magic Shop in Toledo, living magic day after day and constantly performing whatever tricks the magicians who were the shop's customers wanted to see. He then became chief demonstrator at Harold Sterling's shop in Detroit, and while still in his teens became manager of Abbott's shop there. Later on, for a time, Fox owned and operated his own Detroit magic shop.

Karrell Fox was among the first to bring magic into trade and industrial shows in a big way, and they are an important part of his creative and performing activities. He may appear at a trade show as a comedy magician, illusionist, close-up performer, or hypnotist, or in one of his character roles. But whatever magic he uses, the important trick, he says, is not only to get the attention of the moving crowd, "but to stop them and to hold them." As shown here, Fox tailors his magic to fit each type of audience and trade-show situation.

create really large-scale magical industrial shows. Being in Detroit, the center of the auto industry, Fox worked out a presentation for the Ford Motor Company, and he also managed to gain an appointment to discuss it with the son of Henry Ford. His showmanship during that interview was something the motor magnate never forgot, and was the start of a long and close relationship with the company.

Fox found an opportunity to show Ford a trick. He had Ford choose a card and return it to the pack; but then the trick apparently went wrong and he failed to find the card Ford had chosen. Pretending to be embarrassed by the "mistake," Fox asked Ford if he could at least see the famous garden on the balcony behind the desk. Ford drew aside the curtains and stared in amazement at what he saw outside his window. There, spelled out across the sky by a skywriting plane, was the name of Ford's chosen card.

More than three million dollars went into "The Magic World of Ford" shows that Fox created, produced and supervised—big traveling shows that toured the country for four years, with four separate units out on the road at the same time. Fox went on to produce shows for other auto manufacturers, and to perform for them himself at auto shows and dealer meetings. He has since been doing magic for some of the same companies for more than twenty years.

Fox tailors his trade-show appearances to each situation. He may perform a commercial version of his own style of comedy magic, may present an illusion, close-up magic, appear as a hypnotist or in one of his character roles. "You've got to have an outstanding 'something' to get the attention of a rapidly moving trade show crowd," he says. "It takes a certain kind of magic, not only to stop them, but more important, to hold them."

Another side of his business with auto makers and other companies is creating and supplying tricks, games, and novelties as advertising giveaways and premiums. He has supplied such things as a million trick pencils for one promotion, hundreds of thousands of sets of a three-card trick for another. He is constantly developing fresh ideas that can be put to promotional uses.

As an entertainer, he is a favorite at private parties of automobile executives. Recently while performing in another show in the Bahamas, he was asked by the president of an auto company to entertain at a party in Florida. When Fox explained his tight schedule, a helicopter was sent to pick him up in the Bahamas and lift him to the door of the Florida hotel where the company president's party was being held. He entertained at the party and was helicoptered back to the Bahamas in time to do his regular show.

Fox gives a lot of inspirational pep talks, filled with comedy and magic, at gatherings of salesmen. That activity grew out of his younger years of listening to many other speakers at sales meetings while he was waiting backstage to present his magic. Some of the speakers were

As a "foxy-grandpa" type of wizard, Karrell Fox gently leads children's audiences into a fantasy of magical make-believe in his story-book characterization of Wow the Wizard.

excellent educational lecturers, but they were seldom entertaining. Fox took the concept of sales motivation and added entertainment to it.

In another direction he has turned his knowledge of hypnotism to educational use, in the training of professionals in hypnosis for medical and dental purposes. He also lectures on hypnotism to college groups and presents a college concert program called "A Hypnotic Happening."

As a children's entertainer, Fox first established his role as Milky the Clown on Detroit television by taking over an already long-running TV kid show for a sponsoring milk company and building the character into a clown familiar to thousands of youngsters. For five years he

presented a regular weekly one-hour television show as Milky, creating a dozen or so new tricks for each program, and making hundreds of personal appearances.

When he appears as Wow the Wizard in other children's shows, he is transformed into an entirely different character, wearing a silvery white wig and costumed in a tall and pointed medieval wizard's hat and long-flowing purple robe patterned with half-moons and stars. With his eyes twinkling behind grandfatherly half-glasses, he is a quiet-spoken, warmly friendly old wizard, who gently leads the children through magical adventures in which they take part.

Some years ago a writer for a magic magazine suggested that Fox looked and sounded a little like W. C. Fields, which gave him the idea for creating his impersonation of Fields. He owns one of the largest private collections of Fields memorabilia and has impersonated him in television and radio commercials, films, and stage productions. He has also built his characterization into a popular college lecture-circuit program, "An Evening With W. C."

For his full-evening programs of mentalism for college audiences and other groups, Fox again changes his performing style. He invites them to join him on an imaginary "Journey to the Center of the Mind," and his approach is that of the lecturer, not the magician doing tricks. For his mental routines, he uses only ordinary-looking props, and avoids even the slightest suggestion of anything "tricky" or "magicky" in his entertainingly straightforward presentation.

In all his roles, his magic is novel and visual and his methods are ingenious and freshly original, but his personality transcends the tricks. Genuinely witty, he is never brash and smart-alecky. He comes across as a pleasantly good-humored, easygoing, and warmly friendly individual whose aim is not only to make people laugh but to make them happy. Reviewers have said that Fox could appear on a stage and do nothing at all and the audience still would like him.

"You have to really reach the audience and that goes beyond the tricks themselves," he says. "When I finish an act, I don't care if people forget what tricks I did as long as they remember me as an entertainer."

He has planned some of his acts so all the magical props for each of them fit into a single attaché case, and he can switch roles almost as easily as he can switch carrying cases. But he has never ceased adding new faces and facets to his talents. He has a thirst for new experiences, for exploring everything he gets into, a creative enthusiasm for working on his ideas until he extracts whatever is practical.

Fox has appeared on top U.S. and British television variety shows, has worked with television and film stars, has been a stage and nightclub show producer and a director of magical effects for movies. But he has no real desire to become a permanent part of the glittering show business worlds of Hollywood or Las Vegas. He has done too well right at home, with his activities centered in the Detroit area, to be tempted away for very long from the good life his magic has made there for him.

He thoroughly enjoys his family life with his wife, former professional dancer Lynn Voss, and their two sons, at home on a two-acre wooded estate in Farmington, Michigan, in the thirteen-room house they call "The Fox's Den."

Fox has redesigned the interior himself so the walls and floors of the rooms reflect the mood colorings of a hidden lighting system. A basement room converts into an impromptu magic theater for entertaining guests, who often include visiting magicians. In the basement there is the lair that is Fox's office, where he puts in a lot of hard work at home on the projects he also considers fun, since magic is still his favorite hobby and one in which all the Foxes share.

He is a member of fourteen national and international magic societies, a winner of seventeen trophies and many other awards and honors, counts hundreds of magicians among his friends. He has helped many of them in their careers, and loves to do magic for other magicians and to talk magic with them, whether they be professionals or beginning amateurs. "There's nothing wrong with being an amateur or a hobbyist in any profession. That's how we all started out," he says. "The more amateur magicians there are, the more magic shops and books on magic, the better it is for all of us. The fact that the public is becoming more magic-conscious all the time is a healthy situation."

He believes that one of the benefits of the growth of magic as a hobby will be in forcing "those who call themselves professionals" to be far more professional about it. "They will have to spend more time developing new tricks and routines, and much more time with the 'three P's'—practicing, perfecting, and polishing."

But he also feels that the person who buys a few magic props and gives a few shows shouldn't suddenly start calling himself a professional, that he shouldn't be reluctant to admit he *is* a hobbyist. "The person who likes to paint pictures and does it as a hobby doesn't claim to be a professional artist, and the one who sings at parties or in church doesn't call himself a professional singer. So why should the kid or adult who does a few tricks consider himself a professional magician?"

Among the most inventive of magicians, Fox generously shares his secrets, and the tricks he explains in his convention lectures, books, and writings for magic magazines are right out of his own shows. "I have always believed in sharing ideas that have worked out for me with my fellow magicians, just as so many of them have shared their good ideas with me," he says. "That's what makes this magic business of ours progress, and the sharing that we all do is also one of the reasons you will find more real friendship among

As a close-up magician, Karrell Fox is a favorite entertainer of auto magnates and other V.I.P.'s at private parties and in the "hospitality suites" provided by big corporations for their top customers.

magicians than those in most other professions."

He finds creative inspiration for new tricks almost everywhere. An idea that can be developed into a trick may be suggested by some comic bit of business in a movie he sees, by a story he hears, the tagline of a joke, by some experience or incident in his daily life. He keeps a "things to think about" notebook of ways to change or simplify effects. Browsing through a gift shop or variety store sets his mind turning with ideas for making magical use of new products or gadgets that are on display.

"First I come up with the effect that I want to achieve, the climax that the trick will have," he says. "Then I figure out the simplest and most direct way of getting that effect."

Simplicity of method is the keynote of all his magical thinking. He eliminates fussy, elaborate, and involved methods by which a trick might be done and has the ability to create a method that is so subtle and so very simple there is hardly any trickery to detect. Spectators, who usually imagine that there must be some far more complex explanation, are left with nothing to discover.

"The further you delve into magic, the more you will realize it is the simple means that create the most profound effect for an audience," Fox advises. "Never get so involved with the method that you forget the effect. The simpler the method, the more time you will have to perfect your showmanship—to make it not just a trick but entertainment."

Frank Garcia

Known as "The Man with the Million Dollar Hands," Frank Garcia has spent more than half his life training those hands in the skills that have brought him recognition among magicians as an expert at sleight of hand and manipulative magic.

He earns a good living mainly from close-up magic, performing it, teaching it, and writing about it. But making a commercial success of it has required not only sleight of hand but what Garcia calls "sleight of mouth," amusing patter, presen-tation, and the showmanly ability to be entertaining.

Garcia knows all the intricate moves and fingerings, knows at least thirty different ways to double-lift cards from the top of a pack to show two as one, and he enjoys doing magic for magicians. But when he performs for the public his skills become the carefully hidden means by which the magic seems to happen almost effortlessly.

"I firmly believe it is the effect that counts," he says. "All good tricks and routines must have an easily followed plot. The ultimate test of any trick is not in how cleverly it may be accomplished, but in the audience reaction to its performance."

During his years in show business,

Frank Garcia, whose "million-dollar hands" have brought him success and recognition as a close-up magician and expert on methods of crooked gamblers, was too poor as a boy to afford apparatus. But with a love of magic and a pack of cards, he taught himself his early skills at sleight of hand.

Garcia has appeared as a stage magician in many theaters, nightclubs, and on television shows, manipulating cards and billiard balls and performing other polished feats of stage sleight of hand. He occasionally still does, but his close-up work and writing keep him too busy to make as many stage appearances as he once made.

He is a popular close-up performer at trade shows, at the private parties of wealthy and prominent people, and in the "hospitality suites" where big corporations entertain their important clients. He is also a well-known authority on gambling and the detection of crooked gamblers, has written and lectured extensively on the subject, and gives demonstrations exposing the methods of the cardsharps and gaming table cheats.

Born in 1927 in New York City, where he has always made his home, Garcia lives with his wife, Lillian, in a comfortable apartment in the midtown Manhattan theatrical district. His parents had come to New York from Spain. Garcia began handling cards at the age of four, not as a magic-minded toddler, but because his merchant-seaman father, an inveterate card player and gambler, taught him poker and other card games, and kept him amused by explaining how dice should be rolled for the game of craps.

When he was about nine his family took him to a Spanish theater in the Bronx to see a magic show. It was performed by David Bamberg—the last of six generations of the Bamberg family of famous magicians—who had assumed the stage name and Chinese characterization of Fu Manchu to gain fame throughout South America as the continent's most celebrated illusionist.

"I knew right then that what I wanted to do the rest of my life was magic," Garcia recalls. He soon acquired two or three inexpensive tricks. "I performed them so often that I wore them out." A little later he saved his dimes and pennies and bought secondhand copies of two magic books, one of which luckily happened to be the "bible" of card handlers, S. W. Erdnase's *Expert at the Card Table*. Garcia also just about wore out the books, trying to learn everything in them.

"I couldn't afford any big equipment, so I relied on a deck of cards and a few coins," he says. He was performing shows before he was in high school, free shows for anybody who would watch. "I think the beginning magician should work wherever he can," he believes. "I did hundreds of shows without even thinking of being paid, just because I wanted the experience."

Garcia had an unusual talent for drawing and his schoolteachers advised his parents to encourage him to pursue an art career, which he did for a time, but the only pursuit that really interested him was magic. He was obsessed with learning the techniques of sleight of hand and taught himself to do all his tricks with either hand with equal facility.

"I was so in love with doing magic, I wanted to be able to do with my right hand whatever I could do with my left," he explains. "It took a long time to become skillful at cards, and I'm still working at it. You never learn all there is to know and you have to keep practicing the scales."

He was fourteen before he ever knew there was such a thing as a magic shop, but he finally discovered the Manhattan shop run by the late Max Holden. He became a frequent visitor, exchanged ideas with other amateurs, and was surprised to discover that his own self-taught skill with cards impressed some of the top card experts. They encouraged him and gradually became his friends. Holden welcomed him as a shop visitor even though Garcia still had little to spend for store-bought tricks. In those beginning years, the shop served as his first magic club.

When the attack on Pearl Harbor started World War II, Garcia still wasn't fifteen, too young for military service, but he offered his magical services by joining the American Theater Wing and performing dozens of free shows at USO canteens. At one of the canteens, he was asked to demonstrate some of the methods crooked gamblers use. He had no planned program, but agreed to show the servicemen what he could. He kept them entertained, amazed, and eager to see more for almost two hours before he finally put away his pack of cards, having also discovered a future career for himself, exposing crooked gamblers.

Garcia began performing magic professionally after he graduated from high school in 1945, but found he was still giving more free shows than those he was being paid for. He went to work at Holden's magic shop in 1948, at the age of twenty-one, and soon became the shop's manager. He had pioneered in early television by appearing with comedian Morey Amsterdam in 1948 and later was on the "Broadway Open House" program, the forerunner of the "Tonight" show.

He gave up his magic-shop job to return to full-time performing, took

---

Garcia played in vaudeville and night clubs as a stage magician after becoming a full-time professional at the age of eighteen and was a pioneer performer in early television. But he gained his first real success with an act exposing card-game cheats. He traveled the country with it, worked with police departments and government agencies, and performed as a magician aboard cruise ships while secretly acting as a gambling detective.

to the stage to tour what was left of the vaudeville circuits, did five shows a day in the Loew's and RKO theaters around New York, and made the bill at the Palace on Broadway, then in its fading glory but still the goal of all vaudevillians. During those years, he learned his performing the hard way, playing nightclubs, hotel supper rooms, vacation resorts, club dates, whatever was available.

He learned to handle drunken hecklers, to hold the attention of male audiences who were eagerly waiting for striptease dancers to appear, to put across his magic in elegant or sleazy surroundings, to entertain no matter how he felt or how tired he was by the time a third show took to the floor at two in the morning. "Some of the spots were good and some were bad," he says. "But I did them. I played them all. I paid my dues."

Still it was a long climb to the top and he felt he wasn't really getting anywhere until he finally decided to center his performing around his close-up skills and his knowledge of gambling. He put together a gambling act and developed a projector that would greatly magnify his hands in full color on an overhead screen, so everybody could see the tabletop manipulations he performed as he explained how crooked gamblers operated.

It was an immediate success. He became a featured act, earning top money, traveled all over the country with it, and appeared on the most popular national television shows. He worked with the New York Police Department, with special detective squads investigating gambling, with the FBI, and other U.S. and Canadian government agencies; he lectured to them and became an expert witness often called to testify before grand juries.

The Defense Department gave Garcia a captain's commission in 1957 and sent him to Germany, France, and Scotland as a lecturer for the U.S. Air Force. The Royal Canadian Mounted Police sent him on tours of Canada. Meanwhile he wrote a best-selling book on the subject, *Marked Cards and Loaded Dice.*

During a good part of each year from 1961 to 1967, he traveled the seas, combining magic with being a gambling detective. Various steamship lines, anxious to clean up widespread shipboard gambling, hired him to pose as an entertainer, staging regular magic shows for the cruising passengers and using that as a screen while he carried out his other job of detecting and stopping crooked gambling.

"I was threatened many times—sometimes threats against my life—but I was lucky in warding them off, and also was successful in putting many cheats off the ships," he says. "I met some of the best card handlers in the business, some of whom later became my friends and some who are not friends, understandably because I was exposing their trade."

In more recent years, his gambling demonstrations have found new audiences among young college-student groups. But much of his performing now is of commercially-themed close-up magic at trade shows. Booked through a Chicago theatrical agency that specializes in such shows, Garcia travels from New York around the country to make twenty-five or so well-paid trade show appearances each year, promoting products and industries with magic.

In one form or another, his devotion is clearly to the close-up magic that was his first love. "If magic is an art, close-up is where the real magic is," he says. "Making personal contact with the people you entertain—working with your hands and your wits."

A big man, but physically graceful, genial, soft-spoken, and with a charming sense of humor, his skilled hands are seldom without a pack of cards or some other magic prop in them. He is almost always at work on new tricks and routines. As an all-around professional with long practical experience, he also has the ability to communicate what he has learned to other magicians, through his writing, lectures, and direct teaching.

Regarded as one of the best teachers of magic, he now confines his personal teaching to private individual instruction, coaching and giving polish to those who already have some skills. He gives eight or nine lectures a year at magic clubs and conventions—from which he has received honors and awards—and has lectured to European magic groups. Many of the tricks he has created or improved upon are marketed by magic dealers.

Card tricks can be just card tricks, but when Garcia does them they're magic, and it's not all in his hands. His card plots are simple and direct and build to a logical climax. He presents them with a charm that makes even people who don't like card tricks enjoy his.

During the past several years Garcia has deliberately limited his public performing to concentrate on his writing. He is a prolific author of specialized books for magicians, many of which he profitably publishes himself. Each deals with a specific type of magic or with one particular classic effect in all its variations, moves, routines, and presentations. Highly popular with magicians, clearly written, detailed, and practical, they are best-sellers of their kind.

For beginners at sleight of hand, Garcia's advice is to follow the old axiom that "the first rule is *practice,* the second rule is *practice,* and the third rule is to *practice again."* But he also feels that newcomers to magic often fail to realize how important it is to do all they can to make audiences like them personally.

Young performers especially may neglect such things as personal appearance, good grooming, or the simple matter of having clean hands and fingernails; or because of ner-

vousness they may "put on snobbish airs" or fall into a standoffish attitude. "If you make an audience really like you, you can do no wrong," says Garcia. "They'll like almost anything you do."

Jeff Sheridan

Jeff Sheridan never speaks when he performs, but his audiences clearly understand everything he never says. His magical training grounds have been the parks and sidewalks of New York, where as a street magician he revived the tradition of the wandering conjurors who down through the ages entertained in the marketplaces and public squares before magic moved indoors into the theaters.

Sheridan has also brought his magic indoors, into concert and lecture halls, theaters and nightclubs, but he has kept the distinctly original style of performing he developed on the streets.

Many magicians present their stage and nightclub acts without patter, silently performing manipulative magic or more spectacular tricks and illusions to musical accompaniment. What makes Sheridan unique is that what he does—in silence—is audience-participation magic, close-up and in direct contact with his spectators, drawing them personally into his silent routines.

All without saying a word, he borrows things from them, gets

Garcia demonstrates the old shell game, but even with walnut shells this big you'll never guess which one the ball will be under.

Jeff Sheridan, who directly involves spectators in all his magic. He communicates eloquently with his audiences without ever saying a word. Sheridan revived the ancient art of street magic in New York, created his own "personal theater" in Central Park, and won an award from the Municipal Arts Society for enhancing the cultural life of the city. After thousands of street performances, he has brought his silent artistry indoors to night clubs, theaters, and concert halls.

them to act as volunteer assistants, leads them to do what he wants them to do, to respond as he wishes them to respond. Always dressed totally in black—in a simple turtleneck shirt and slacks—using the simplest of props and the most basic effects, Sheridan relies almost entirely on sleight of hand and an artistry of presentation tested in thousands of street performances.

A critic for *Variety*, praising his unusual act while Sheridan was playing at a New York night spot, The Bottom Line, in 1978, pointed out that he does it all "in mime, using gestures, expressions and prestidigitation for communication." Commenting on his silent ability to involve the spectators and "talk" to them without saying a word, *Variety*'s critic wrote: "Silence may come from the stage, but laughter and mitting come back from the crowd. Sheridan's high-calibre performance and bright spirits deservedly win over a skeptical youthful rock throng."

Born in the Bronx in 1948, Sheridan took up magic at the age of nine after an uncle had fooled him with some card tricks, which started him looking through the magic books in the public library to find out how they were done. He found other tricks in the books, learned to do some of them, and soon was amazing his neighborhood friends.

"I used to hide myself in my room and practice," he remembers. "I didn't have much else. I was a pretty inhibited kid, never into sports or anything like that. But with magic, I had my own expertise."

He later joined a young magicians' club, the Future American Magical Entertainers, better known as FAME, which was sponsored by the city as a recreational youth project and held its meetings in a school gymnasium in midtown Manhattan. Its members included a number of excellent young magicians, some of whom became well-known professionals.

Sheridan's ambition to become a magician was the only constant thing in his nomadic childhood. Before he was fifteen, when his parents separated, he had lived in seven different homes. He went to five different high schools, became a school dropout, but later finished his schooling at night classes while doing magic during the days. "I don't remember ever really wanting to be anything but a magician," he says.

He worked up an act he did in a small neighborhood Bronx nightclub and did some other shows. He had no money for flashy equipment and couldn't see himself as the traditional stage magician in top hat and tails. So he developed his own style of silently performing sleight of hand with audience participation.

"I never felt comfortable speaking before a group, and with magic I could never concentrate on two things at once," he explains. "But more than that, I felt that speech interfered with the illusion. Magic is about images. It's about changes. With speech, the purity of the image is lost. The magic becomes accessory to the talk and too often it all descends into sideshow comedy."

He took an office job for a while, working a photocopying machine for a Wall Street firm. But he hated the dull routine of office work, and it made him more than ever determined to earn a full-time living somehow as a magician. He set out on his own at the age of nineteen, moved into a cheap room in the section of lower Manhattan known as Little Italy, and tried to support himself doing magic.

The opportunities for his kind of silent magic were limited. There weren't any theaters with variety shows to provide experience. Most nightclubs wanted singers and comedians, or at least magicians with funny patter or pretty assistants they sawed in half.

Sheridan did some party shows, gave lessons in sleight of hand, got a few small nightclub bookings. The manager of one club told him his silent act was bad for business—not that it wasn't clever and entertaining, but the customers became so interested watching what he was doing that they stopped drinking while he was on.

"There was nowhere for a young magician to develop," he says. "I took my magic to the streets because that was the only logical thing for me to do."

He started his street magic in Central Park almost by accident. One afternoon in 1967 he happened to be in the park near the Bethesda Fountain, then a gathering place for the young counterculture, and a camera crew was filming a documentary. He always carried a pack of cards and he decided to liven up the youth scene by performing a few card tricks.

As he fanned the cards, manipulated them, made them vanish and reappear, a good crowd gathered. He suddenly discovered he had an audience eager to see him do his magic in his own way, and also willing to reward him afterwards by dropping some money into his little black bag.

It was no way to quick fame and riches, but in time it brought him a measure of both, and meanwhile gave him the means to continue his profession. Becoming a street entertainer embarrassed him somewhat at first; he knew there were people who might condescendingly group him with street beggars seeking handouts, and he wondered what relatives or friends would think if they saw him. But the knowledge that he was providing honest entertainment, and the obvious enjoyment of those who watched, overcame that embarrassment.

"It was the most honest thing I ever did," Sheridan says, looking back. "They watched the show first and then paid only whatever they wanted to pay for seeing it."

Street magic had a long history as part of the ancient conjuring art, and in other cities, especially in Europe, there were still street magicians around, as there soon would be again on the streets of New York. But when Sheridan started in 1967, he wasn't aware of any others. He was the first in many years to bring street magic to real prominence again in New York and to important recognition as a performing art. As far as he knew, he certainly was the only nontalking street magician.

His decision always to dress only in black grew out of necessity, but added to his visual presentation. "I wore black when I was getting started because it stood up well to the dirt of the streets," he says. "All I could afford was inexpensive slacks and two-dollar turtlenecks. After I was more successful, I could afford better-fitting stuff, but still black and simple."

Sheridan performed for sidewalk crowds at various places around the city, but Central Park was where he established himself as something of an institution. He annexed part of the park as his own showplace by transforming the park's Walter Scott statue into a "theater."

The statue formed what those who later wrote about him in theatrical arts magazines described as a "natural proscenium space." It served as a backdrop, centering people in front of him and cutting off the view from the rear. The statue's base also provided a natural platform that became his stage, where he could be seen more easily and draw larger audiences.

He set up no tables or equipment, made no speeches and staged no ballyhoo, and park police tolerantly accepted his use of the statue. "I thought of it as my personal outdoor theater," he recalls, "and I didn't pay rent, which was nice."

Sheridan began a steady ten-year run of continuous appearances at the Walter Scott statue, regularly putting on his shows there every Sunday from early spring into late fall. He sometimes did fifty or more shows a day, each limited to a carefully structured five-minute act because "people outdoors have other things to do and are not going to stop longer than that."

Over the years of performing and working on his routines until they became part of himself, he gradually created a kind of magic that seemed as if it were happening right then for the first time. But it was precisely crafted, each move and gesture analyzed and planned for a specific audience reaction.

"It takes time for a magician to realize who he is and what he has to offer," he says. "Anybody can buy the props, but nobody can buy the art of presentation. You must create a personal magic, so the sense of illusion cannot be separated from the performer."

At his Scott statue "theater," Sheridan would first draw an audience by arousing curiosity. He would stand silently, not moving. Then one hand might go up and produce a fan of cards. He would begin to get involved in doing some manipulations, but as if for himself, absorbed in what he was doing and purposely ignoring the people, noise, traffic, everything around him. By being oblivious to the audience, he would make people wonder what was going on, and they would move closer to find out.

Staring into a void, as though not seeing anyone, he would hold up a rope, magically link the handle of a pair of scissors to the rope and unlink them again. "I start by not relating to anyone but myself," he says, "and then I begin to relate to the audience, but only one to one." Scanning the audience, he would fix on one person's eyes, usually a young woman, and indicate silently that she should take the scissors and cut the rope.

Strange things would happen to the cut pieces of rope, so that at first the trick seemed to go wrong, with Sheridan eloquently pantomiming his shyness and confusion, playing only to that one woman spectator— but with the audience held watching and amused.

As the trick finally succeeded and the rope was restored, he would smile at her happily, and without pausing would hold out his hand to shake hands with her. When she took his hand, he would pull her up to the base of the statue, keeping her hand as he drew her up to his "stage" and turned her to face the audience.

"That's how I get a volunteer," he says. "I never ask, and they always come, which gets another response from the audience. I never let go of that hand, no matter what happens."

When he had her beside him, he would lift the palm of her hand and brush it off as if it had become a bit dirty. Reaching down into the black bag at his feet, he would remove a small brightly-colored sponge and wipe her hand with that. As the audience laughed, the sponge magically would become two sponges, which led into a routine of the sponges vanishing, reappearing, and penetrating her hands.

In perhaps less than two minutes, he had attracted an audience, involved a pretty spectator in the humorous byplay, gotten her to be his assistant, and had performed two entertaining and visually surprising tricks, linking the tricks together with a natural continuity that set the scene for the rest of his performance.

70

Because he never talked, some thought he was a mute and others that he was from some faraway foreign land and couldn't speak English. At first when somebody congratulated him after a performance, he said, "Thank you," which usually produced a squeal of surprise and the shout, "You talked!" But he realized people were disappointed when he spoke. They had all sorts of romantic notions about him, and he learned just to smile or nod to whatever they said and to let them keep their fantasies. "I didn't want to spoil it for them by telling them I was just a kid from the Bronx."

As Sheridan's street magic skills grew, along with his celebrity as an entertainer in Central Park, the coins and dollar bills people dropped into his little black bag increased, until on a single good day he might collect several hundred dollars. He also found other tokens of appreciation in his black bag, given by those who had little money: a flower, a trinket of jewelry, polished pebbles some child had clutched in hand as a prize to donate for the magic brought into his life.

Performing-arts groups took an interest in the living theater he had created at the statue in the park. He became the subject of analytical articles in drama journals. Television news cameramen frequently pictured him. There were newspaper feature stories, write-ups in national news magazines. He received an award from the Municipal Arts Society of New York for enhancing the cultural life of the city, became an instructor at the Silent Performer Workshop, and the co-author, with writer Edward Claflin, of the book *Street Magic,* an illustrated history of the art.

With his growing success, Sheridan had moved into an uptown apartment, west of Central Park, joking that "I like to be able to walk to work." Although he uses few visible props himself, the apartment shelves are filled with antiques and more modern equipment, with his magic books, and on the walls of the rooms are his posters of past great magicians. When not keeping his silence as a performer, he can be very articulate about the art of magic—and he does regard it as an art.

Sheridan's concept of magic as basically a visual art has made him a student not only of mime and the other performing arts but also of the visual arts of sculpture and painting. He thinks of magic in terms of images rather than just tricks. When he puts together a new routine he tries to combine the familiar objects he uses as props in an unpredictable and unfamiliar way to give a "surreal" quality to his performance, as a painter might combine known forms and figures in patterns compellingly different from everyday reality.

"The conjuror is every man's surrealist," he says, "a lone performer who produces something out of nothing and creates new visionary experiences with seemingly ordinary things." Among painters Sheridan admires is Salvador Dali.

"There's a strong element of the conjuror in Dali."

For his hour-long indoor concert programs of silent magic, he has blended together and expanded his short street magic acts and added effects he couldn't properly present without more of a real stage than his "outdoor theater" in the park. He gave the new format its first trial run with a series of *Evenings of Magic in Concert* at the New York University Theater in 1977, presentations called "Visual Alchemy."

"I wanted to get back to the very basic primitive things," he explains, "the primal, where magic began, visual experiences with fire, smoke, water, energy."

The new concerts marked something of a turning point in Sheridan's then twenty-nine-year-old life. "I spent my twenties on the streets," he says, "and I'll probably spend my thirties in the theaters." But the years of street magic defined his style and he doesn't intend to give it up entirely. He feels the need to maintain contact with his street audiences. "I'm still going to try to make it back to the Walter Scott statue on as many Sundays as I can. It's been like home to me."

For Further Reading

General

Recently published for the general public, these introductory books on tricks and performing can be obtained through most regular bookstores and should be available in some public libraries.

Anderson, George B. *Magic Digest.* Northfield, Ill.: Digest Books, 1972. Paperback. Dozens of standard tricks of all types clearly explained, plus much other advice and information about magic and magicians.

Christopher, Milbourne. *Milbourne Christopher's Magic Book.* New York: Thomas Y. Crowell, 1977. A famous magician teaches presentation and performances, misdirection, showmanship, and how to do many practical, novel and entertaining tricks.

Garcia, Frank, and Schindler, George. *Magic with Cards.* New York: David McKay, 1975. With the emphasis on entertaining presentations, explains more than one hundred card tricks with an ordinary deck.

Hay, Henry. *The Amateur Magician's Handbook.* New York: New American Library, 1974. Paperback. Explains classic and standard tricks, with and without special apparatus, and basic sleight of hand.

Lewis, Angelo John [Professor Hoffmann]. *Modern Magic.* New York: Dover Publications, 1978. Paperback. A reprint of the century-old classic, the first book in English that really taught how to do magic—and which inspired generations of magicians. Complete and unabridged, with an introduction by Charles Reynolds.

Lewis, Shari, and Hurwitz, Abraham B. *Magic for Non-Magicians*. Los Angeles: J. P. Tarcher, 1975. Simple but effective tricks without store-bought apparatus or difficult sleight of hand.

Lorayne, Harry. *The Magic Book*. New York: G. P. Putnam's Sons, 1977. Teaches basic sleight of hand for performing close-up magic with ordinary things. Expert instruction in the best methods of doing many standard tricks with cards, coins, matches, paper, strings, etc.

Nelms, Henning. *Magic and Showmanship*. New York: Dover Publications, 1969. Paperback. Staging, presentation, and theatrical techniques applied to performing magic.

Scarne, John. *Scarne on Card Tricks*. New York: New American Library, 1974. Paperback. Many good card tricks, mostly requiring no intricate sleight of hand.

Magic Books by Bill Severn

Here is a chronological listing of my own books on magic and related subjects, published by David McKay Co., Inc., New York; they can be obtained through general bookstores or may be found in public libraries.

Magic Wherever You Are. 1957. Magic for the living room, dining room, outdoors, etc., not performed as acts, but as unexpected "happenings" to surprise your friends.

Magic and Magicians. 1958. A brief history of magic, the world of magic and magicians, biographies of famous past magicians and modern performers.

Shadow Magic. 1959. The story of shadow shows, with instructions and scripts for staging human shadow plays, hand shadows, shadow puppets.

Rope Roundup. 1960. Re-issued 1976 as *The Book of Rope and Knots*. Includes knots and ties, trick knots and puzzles, and rope magic, plus rope-spinning, stunts, games, making things, and a history of ropes and their uses through the ages.

Magic with Paper. 1962. Tricks with all sorts of things made of paper: tissue, newspapers, magazines, cardboard, cartons and tubes, bags, envelopes, cups; also utility props and devices, paper-tearing designs.

Magic in Your Pockets. 1964. Tricks with things that can be carried around in your pockets; emphasis on simple methods and unusual props and presentations.

Magic Shows You Can Give. 1965. Instructions for putting together, staging, and performing complete acts for club, stage, briefcase, and kid shows, with routines explained in the form of step-by-step word and action scripts.

Packs of Fun. 1967. Unusual things to know about playing cards and ways to have fun with them. Includes card tricks, card handling, puzzles, gags, stunts, games, fortune-telling, mind reading, and the lore, legends and history of cards.

Magic Comedy. 1968. Comedy tricks, props, stunts, routines, skits and sketches; stage, kid show, close-up, magical party fun, magic clowning, master of ceremonies material; comedy wands, flowers, other devices.

Magic Across the Table. 1972. Tabletop magic with pads, pencils, bottle caps, chewing gum, things from around the house, from the kitchen, etc.; not standard impromptu stunts but unusual tricks prepared in advance for showing to a few friends seated with you at a table.

Bill Severn's Big Book of Magic. 1973. Some fifty routines for magic with cards, ropes, coins and bills, handkerchiefs, close-up, platform and stage. An exploration of each type of magic, biographical and historical sketches of its famous tricks and celebrated performers; the world of magic and magicians; paper-tearing designs and chapeaugraphy; how to learn, routine, stage, and perform magic.

Bill Severn's Magic Trunk. 1974. A slipcased set, in the form of a "magic trunk" of paperback editions of four previously published books: *Magic with Paper; Magic in Your Pockets; Magic Shows You Can Give; Magic Comedy.*

Magic in Mind. 1974. An introduction to mental magic, its theory and performance, with new tricks and presentations; close-up and platform effects of make-believe mind reading, ESP, mind control, telepathy, mental visions, predictions, accomplished by simple methods.

Bill Severn's Magic Workshop. 1976. Twenty-five make-and-do magic workshop projects and more than sixty tricks that can be performed with the props constructed from materials found around the house and put together without special tools or skills. Utility props, secret gadgets and gimmicks, to encourage the amateur to develop his own new presentation.

Magic with Coins and Bills. 1977. Basic sleight of hand with coins; "do anywhere" tricks; novel money magic with prepared coins and bills made at home; close-up and stage routines; "gag" bills and comedy effects.

50 Ways to Have Fun with Old Newspapers. 1978. Games, puzzles, hats, cutouts, paper designs, making things, etc., including a chapter of unusual magic tricks with newspapers; easy-to-follow text and many detailed illustrations.

Bill Severn's Big Book of Close-Up Magic. 1978. A large collection of tricks of all kinds for performing while standing or seated close to those watching.

Magic Dealer Publications

These are *not* available in general bookstores or in most public libraries. They can be obtained from magic dealers or direct from the publishers.

Courses in Magic

Tarbell, Harlan. *The Tarbell Course in Magic.* n.d. 7 vols. Louis Tannen, Inc., 1540 Broadway, New York, NY 10036. A complete course in the tricks, methods, principles, presentation, and performance of almost every form of magic. Started in the late 1920s as a mail-order correspondence course, Tarbell's carefully taught lessons were greatly expanded with material collected during the more than thirty years of publication of these seven volumes in book form (1941–72). Their special value for serious beginners is in their explanation of everything in detail, without assuming any prior knowledge of what is being taught. The "meat" of the lessons is in the first six volumes, but the seventh includes a cross-index to the entire set as well as some interesting additional tricks.

Wilson, Mark. *The Mark Wilson Course in Magic.* 1975. Mark Wilson, P.O. Box 440, North Hollywood, CA 91603. Probably the best one-volume course in magic ever written. Clear, step-by-step instructions for putting together, learning, and presenting several hundred tricks, explained in a way that provides a good basic knowledge of modern techniques and methods. Covers a broad range of magic with a professional approach, and includes many effects with props that can be as-

sembled at home, as well as some with standard small apparatus. More than 2,500 illustrations, 472 large spiral-bound pages.

Encyclopedias and Specialized Books

Adair, Ian. *Encyclopedia of Dove Magic,* 4 vols. 1968–77. The Supreme Magic Company, Ltd., 64 High Street, Bideford, Devon, England. Almost anything a magician could want to know about magic with doves is covered in the hundreds of pages of these four large volumes. Even for the magician not interested in dove tricks, they provide a good reference library of modern methods and apparatus that can be adapted to many other forms of magic.

Anderson, Gene, and Marshall, Frances. *Newspaper Magic.* 1965. Magic, Inc., 5082 N. Lincoln Ave., Chicago, IL 60625. Tricks and routines with newspapers, plus paper-tearing designs, comic paper hats, several complete acts, and Anderson's famed version of the Torn and Restored Newspaper as featured by Doug Henning.

Anthony, Norman. *Basic Card Techniques.* n.d. Louis Tannen, Inc., 1540 Broadway, New York, NY 10036. Basic card handling, manipulations, trick cards and devices, clearly explained for the beginner in card magic, along with an excellent chapter on presentation of all kinds of magic.

Bobo, J. B. *The New Modern Coin*

Magic. n.d. Magic, Inc., 5082 N. Lincoln Ave., Chicago. IL 60625. The most complete book of coin magic. More than 500 pages, over 600 illustrations, and clear instructions for 110 coin sleights and the entertaining presentation of 312 coin tricks. Covers basic techniques, simple and advanced sleight of hand, sleeving, coin classics and their variations, coin boxes and apparatus, trick coins, stage magic with coins, coin acts and close-up routines, and modern developments in coin magic.

Fitzkee, Dariel. *Magic by Misdirection.* Reprint of 1945 original. Lloyd E. Jones, 4064 39th Ave., Oakland, CA 94619. A detailed study of the psychology of magical deception, with practical illustrations of tricks using the principles analyzed.

Fitzkee, Dariel. *Showmanship for Magicians.* Reprint of 1943 original. Lloyd E. Jones, 4064 39th Ave., Oakland, CA 94619. The standard work on how to make magic more appealing and entertaining through showmanly presentation: choice of material, style, timing, pointing, pacing, building to climaxes, etc.

Griffin, Ken and Roberta. *Illusion Show Know-How.* Abbott's Magic Manufacturing Co., Colon, MI 49040, n.d. Practical advice (not explanations of tricks) for any magician interested in performing stage magic. Deals with routing, planned stage action, packing, showmanship and presentation, audience reaction, handling volunteer assistants, staging illusions, wardrobes,

construction of props and scenery, lighting, stage terms, and much more.

Holden, Max. *Programmes of Famous Magicians.* n.d. Magic, Inc., 5082 N. Lincoln Ave., Chicago, IL 60625. A booklet listing the programs of over one hundred famous magicians, showing what tricks they used and how they routined their acts.

James, Stewart. *Abbott's Encyclopedia of Rope Tricks.* 2 vols. 1941, 1962. Abbott's Magic Manufacturing Co., Colon, MI 49040. The definitive work on rope magic. Tricks, routines, principles, methods, and devices, gathered from magicians, dealers, books, magic magazines; carefully edited and explained to present a great variety of effects, such as cut and restored ropes, knots, ties, escapes, penetrations.

Marshall, Frances. *Kid Stuff.* 5 vols. 1954–75. Magic, Inc., 5082 N. Lincoln Ave., Chicago, IL 60625. A series of books that amounts to an encyclopedia of performing magic for children, with contributions by many leading entertainers in the field. The four paperbacks and one large hardbound volume total nearly a thousand pages of tricks, routines, scripts, special material, advice, and information.

Marshall, Frances and Jay. *The Success Book.* n.d. 2 vols. Magic, Inc., 5082 N. Lincoln Ave., Chicago, IL 60625. Explores almost every branch of magic and its varied activities, and suggests many ways of achieving satisfaction, profit, and success. Encyclopedic in coverage and filled with practical advice on such things as personality, appearance, clothing, selection of tricks, presentation, staging, assistants, patter, packing, working with animals, booking shows, publicity and promotion, specialized fields of magical entertaining, magic dealers, books and magazines, etc.

Rice, Harold R. *Encyclopedia of Silk Magic*. 3 vols. 1948–62. Silk King Studios, 604 Evening Star Lane, Cincinnati, OH 45220. Hundreds of methods and variations, routines, and presentations for performing with silk handkerchiefs. Full explanations of nearly all known appara-

tus and devices used in such tricks: non-apparatus methods, knot-tying, dyeing silks, various silk folds. This is the standard reference work on silk magic, a comprehensive library of more than 1,500 pages, several thousand illustrations.

Taylor, Tony. *Spotlight on 101 Great Magic Acts*. n.d. Micky Hades International, Box 476, Calgary, Alberta, Canada T2P 2J1. Another collection of programs of famous magicians, and performances seen over the years by the author, with biographical notes, comments by the press, other material. A good source of information on the routining of acts.

3

WOMEN IN MAGIC

Probably the first woman to perform magic professionally in America was Mrs. John Brenon. Little is known about her, not even her first name. But it is known that she entertained New Yorkers with magic back in 1787, the year the constitution of the new United States was being drafted.

She appeared with her husband, a magician and ropewalking aerialist from Dublin, who featured a version of the bullet-catching trick—having a pistol fired at him from the audience while he balanced himself on a rope and magically caught the shot in his handkerchief. Mrs. Brenon's magic apparently was less sensational, but it was noted that she did perform with "dexterity of hand."

Over the years since then America's women magicians have impressed audiences with every kind of magic. Male performers have always greatly outnumbered them, but women have successfully performed on stage and in close-up, as club and party entertainers, mentalists, comic magicians, magic clowns, skilled sleight-of-hand manipulators, escape artists, and illusionists.

Other women, while not magicians themselves, have been partners in magic acts whose success has greatly depended upon them. Many have first become interested in magic as assistants in the shows of a husband, father, brother, or boyfriend. There have also been acts with women as the performers and men as their assistants.

Women have worked in, run and owned magic companies; have made props and equipment, designed costumes and scenery. They have written scripts for magic shows and for the presentation of magic at trade and industrial shows. There are women teachers of magic, lecturers on magic, writers for magic magazines, collectors of books, posters, and apparatus. Hundreds of women have joined in all of magic's varied hobbies and activities for the same reasons most men do: sometimes for profit and mainly for fun.

If the world of magic has been mostly a man's world, by tradition and simply because most magicians are men, women have been welcomed into it. They attend magic conventions in great numbers, are featured performers in convention shows, take part in convention contests and frequently win them. For years women have been among elected officers of magic clubs. Here and there a few clubs still have only male members, but they are very few, and the national and international societies have had women members almost from the start.

The Society of American Magicians, oldest of the magic societies, elected its first woman member, Madame Redan of Boston, in 1903, a little more than a year after it was organized. In 1904, SAM admitted its second woman member, Adelaide Herrmann, widow of the famed Alexander Herrmann; she herself was to become the most famous of women magicians.

Adelaide Herrmann

She was Adelaide Scarcez, a twenty-two-year-old London-born professional dancer, when she married Herrmann in New York in 1875, in a ceremony performed by the city's mayor. As Herrmann's

---

Adelaide Herrmann, wife of Herrmann the Great, and herself the most famous of women magicians, wrote on the back of this picture: "This is how I used to look when I assisted my husband years ago. The picture was taken in Paris when we played the Eden Theatre." ROBERT LUND COLLECTION— AMERICAN MUSEUM OF MAGIC

Adelaide Herrmann performed magic for half a century, first in the shows of her world-famed husband, next with her nephew Leon, and then on her own in vaudeville theaters for some thirty years. She topped the bills with her own performance and was advertised as "The Greatest of the Herrmanns." She made a note on the back of this picture that it was taken while she was playing the Haymarket Theatre in Chicago, but no date was given. ROBERT LUND COLLECTION—AMERICAN MUSEUM OF MAGIC

chief assistant in the spectacular illusions they presented, and as a featured dancer, she toured with her husband for more than twenty years. Internationally recognized as the greatest magician of his time, Herrmann built his big shows into one of the top attractions of the American stage, and earned not only theatrical fame but hundreds of thousands of dollars.

Herrmann lived up to his success in a befitting style, with a palatial home, horses and carriages, a yacht, and a luxurious private railroad car in which he and Adelaide traveled the country. But he suffered disastrous financial losses in theatrical real estate investments and in Wall Street. There was little money left when he died of a heart attack in 1896, while on his way to play an engagement in Pennsylvania.

Adelaide cabled his nephew, Leon Herrmann, also a magician and then in Paris, to come to the United States and help her keep the show going. She became the star of it, with Leon featured, but after a few successful years they had disagree-

Adelaide Herrmann, the "peerless and inimitative Queen of Magic," as she appeared in New York before World War I. ROBERT LUND COLLECTION—AMERICAN MUSEUM OF MAGIC

ments and went their separate ways. Leon appropriated the "Herrmann the Great" billing for a show of his own. Adelaide billed herself as "The Greatest of the Herrmanns," and began a new career in vaudeville.

The unusual magic acts she created kept her a headliner in the variety theaters for some thirty years. She played in Europe at times—in London's Hippodrome, Berlin's Wintergarten, the Folies-Bergère in Paris—and made other foreign tours. But she achieved most of her fame in the United States, as a perennial star of the Keith vaudeville circuit.

A 1910 program for Keith's Theater in Columbus, Ohio announced that the "peerless and inimitative Queen of Magic" would play the role of "Cleopatra the Egyptian Sorceress" in presenting "many new and marvelous magical creations." Seven years later, at the age of sixty-four, Adelaide Herrmann was again appearing as Cleopatra, which prompted a theatrical trade paper to comment that she seemed to have discovered the Fountain of Youth.

Another of her long-popular magical sketches was built around the story of Noah's Ark. A long ark-shaped box was shown empty, buckets of water representing the flood were poured into it, and she then produced from the ark all sorts of birds and animals in pairs. When the front and back doors of the ark were opened wide, the water had vanished and the ark was completely filled with a reclining young lady.

Year after year, she continued

Adelaide Herrmann producing a live duck from an also magically produced mass of colored ribbon streamers. At the age of sixty-four, she was still playing the role of "Cleopatra the Egyptian Sorceress" in some of her vaudeville appearances. She was seventy-five before she retired from active performing, still a star. ROBERT LUND COLLECTION—AMERICAN MUSEUM OF MAGIC

her tours, topping the bills and appearing in nearly every major city in the country. There were predictions that her career was over in 1926 when a fire that swept through a New York theatrical warehouse killed sixty of her trained animals and destroyed most of her magic equipment. She was seventy-three, and as she stood weeping outside the burned warehouse, she told reporters, "This finishes it all. I should have quit a year ago."

But two months later, Adelaide Herrmann was back on the road with a dazzling new act, *Magic, Grace and Music*. Audiences loved her as they always had, and still a star, she went on entertaining them for two more years. Her final performance was at the Keith Orpheum Theater in Brooklyn in 1928. A large part of her last years were spent in her Manhattan hotel suite, sorting through the memorabilia of half a century of performing magic, for a book she hoped to write but never got written. She died in 1932 at the age of seventy-nine.

Talma

The most famous of women sleight-of-hand performers was Talma, the "Queen of Coins," who claimed to be able to palm thirty of them in one of her small hands, and who was advertised as "the only lady palmist in the world."

She was Mary Ford, a pretty six-teen-year-old English girl when she became an assistant in 1890 to celebrated illusionist Servais Le Roy, who taught her magic, gave her the stage name of Mercedes Talma, and later married her. After touring America and Europe as his assistant, she became eager to have an act of her own, and with Le Roy's help she began "five years of diligent study," devoting her "whole time" to learning coin manipulation.

When she first appeared as the

"A good many women have the faculty of making money fly, but Talma's art lies in her ability to call it all back again," a reviewer wrote of the beautiful Mercedes Talma, the "Queen of Coins," shown here in street attire around the time her coin manipulations first made her a London sensation in 1899. ROBERT LUND COLLECTION—AMERICAN MUSEUM OF MAGIC

82

"Queen of Coins," at the Oxford Music Hall in London in 1899, she was an immediate sensation. Critics wrote of her "wonderful dexterity, ease and grace," her "undeniable artistry," and of the hearty applause that greeted her "astonishing art of juggling with coins." They also took note of her "personal attractions," saying she looked like actress Maude Adams, was "dainty and petite and bubbling over with good spirits and vivacity."

"The few men who are experts in her line have the advantage of bigger hands," one reviewer wrote, "but Talma wears a five and a half glove, and can do everything it is possible to do with coins." She packed the theater for months, and "with the simple aid of her own deft fingers . . . has managed to coin money for the management ever since she first stepped on the stage."

A theatrical journal reported that she was the talk of London's amusement seekers, with everybody asking, "Have you seen Talma?" There were illustrated magazine articles, newspaper features, and interviews; she was so much the hit of the season that American correspondents in London cabled stories about her to their papers in the United States. The correspondent for the *New York Journal* wrote a detailed description of Talma's act:

"With her supple hands, she tosses up a few coins, catches them and tosses again and again, until a perfect shower of gold and silver pieces appear in the air. . . . It is the rapidity with which she keeps them in motion that makes a half dozen pieces actually appear like half a hundred. It looks as if she were picking them out of the air. If any man were skillful enough to do this act it would be said that he had the coins up his sleeves. But Talma has no sleeves . . . she depends solely upon the suppleness and dexterity of her arms and hands to make the coins increase and multiply and appear and disappear at will.

"For a quarter of an hour, she introduces surprise after surprise, scattering the shower of gold and silver pieces in all directions, apparently keepng the air full of them, and all of a sudden bringing them all together again in her little closed palms. . . . The pretty conjuror has perfect self-possession and in her most difficult of feats preserves a gracefulness of motion. . . , A good many women have the faculty of making money fly, but Talma's art lies in her ability to call it all back again."

Talma repeated her success as the "Queen of Coins" at other British music halls, and was a star attraction at theaters in France and Germany. Le Roy then created a big three-star show, combining his and Talma's talents with those of a hilarious magic comedian, fat, balding, rumble-voiced Leon Bosco. As Le Roy, Talma and Bosco, the "Monarchs of Mystery," they toured Europe, South Africa, Australia, the United States, and South America.

Her coin act was a feature of the

show, but she also performed other magic in it and played a leading role in the sketches and novel presentations Le Roy designed for the illusions he invented. She made a habit of always carrying a few of her silver coins in a pocket when she traveled, and enjoyed astonishing cabbies and shopkeepers by seeming to pluck the money out of the air to pay them.

Once, while touring in South Africa, according to her own account of the adventure, she unintentionally started a near-riot by producing some coins from a man's beard, which caused his companions to seize him and search for the source of his unexpected wealth. Later, when she was appearing in New York, two toughs accosted her on the street and demanded her money. Talma reportedly fell back a step and began to catch coins from the air and throw them at the thieves—which so disconcerted them that they fled.

She and Le Roy returned to London in 1910, where they operated a magic-supply company for a time, selling tricks and illusions to other magicians. The original Bosco was in ill health and was replaced in the show by other performers playing his role, and they began another Le Roy, Talma and Bosco tour early in 1914 in Australia.

Talma again conjured with coins, magically produced foaming glasses of beer, and in a spectacular scene that recreated the court of the Roman Emperor Nero—filling the stage with twenty actors costumed as Roman soldiers—she was seized and thrown into a lion's cage, but was saved when the lion vanished in a cloud of smoke.

She also became the first woman not only to float in midair but to vanish while floating there. Le Roy "hypnotized" her, covered her with a thin cloth, sent her soaring into the air, whipped the cloth away, and she was gone. That *Asrah* levitation, with its startling climax of Talma's midair disappearance, was the greatest of Le Roy's many inven-

---

Talma claimed she could palm thirty coins in one of her unusually small hands. She tossed a few coins into the air and kept juggling them until they seemed to have multiplied "into half a hundred gold and silver pieces," which then vanished until she reclaimed them by magically plucking them out of the air once more. "For a quarter of an hour, she introduces surprise after surprise," a critic said, "and in her most difficult feats preserves a gracefulness of motion." ROBERT LUND COLLECTION— AMERICAN MUSEUM OF MAGIC

With her husband, magician Servais Le Roy, and with magic comedian Leon Bosco, Talma performed her coin manipulations in a big three-star magic show that toured the world and later played the vaudeville theaters for years. She appeared in America's leading vaudeville houses up through the 1920s. ROBERT LUND COLLECTION— AMERICAN MUSEUM OF MAGIC

December 1914. They toured North and South America with the big show, and alternately presented a condensed version of it in vaudeville, where they were a hit attraction for years, playing the Palace on Broadway and other top U.S. vaudeville theaters.

Talma starred with Le Roy in a succession of various illusion shows and vaudeville acts all through the 1920s. He was severely injured when struck by an automobile near their Keansburg, New Jersey, home in 1930, and although he recovered, they retired from active performing. The "Queen of Coins" died in 1944 at the age of seventy. Le Roy was eighty-eight when he died in 1953.

tions, and was later copied by other famous magicians.

After presenting the show in New Zealand, they had planned to take it to Asia, but the First World War changed their plans and they sailed instead to the United States, where they opened in San Francisco in

Jane Thurston

Jane Thurston made her first stage appearance with the great Howard Thurston in 1928. She was his stepdaughter, but as close to him as a daughter of his own, and he hoped to make her a magician who someday might succeed him and carry on the Thurston name as the greatest in magic. He was nearing the end of his long career when he brought her into his shows with a magic act of her own.

She was coached in magic by Herman Hanson, himself an accomplished magician and former vaudeville performer, who was also Thurston's all-around creative con-

Jane Thurston, stepdaughter of the great Howard Thurston, was sixteen when she first performed her own magic act as a featured attraction in his 1928 shows. She combined magic with singing and dancing in a variety of magic acts she presented until the Thurston shows ended in 1935. One of the special songs she sang was "My Daddy's a Hocus-Pocus Man," and the shows were advertised as "Thurston the Famous Magician and Daughter Jane."

sultant and stage manager. An attractive sixteen-year-old girl with versatile talents, she combined her magic with singing and dancing. She produced silk handkerchiefs, bowls of water and goldfish, performed a variety of other tricks, tap-danced, and sang "My Daddy's A Hocus-Pocus Man." Audiences and critics liked her and she was publicized in newspapers and national magazines as "The Maid of Magic."

Jane Thurston had a new act in each season's show for the next three years. By 1931 she was presenting a "black art" act in which she magically caught large butterflies that danced above her head; transformed a disembodied figure into a live man; and performed a floating-ball routine, making a man and a row of dancing girls suddenly appear on a tightrope, and then floating herself into the air on a large ball as the man and girls flew in space around her. The show was advertised as "Thurston the Famous Magician and Daughter Jane."

But that was the last of the great full-evening Thurston shows. With the nation plunged into financial depression, many legitimate theaters closing, and the competition of talking pictures, radio, and other inexpensive entertainment, the whole pattern of show business was changing. Thurston's elaborate road show, with its big traveling cast and freight cars full of equipment, was no longer profitable. He closed it down in 1931 after a final performance in Boston and organized a condensed one-hour unit for presentation in the large theaters that offered a stage show and a feature picture for one low admission price.

The circuit-touring Thurston shows were still a top theatrical attraction, frequently breaking box-office records, and as they played on into the mid-1930s his daughter's magic was prominently featured. She was with him at the Valencia Theater in Jamaica, New York, in April 1934, when word reached them between shows that her mother, Leotha Thurston, had suffered a heart attack at their home in Beechurst, Long Island.

Thurston asked Jane to go on with the show, with Herman Hanson substituting for him on stage, and hurried to Beechurst, but by the time he reached his wife's bedside she had died. As newspapers reported it: "Thurston's Wife Dies And Their Daughter Gives Their Act. . . . Mr. Thurston left the theatre immediately and the scheduled performances were carried on by his daughter Jane and his company."

Her part as a performing magician was expanded in the 1935 show. Thurston, although in apparently vigorous good health at the age of sixty-five, had announced that it was to be his farewell tour. An illusion had been constructed to present Jane to audiences as the magician of the future, in a giant-sized magic book with large pages that were turned. On the first page was a picture of Harry Kellar, the great magician of the past whose show Thurston had taken over as Kellar's successor more than twenty-five years before. Another page pictured Thurston himself as the magician of the present. When the final page was turned, Jane appeared and stepped out to the stage.

On October 6, 1935, after the last of that day's four performances at the Kearse Theater in Charleston, West Virginia, Thurston collapsed. He had a paralytic stroke. In the hospital, as the Associated Press reported, "he turned over the wand to his 23-year-old daughter Jane." He

asked her to reorganize the show, with Herman Hanson's help, to "take over the center of the stage" and complete the tour without him.

She and Hanson finished the engagement in Charleston, and as Thurston wished, they then returned to New York to work out a new show with Jane as the star attraction. But it was never to be. There were financial difficulties, other entanglements, and theaters had no desire to book a Thurston show without Thurston himself in it.

Thurston recovered sufficiently to walk with the aid of a cane, and to talk about possibly performing again when he regained his health. But he suffered another stroke and died in Miami Beach in April 1936, and by then the show had been put in storage. Jane Thurston retired to private life and never publicly performed again. But for seven years she had been a magician in the greatest of magic shows—and had earned her place in the history of magic.

Celeste Evans

One of the best-known and most successful of today's professional women magicians, Celeste Evans had no magically famous father or husband to guide her footsteps in the paths of magic. She made it on her own, teaching herself her first magic from books she read as a child in her family's home in White Rock, British Columbia. After seeing a magic show performed by Canadian magician Alan Lambie, she was so inspired that she put away her dolls and decided to become a magician.

With few other sources of amuse-

ment available, she amused herself for hours practicing sleight of hand with cards and other simple magic props she acquired. Soon she was amusing friends with her magic, and while in her early teens began giving party shows. Having also learned stenography in school, she moved to Vancouver to take a business office job. There she became acquainted with other magicians, took some magic lessons to polish her skills, and impressed some of Vancouver's most expert magicians with her ability.

Her first experience as a full-time professional magician was with a traveling tent show. She became a popular club-date performer and then was booked to entertain Canadian troops in Japan and Korea. Later bookings had her performing for UN forces patrolling the Gaza Strip, the Congo, and other trouble spots of the world. She has also toured India and other parts of Asia, and has made at least half a dozen tours of Europe.

For a time, Celeste Evans lived in New York, but theatrical agents kept her busy performing her magic all over the country and the world, in major hotels and nightclubs, in stage shows, and on television. In 1962 she married her manager, Harry Breyn, and made her home in Chicago. They became the parents of a son and daughter.

A statuesque brunette, costumed in elegant formal evening gowns, Celeste Evans brings an air of sophisticated sorcery to her manipulative sleight-of-hand routines, her colorful conjuring with silk scarves, her productions of doves and of a live poodle dog. She is also a charming performer of audience-participation magic in which she amusingly draws spectators into the act.

Behind the glamor is a sure sense of showmanship gained in hundreds of performances before audiences of every kind, and a constantly practiced technical skill admired by other magicians. Celeste Evans has won their applause at magic conventions and has received many honors and awards from magic societies.

Frances Marshall

Among the most knowledgeable of magicians, Frances Marshall knew nothing about magic when she first went to work in a Chicago magic shop at the age of twenty-one. That was back in the depression year of 1931 and she took the job even though it paid only twenty-five cents an hour. She was hired mainly because she could type.

Ever since, she has been performing magic, making magic, selling magic, writing about magic. She has been surrounded by magic and by magicians every day of her life. She married the owner of the magic shop, Laurie Ireland, and was "thoroughly indoctrinated with love and respect for our hobby and profession." During the years of helping him run the company—of which she became the owner after he died—she also became an accom-

Frances Marshall, who probably knows as much about magic and magicians as anybody could know, has been sharing that knowledge and experience with others most of her life. With her husband, Jay Marshall, she operates a large magic company. She has been an active performer herself for more than forty years, is a prolific columnist for magic magazines and the author of a score of books on magic, and counts among the friends she has helped hundreds of magicians of every talent throughout the world.

plished magician, one of the best of children's entertainers.

The widowed Frances Ireland became Frances Marshall in 1955 when she married prominent professional magician Jay Marshall, a well-known stage and television performer, comedian, ventriloquist, and multi-talented show business personality. The new firm they built together, Magic, Inc., has a building of its own in Chicago, housing their home, business, workshops, library, collections, club meeting room, and half a hundred varied magic activities.

"I went into magic for what magic could do for me," Frances Marshall says. "What I could do for magic became a lifelong compulsion, because magic has given me a life so full of true riches that I can never repay it all. I count my friends from one end of the earth to the other. I have memories of wonderful things that have happened to me, places I have been, people of all levels I have met, beyond any dreams I might have had in my youth."

One of her youthful dreams was to be on the stage and another was to be a newspaper reporter. She has been on many stages, large and small. And although she never got to work for a newspaper, millions of her words have been published in columns she regularly writes for various magic magazines—and also in nearly a score of books she has written on magic. Her monthly column, "Around Chicago," has appeared for more than thirty years in *The Linking Ring,* the magazine of the International Brotherhood of Magicians, of which she is an associate editor. Another of her popular columns, "For Women Only," has long been a feature of *The New Tops* magazine. Still another, "It's Never Too Late," is dedicated to magic's many active senior citizens, men and women who in their retirement years have found new freedom to pursue the joys of magic as a hobby. Writing the columns is her own hobby-within-a-hobby—which all began because so much interesting news about magicians passed through the magic shop that she decided "it was a pity not to pass it on."

Once, she humorously listed her occupation as "magic shop slavey," but running one of the busiest of magic companies with her husband is work she thoroughly enjoys. It involves her in daily consultations with magicians and in a never-dull variety of other tasks. Often she makes up the first sample of a new trick with her own hands, especially when it requires sewing. "I have always sewed," she says, "but years ago I gave up on clothes and settled for magic."

She has described her home as being confined "to an open space around the kitchen table, sink and stove." Stretching out from there in all directions are books, props, boxes of things, mountains of paperwork, files of correspondence. Outside the kitchen window are the plants of her "roof garden," one of the few of her other hobbies not directly connected with magic. The guest room usually is occupied by some well-known visiting magician.

When she isn't home she is likely to be in the company of magicians elsewhere in the country or in some foreign land, attending club meetings, informal gatherings, conventions. She no longer performs for the public as frequently as she did for some forty years, but no matter how busy she may be with other things, she still keeps her hand in. "I feel I must put on the costume and get out in front of an audience now and then to see what today's audiences are really like."

More than two hundred of Frances Marshall's friends gathered in Chicago in November 1976, to celebrate her sixty-fifth birthday and her forty-fifth year in magic. Because she wanted it to be not only a celebration in her honor but one in which her friends could share, she turned the anniversary party into a two-day magic fest for them.

Top magicians took time out from busy professional engagements to present their acts in a church social hall and a nearby school auditorium. They came from across the country, and some from Europe, to share their talents and expert knowledge in demonstrations and lectures. A flood of telegrams and letters wished Frances Marshall a continuing long and active magic life. With the celebration over, she accepted the good wishes and went back to work, observing: "You only get out of magic whatever you put into it."

Janet Clinton, who got her start performing on New York television at the age of eight, became a popular magician in the Boston area and then moved to Alabama and Virgina to become "the South's Leading Lady Magician."

Janet Clinton

Often billed as "The South's Leading Lady Magician," Janet Clinton began her career performing on New York television at the age of eight. At the time, she was the youngest magician ever to appear on television. She remembers the makeup felt like "brown mud," and that studio lights were so hot she feared her costume might smolder.

Encouraged in her youthful magic activities by her father, Frank Clinton, himself an accomplished amateur magician, she won several television talent contests, including one in which she outperformed thirty-eight other weekly winners. Soon she was appearing on all the New York stations, and at the age of ten was offered a featured spot on two weekly programs. That was the beginning of many television shows, in Michigan, Illinois, Massachusetts, Alabama, Mississippi, and elsewhere.

She also began winning contests

91

at magic conventions. Stories about her success as a "girl magician" were published in *Cosmopolitan, American Girl, Junior Scholastic,* and other national magazines. She was a busy young performer during her years of finishing school at Packer Collegiate Institute in New York, and at Tufts University in Boston, where she graduated with honors. After she married, she kept Janet Clinton as her stage name, made her home in Massachusetts, and became a popular magician in the Boston area. Costumed in a feminine version of the traditional top hat and tails, she presented stage magic and illusions for adult audiences, performed on television, at company sales meetings, clubs, parties, picnics, store openings.

"I enjoy stepping out on the stage," she says, "and seeing an audience of strangers—each with his or her own worries, thoughts and problems—gradually become a harmonious group, all of them having fun *together* through magic."

But she found her greatest satisfaction in entertaining children and that has become her specialty. Gradually she developed her own character role as "Pixie." Wearing a high-pointed conical hat and costumed to portray a mischievous magical sprite who might have stepped out of the pages of a children's story book, she draws the youngsters actively into all the magic that they help to make happen. At other times she performs for them as a magic clown, dressed in red, yellow, and blue satin and with hair all colors of the rainbow. "My own style of being a

Janet Clinton as a magic clown. "My style is gentle clowning," she says, "not the slapstick and bop-them-on-the-head type of clowning."

clown is *gentle,*" she explains, "not the slapstick and bop-them-on-the-head type of clowning, which would be contrary to my personality."

Some of her most rewarding personal experiences in magic have come from entertaining children in hospitals. She recalls a little boy, seriously burned in an accident, who was wheeled in to see her show with his head and body encased in a protective plaster cast. He lay silent, withdrawn, hardly watching at first.

But then he began to laugh, call out, join in the fun, and afterwards he chattered unceasingly, full of enthusiasm, full of questions.

"After they took him back into his room and I was all packed and ready to leave," Janet Clinton remembers, "three of the nurses came over and told me that little fellow had been in the hospital eleven days and had refused to utter a word to anyone—until the show. It made me feel that sometimes there's a real magic in what magical entertainment and fun can do."

On the more commercial side of magic she has enjoyed the creative challenge of working out practical methods to meet some of the unusual requests made by sales executives for big corporations. Hired by a national food company to entertain its top salesmen meeting at a swanky resort hotel, she was given a list of the magic the company had dreamed up to inspire sales enthusiasm for a new line of substitutes for beef, chicken and ham—all made of soybeans.

Taking it for granted that a magician should be able to do anything, the company had four main requirements for the show. She was asked to turn soybeans into live cows, chickens, and pigs; change the animals into beef, chicken, and ham products; then transform those into money; and finally to show a photograph of a veteran employee and change the picture into the man himself.

"I fashioned the show around those requests and added other related ideas," she says. "But there was one exception. I didn't produce live cows or pigs—only chicks. I still wonder what the hotel personnel would have done if I had arrived there with cows and pigs."

Active in half a dozen societies of magicians, clowns, and professional entertainers, she was secretary of the Boston Ring of the International Brotherhood of Magicians. She was slated to become the ring's vice-president when she moved with her family to Mobile, Alabama, and began the transition that was to make her "The South's Leading Lady Magician."

After performing in New York and Boston, she found Mobile "quite a change" and was faced with establishing herself as an entertainer in an area where many of the people she met seemed rather surprised at first to discover she was a woman who went around presenting magic shows. But eventually she was averaging five or six shows a week, performances of all kinds as before, but specializing in children's entertaining. During the nine years she lived in Mobile, "Janet Clinton as Pixie" became so well-known that wherever she went, youngsters would call out, "Hi, Pixie!"

"Their recognition continually pleased and amazed me," she says, "as I always thought I looked and was very different out of costume, merely pushing a grocery cart or getting the car filled at the gas station."

But Janet Clinton has always found magic to be a real "friend-maker," which has helped her to meet "delightful and warm people,

In her magical character role as "Pixie," Janet Clinton became so well-known to the children of Mobile, Alabama, that even when she was in street clothes they recognized her wherever she went with delighted shouts of "Hi, Pixie!" As part of her shows, she taught her young audiences to applaud with a special "Pixie clap" of their hands to make the magic happen, and that became a citywide fad of Mobile's small fry.

magicians and lay folk alike," and it has also been "an unbelievable personality expander and booster for me as well as for my children." Her husband is not a performer, but "he's an encourager, prop carrier, and he loves to stand in the wings to watch the shows *and* the audiences."

When her daughter Kristen was born, doctors said she might never be able to speak, but Kristen had excellent medical care and speaks in all her own magic shows, after taking up magic as a hobby at an even younger age than when her mother first started. When Kristen was only seven she won first place in a junior contest at a convention of the Society of American Magicians. She won again at the age of nine, and a third time when she was eleven. Now a teenager, she gives shows at libraries, schools and churches.

"She has a quiet personality, as I have offstage," her mother says, "but in costume, with an audience and a show, which is fun to perform and entertaining for those watching, a new world opens up."

Kristen's brother Rocky, seven years younger, has also donned clown costumes and done balloon sculpturing at picnics, grand openings of stores, and other events with a young audience to be kept entertained while his mother is setting things up for another performance. "Rocky is outgoing and enjoys people," says Janet Clinton, "and magic has been an easy and natural expression for him." Janet Clinton and her family moved from Mobile to Norfolk, Virginia in 1977, and the garage and another room in the house were turned into magic rooms, so they could continue their magical lives and her performing career from there.

"I am really grateful to magic for being the sort of a hobby which helps us to express our personality in an entertaining way and which also adds a new dimension to it," she says. "It provides confidence and a feeling of 'being special' to the shy child or adult and is a wonderful outlet for the more extroverted person. Magic has contributed to all our lives in different ways."

Janet Clinton as she usually appears when performing for an adult audience costumed in her version of the traditional top hat and tails. With a busy family and social life, and as a mother of two children who are also active magic hobbyists, she still manages to perform an average of five to six magic shows a week.

95

Dorothy Dietrich

Dorothy Dietrich got her start in show business as a puppeteer, entertaining children with puppet shows in her native city of Erie, Pennsylvania. Her first summer job in New York was giving outdoor puppet shows sponsored by the Parks Department. She still includes puppets in some of the shows she gives for children, but her ambition since childhood was to become a magician, and she has succeeded in be-

Her brother fooled Dorothy Dietrich with some magic tricks when she was a little girl, so she learned some of her own and then always wanted to be a magician. But she started in show business as a puppeteer before achieving her ambition by becoming a busy professional mystifier.

coming a busy full-time professional.

It all began when her brother George took up magic as a hobby and fooled her with his tricks. Not to be outdone, Dorothy went to the Erie public library, dug out the available magic books, taught herself some of the tricks in them, and soon proved that there was more than one aspiring magician in the family. Among the books she read was a biography of Houdini, who became a childhood idol, a fact that later influenced her desire to perform straitjacket escapes.

"I was always interested in magic," she says. "I liked to see the look on people's faces when I did some trick that fooled them." For a time the puppets took precedence over magic. But puppetry and magic have always had a close affinity, and while giving her puppet shows in New York she became associated with people in magic, which renewed her ambition to be a magician. "I knew it was what I always really wanted to do, and I also knew that if I hoped to get anywhere I had to work at it."

Dorothy Dietrich's puppetry had given her a sense of showmanship and a knowledge of how to create entertaining presentations. But she also took lessons in dance and theater as she developed her magic skills and worked out routines suited to a feminine style of performing. She appeared as often as she could wherever she had a chance to break in—at charity affairs, hospitals, parties, small clubs.

"It was hard for me starting out

With her personality unusually restrained, Dorothy Dietrich is shown here about to escape from a strait jacket, a desire she says was influenced by her reading of a biography of Houdini when she was a child.

and college auditoriums, trade shows. On television she won attention as a woman who, instead of allowing herself to be sawed in half, reversed the traditional illusion and severed into two parts the male hosts of talk shows and network specials.

She became the featured attraction at the Magic Towne House in New York and also became busily involved in the management and direction of all its activities. She staged and took part in the adult and children's shows regularly presented in its intimate theater. She helped with promotions, ticket reservations, and the operation of its magic shop and magazine. She provided magicians for outside shows.

"Whatever you think of as busy, I keep ten times busier," she jokes, admitting that she maintains an "insane" working schedule, often putting in eighty hours a week. "But I enjoy what I'm doing."

A reviewer for *Cue* magazine wrote that her afternoon Magic Towne House shows for children were performances to "enjoy, enjoy." The same reporter commented that unlike some of the more somberly mysterious male wonder workers, Dorothy Dietrich was "non-threatening to the little kids who comprise much of her audience." Looking hardly more than a grown-up little girl herself, suggesting—in her costume, appearance, and manner—a friendly big sister, she leads the children through routines in which they take part, producing such surprises as

because as a woman magician I wasn't taken seriously at first," she says. She had to convince people she was a really good magician and not just a pretty girl who wanted to do a magic act. "I stuck to it, and little by little people began to accept me."

The recognition gradually put Dorothy Dietrich and her magic into resort hotels, nightclubs, school

Comedian Bill Cosby ponders where the dove produced by Dorothy Dietrich could have come from during an ABC television special.

silks and doves, and even a rabbit for them to pet.

In the same room a few hours later, for a nighttime adult audience, she is a completely different performer. In a brief satin costume, moving to the pulsing beat of disco music, looking not at all like a little girl, she mixes baffling magic with an easy informality, exchanging jokes with the audience, topping good-natured heckling in a way that guarantees laughter.

Choosing some outspoken man in the audience to be her "victim," she dares him to come up and be sawed in half. Usually she gets someone who can be coaxed into acting up to the challenge, so that he joins in the fun with feigned fear. As she puts him into an open framework and applies a power saw to his midsec-

tion, she tells him, "Don't worry. If this doesn't work, I'll send you home in two taxis."

When she first contemplated sawing men in half, she discovered that the standard apparatus for the illusion wasn't designed to accommodate wide-waisted males, and so she had to have the device specially enlarged. She has also made over other tricks, such as those calling for the use of pockets, jackets, and other hiding places that male magicians take for granted, but which aren't available to a woman in a close-fitting costume. She has redesigned most of her props to not only provide substitute areas of concealment but to also make them more feminine in style and decoration.

Her main hobby is doing magic,

planning magic, and talking magic with magicians. But other hobbies include palmistry, handwriting analysis, a collection of more than two hundred puppets, and collecting magic posters and books. Her advice to beginners is to read everything they can about magic, to see as many magic shows as they can, and then to practice and perform as often as possible for family, friends, and anybody else who will watch.

"It's fine to practice before a mirror, but you can master a trick in practice and still fall apart when you do it in front of people," she says. "You have to do magic with an audience, so you can get a playback from them."

Shelley Carroll

Singer, dancer, aspiring young actress making the rounds of Broadway theater auditions and booking offices, Shelley Carroll never thought of becoming a magician—until it struck her that this might be an attention-catching way to showcase her talents. But when she tried magic, she found herself under a spell that turned her toward a full-time career as a professional magician. She likes to say that "it was love at first sleight."

Shelley Carroll has the distinction of being one of the few women among the rising young stars of magic who has gained prominence as a skilled performer of sleight-of-

While linking and unlinking the rings, Dorothy Dietrich brings the audience into her act by joking back and forth with spectators when she is performing informally in the intimate little theater room of the Magic Towne House in New York.

Golf is not her game, but producing eight golf balls at her fingertips is one of the things Shelley Carroll does expertly as a skilled sleight of hand manipulator and professionally trained actress, singer, and dancer who found in magic a way to combine her talents in a unique presentation to make her "different from all the rest."

funeral-directing business the family has operated for more than half a century. But Shelley had a different ambition.

It began when she was seven and her mother took her to see a stage production of *The King and I*, after which Shelley declared that some day she was going to be an actress. Her parents didn't take the childish announcement seriously, but she never had any other ambition. Throughout her school years she was in all her school plays; at the age of ten she had a song-and-dance act she put on at social gatherings. Later, she became involved in community theater. She also won state

hand manipulations. With a minimum of tricky props or elaborate apparatus, she makes cards, golf balls, and other objects appear, multiply, change, and vanish at her fingertips. She does all this with a dancer's graceful style of movement, and with the ability of a trained actress to project her personality as an entertainer.

Her parents named her Carol Lee Shelly, which she later changed to Shelley Carroll after she joined the Screen Actors Guild, because there was another Carol Shelly in the union. She was born in the small Pennsylvania town of Lansdale, near Philadelphia, where her father, an undertaker, hoped his only child would grow up to take over the

Her father hoped she would grow up to be an undertaker, as he is and her grandmother once was, but Shelley Carroll dreamed of success in the Broadway theater, and then fell in love—with magic.

Shelley Carroll
"The Magicienne"

prizes for dramatic poetry readings, and as a high school senior starred in a play that had been entered in a statewide competition with a hundred others. Her performance won her an award as best actress. That brought an offer of a two-year acting apprenticeship at the famed Bucks County Playhouse, but she turned it down to enter Rollins College in Winter Park, Florida, where she got her bachelor's degree as a theater major.

At Rollins, she not only learned stagecraft, lighting, costuming, and designing and building scenery, but gained broad acting and directing experience. She added to this during the summers by acting at regional theaters, dinner playhouses, and in summer stock. Her graduation in 1973 also brought the exciting possibility that a play she had directed might be destined for a major New York production.

The show, a new concept of the *Dracula* story, on which she had collaborated with playwright Robert Arter, won all sorts of awards and critical acclaim and took her and Arter to New York to discuss its possible production there with Broadway producer Morton Gottlieb. But Arter was seriously injured in a crippling accident and her plans for further work on the show were abandoned.

To pay her rent, she now took a job as a bank teller in midtown Manhattan, and during her lunch hour she joined other Broadway hopefuls who were seeking acting jobs at open "cattle call" auditions. Meanwhile, at night, she took sev-eral long strides in her show-business career with singing engagements at such popular nightclubs as Rodney Dangerfield's and the Yellow Brick Road. "But I realized I was just one among a million trying to make it in this business," she recalls, "and that if I wanted to get anywhere I had better find myself a gimmick."

One of the other tellers at the bank mentioned that her kid brother was about to take a course in magic that was being advertised by a school for would-be magicians. "The fact that her brother was twelve years old did not shed a sophisticated light on my aspiring plans for stardom," Shelley says. "But I phoned, found out it was not only for kids, and I enrolled. I simply figured magic was another side of show business I should become acquainted with, since I knew nothing about it."

The magic school was one then being operated by professionals Frank Garcia and George Schindler. Shelley's first class was in January 1974, and she was so "completely enthralled by this strange art called magic" that after that first session she talked to Garcia about her theatrical career, told him she wanted to become a really professional magician, and asked for his help.

Garcia answered that it would "take a lot of hard work, a lot of practice, blood, sweat and tears," but agreed to do what he could for her. Shelley luckily had found one of magic's best, and as it turned out, most generous teachers.

"He took me under his wing,

never charging me a dime for all the painstaking hours he coached me and the props he gave me, and consequently I became his protégée," she says. "He was right that it would take a lot of hard work because all he taught me was sleight of hand. At the time I didn't know the difference, but he kept telling me it would separate me from the other 'lady magicians.' He became my friend and my acting New York father, and because of the way he treated me I hope someday I can do the same for someone else."

Ten months after her first magic lesson, Shelley gave her first public performance, with Garcia and two other magicians, at a benefit show staged by a church in Forest Hills, New York, to raise funds for a children's camp. "It was a far cry from Shakespeare and Neil Simon, but I'll never forget it as long as I live. Never before or since have I been so nervous on any stage as I was that night."

But her act went well, she was a hit with the audience, and as she left the stage, Garcia beamed and said, "See, I've created a monster." From that moment on, she knew magic was to be her future. "I had found what I had been looking for," she says. "I knew that if I worked at magic, I could make it work for me."

Within another six months, by the spring of 1975, Shelley Carroll was a full-time professional, earning her living solely from magic, as she has ever since. Bookings that followed featured her at New York clubs, the Plaza Hotel, the Caravan, took her to the Music Hall in Houston, the Playboy clubs, leading resorts from the Catskills to Hawaii.

Between longer engagements, there were one-night and weekend club dates, and a string of television commercials. She also won the respect of her peers, performing at an annual public show staged by her fellow members of the Society of American Magicians, and also at magic conventions.

She has put a lot of hard work into building her career. "It *is* a business and it must be treated as such," she says. "If you are good enough, believe in yourself, have enough people see your act, eventually you will get your break. But attitude is so important. You have to keep going, keep at your best, even when the going is rough. And you must keep in touch with the agents all the time. They are not looking for you. But it is the entertainer's job to convince an agent he *does* need you and *only* you."

She has made it a rule to put at least one-third of whatever she earns back into the act as an investment. There are copies of photographs to be made (she runs through a hundred of those in a month), publicity releases and brochures, new props, backup props, new costuming, dozens of other expenses. "There have been weeks when I didn't earn a dime, and a few times when I've been hard pressed for rent or food money, but I still have to invest in the act."

Magic, combined with her acting, dancing, and singing, gives her the "added plus" in selling her shows as

Magic with a dancer's grace of movement. Shelley Carroll makes it all look easy, which isn't easy to do.

Shelley Carroll spoofs the Cut and Restored Rope trick.

It takes smart presentation as well as practiced skill at sleight of hand, which is why from her own experience Shelley Carroll advises any woman serious about a magic career to study acting, voice, and dance.

a unique presentation. For her full-length thirty-minute act, she performs fifteen minutes of magical pantomime and dance, "with the heavy stuff up front," then fifteen minutes of comedy and audience participation, and finishes with a "Joel Gray type number" that tells the story of her life as a girl breaking into show business—with a touch of pathos that leaves the audience with something to think

about. Even in shorter presentations, her aim always is to make the audience remember her as a person, not merely a "lady magician."

"It is your personality that sells you to an audience," she says. "If you just do magic tricks, even though they may be the best in the world, people will never remember your name. I believe there must be an emotional bond between the audience and you as a performer. There has to be a real personal relationship, so they like you as an individual, not just for what you do. I consider myself and book myself as an entertainer rather than as a magician."

She feels it is harder for a woman to become a successful professional magician than for a man, partly because agents are used to booking male magicians and their first reaction is to wonder how good a woman magician can be. "You have to overcome their reluctance to gamble on putting you into a show," she says. "But once you prove you are good, then they want you because you do have something different to offer. The fact that there are so few professionals among women in magic is something I don't understand, because it can be made a great selling feature for an act."

Show business is filled with attractive young women, and Shelley Carroll is among them, but her act is based on her personality as an entertainer and her ability at sleight of hand. "There are as many women in my audiences as there are men and as a performer I must appeal to both," she says. "I don't go in for tacky, out-of-place costuming." Usually attired in a full-length tail-coated formal evening suit, her whole approach to the act is to do it "with a touch of class." As she puts it frankly, "I am not selling sex. I am selling my hands."

Look again and the cards may vanish or the cane float through the air. But whatever happens, Shelley Carroll will do it with "a touch of class."

When it comes to secretly using her hands to "steal" hidden things she is about to produce, she believes she has some advantage over male performers. "By the way I move, kick, do a spin-around, the misdirection becomes a natural part of my movements, but a man can't move in the same way without looking terribly unmasculine," she says. "It is true that many props and effects are made for men, not so much in size since there are a lot of men with small hands, but the way they are built or designed to be used is very masculine."

There are two things a woman can do about that, she suggests. "Either have the effect made up to suit her decor, or have a way of handling the props that will look more graceful. It all boils down to the fact that if you are really eager enough to do something, you'll work it out."

From her own experience she is convinced that any woman who is serious about making a career of magic should learn theater, take acting lessons, learn body movement, attend speech classes. "Then learn sleight of hand," she says. "It does take a lot of time and practice, but you will have learned a skill that not many other women have, and you can go just about anywhere in magic from there."

4

LECTURING AND TEACHING

Hundreds of magicians, in addition to performing what the public usually thinks of as magic shows, are involved in doing magic as lecturers and teachers.

Magic is taught to hobby classes of children, adults, and senior citizens. It's taught in high schools and colleges, at recreation centers and summer camps, and by private instruction. It is taught as a tool of communication, as a means of improving personality, as a way of expanding social and business contacts, and for fun.

There are lessons designed for salesmen, corporation executives, theater-arts students. High school and grade school teachers who are magic hobbyists often use magic as an aid in the classroom teaching of reading, math, science, and social studies. It is sometimes used in mental or physical therapy to help the troubled or disabled.

Some magicians tour the college and auditorium lecture circuits with programs about magic or such related subjects as gambling, the occult, and the psychology of deception. Others use magic to illustrate lecture shows about all sorts of themes: public safety, law enforcenent, drug addiction, ecology, and consumer protection.

Lecturing to Magicians

Many well-known magicians lecture about magic to other magicians. They tour the nation's magic clubs, sometimes traveling long distances to appear at several different clubs the same week. Some magic dealers also sponsor lectures, and in some cities there are independently run magic lecture series. At any of the big national conventions, there are likely to be up to a dozen lecturers on the program.

The professionals who do most of the lecturing, and who make a good business of showing other magicians how their tricks are done, usually schedule their lecture dates to fit in with other engagements in a particular area. Some clubs pay for a lecture out of the club treasury, inviting all members to attend; others charge an admission fee. At conventions, the registration fees usually include the lectures. But for special lectures an added admission may be charged.

The magic-lecture business is international, with many European performers lecturing to magicians in America, and Americans lecturing to clubs and conventions in foreign countries. One popular British magician-lecturer, Geoffrey Buckingham, has traveled more than fifty thousand miles during a series of lecture tours of the United States and Canada, and others have made repeated tours, coming up with a new lecture each season.

In addition to whatever fee a lecturer may receive, he profits from the sale of printed lecture notes, usually bought by almost everbody who attends, and also sold by magic dealers around the country. Some lecture notes amount to small magic books in themselves, well-illustrated and giving detailed explanations of everything that was demonstrated. Others are brief and sketchy, with only bare-bones explanations, intended merely to jog the memory of those who may otherwise forget what was said or done.

But lecture-goers also profit, not only from the knowledge they may gain of specific methods, misdirection, showmanship, and presentation but also from watching expert magic expertly performed. They delight in seeing a famous magician work, and in being fooled by him before he reveals his secrets to them.

The average magic hobbyist goes to a lecture hoping he can take home something that is within the limits of his skill and resources, something he immediately recognizes as clever, simple in method, practical, and effective. But even if the lecture material is beyond his immediate skill, he usually admires lecturers who are famed for their dazzling and intricate sleight of hand, because he goes not only to learn magic. He also wants to be entertained.

Howard Schwarzman

"My approach to a lecture is as a show," says Howard Schwarzman, who gives a lot of magic lectures. "It has to be more than an evening of talk and finger-flinging. If a magi-

Professional magic lecturer Howard Schwarzman, who at the age of fifty resumed the full-time magic career he had started more than thirty years before, after having become an expert at magic as a hobbyist during all the years between.

cian is supposed to be an entertainer, then a lecturer who is demonstrating how to do it must do it entertainingly—if he wants to put across what he is teaching."

Schwarzman quit a high-paying sales position late in 1977 and at the age of fifty turned his lifetime hobby of magic into a full-time profession, resuming the career as a professional magician that he had started more than thirty years before. Within less than a year, he had lectured to more than forty clubs and conventions across the country,

and was also involved in trade shows and in close-up and stage performing.

During his years of pursuing magic as a hobby, Schwarzman had become well recognized as an expert at sleight of hand and as an unusually skilled entertainer who frequently appeared at convention shows. He had edited magic books by other experts, was an originator of published routines eagerly adopted by fellow magicians, and was already a popular lecturer long before he turned to lecturing as a profession.

"Besides having great skill, he has a complete understanding of the importance of producing strong effects," Dai Vernon, the dean of magicians most admired by other magicians, has said of Schwarzman. "Whenever Howie does magic, it looks like magic."

Schwarzman has been doing magic almost always—at least since the age of five when an uncle taught him his first tricks. As a youth in New York, he joined the then city-sponsored magic club FAME, gave shows throughout his high school years, and during World War II was a USO entertainer. Drawn into the army himself in 1946-48, he did special services shows.

But when he got out of the army there wasn't enough steady work to be had as a magician, so he reluctantly put his magic on a hobby basis, took a starting job as a door-to-door salesman, and began a sales career. By 1962, living in Baltimore with his wife Laura, he had become a manufacturer's representative for a nationally known men's clothing company. He had also taken up flying, was a fully licensed commercial pilot, and when not selling clothing he flew a plane about the country to do magic. (This is still the way he prefers to travel, piloting himself when there are long hops to be made on his magic tours.) But the pull of magic finally won out over salesmanship and as Schwarzman neared the age of fifty, he decided it was probably then or never.

He now reconverted his hobby into a full-time profession, applied his business training to making a business of magic, made lecturing to magicians his specialty, and at last is successfully doing what he always really wanted to do, "happy and content," he says, with his decision.

Over the years, Schwarzman had seen hundreds of lecturers, some excellent, some good, some dull and boring. The poor ones, he decided, talked too much and didn't demonstrate enough; often, they seemed to be rummaging through a bag of unrelated tricks, flatly presented with rambling explanations. Knowing that magic must be entertaining, whether for magicians or public audiences, he planned and rehearsed his lectures as a show, but with the material programmed for magicians.

What he shows and teaches in his lectures are not just tricks, but full routines. He inserts comedy bits, "inside" jokes, stories out of his own experience or about things that have happened to great performers he has known—to make it more fun, but also to make a point. There is a lot of laughter during Schwarzman's lectures and he tends to make himself the butt of his own jokes. "I take my magic seriously," he says, "but not myself."

After a regular lecture to a magic club, he frequently stays overnight to give private lessons the next day, or to give a separate special lecture to a small group gathered to watch him demonstrate advanced card-handling technique. He also may be booked to do a public show in the same city. But mainly he is a professional magic lecturer and a teacher of magicians.

George Schindler

In his teaching of magic and in his lectures to magic clubs throughout the country, George Schindler urges magicians to think less about fooling people and more about entertaining them. He believes that far too many of today's magic hobbyists become so intent on the mechanics of doing tricks that they lose sight of the real purpose of performing, which is to provide entertainment.

"My tricks and routines are not intended to 'amaze' or 'mystify' anyone," Schindler tells the magicians who hear him lecture. "They are designed to keep my audiences entertained." He explains that he doesn't mean that methods and techniques can be ignored. "They are important to your presentation.

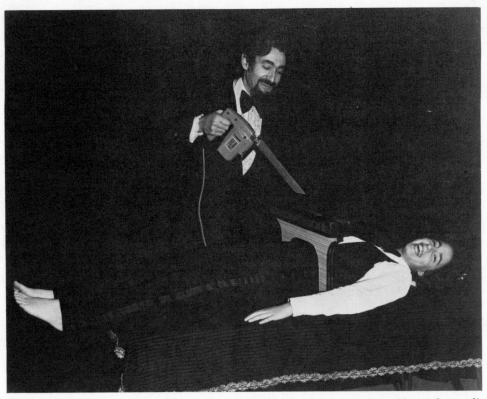

George Schindler, entertainingly dealing here with the magical problem of a split personality, had a boyhood ambition to become a magician, a teacher, or a writer. He grew up to be all three: a professional magician, a teacher of magic, and a writer of magic books.

But they are not important in themselves, as far as the audience is concerned. The primary appeal of magic is entertainment, and that is what should be put first."

Schindler feels that much of the problem comes from judging material from the viewpoint of what pleases other magicians. "As magicians, *we* are entertained by the moves, mystifications, and ingenuity of our fellow magicians," he says. "But *we* are not 'ordinary people,' the kind you perform for outside of magic meetings. The layman who watches you apparently pass some coins through a solid tabletop doesn't care if it was accomplished by this method or that approach. His reaction is what is important, the fact that he is amused, surprised, and pleased, and the end effect should be reached by the simplest and most direct route."

Born in 1929 in Brooklyn, New York, where he still lives with his wife Nina and their three children, Schindler got a toy magic set for his eleventh birthday, soon was earning pocket money entertaining at neighborhood parties, and at the age of sixteen became a performer in nightclubs. He continued his education at Brooklyn College, where he studied to become a teacher. But when he graduated he left teaching behind and became a full-time professional magician, playing clubs, theaters, and cruise ships.

In the early 1950s, he worked at what was then Holden's Magic Shop in New York, demonstrating and selling magic to magicians. In 1955, he left the magic business temporarily and turned to other fields of entertainment. He became a comedian and master of ceremonies in nightclubs, also successfully developed his talent as a ventriloquist, and toured with a partner in an act of music and pantomime.

But magic was his first love, and by 1960 he had brought back his earlier act, combining it with comedy and a fast, witty, ad-lib style of delivery that established him as a "magicomedian." He entertained at resort hotels, played the New York club-date field, added big illusions to the act at times, but also gained recognition for his close-up magic and comedy at trade shows.

In 1973 Schindler was one of the founders of a school for magicians in New York, and although he no longer runs a magic school, he privately instructs many individuals and small groups. He teaches salesmen how to do simple tricks they can carry around in their pockets to help them ingratiate themselves with prospective customers, shows bartenders how to amuse their patrons with magic, and has housewives, business executives, doctors, and dentists among his students. One of the dentists wanted lessons in doing tricks with little balls of cotton and other things used in dental work, so as to ease the fears that some young children have of visiting the dentist.

Schindler has recorded magic lessons on tape cassettes, teaches magic in the books he writes, and each spring stages a weekend of magic for magicians at Grossinger's resort hotel in the Catskills; it amounts to a small convention, with famed guest magicians, lectures, contests, and shows.

Aware from his own childhood experience of how much a magic set can do to inspire interest in magic as a hobby, Schindler helped to create a complete line of magic sets and individually packaged tricks that are marketed in department stores and elsewhere by a major manufacturer of toys and games. He has toured the country and also in England, demonstrating and promoting the sales of the packaged tricks and of his magic books, making the circuits of local television talk shows. He has also staged and produced television magic shows and has made TV commercials. During radio station interviews, he has often performed card tricks for "invisible audiences" of listeners, telling them what to do with their own packs of cards at home so they can wind up fooling themselves with his magic.

In his magic-club and convention lectures, Schindler has made a specialty of demonstrating and teaching what he calls "stand-up close-up magic"—the kind of audience-participation tricks that can be done without the need of a table, so the performer can carry the props in his pockets and freely move about to entertain various groups at a party or other gathering.

Magic clubs like to invite non-magicians to be their guests at after-meeting shows, but they can't invite outsiders to lectures that reveal how tricks are done. Schindler solves that problem to satisfy everybody by first presenting forty minutes of straight entertainment, doing an act exactly as the public would see it, without making any explanations. Then, after the club's invited guests have seen the show and left the meeting room, and only the magicians remain, he takes his act apart and explains the secrets step by step.

Magic Teaching

Many semi-professional as well as professional magicians give private magic lessons, organize classes, offer courses, or operate their own local magic schools, and nearly every magic shop has someone available to give magic lessons.

But the greatest growth in the teaching of magic in recent years has been in the hobby courses sponsored by state universities, community and junior colleges, and high schools as part of continuing education programs for young people or adults; these courses have created hundreds of new magic hobbyists.

Some magicians who are school-teachers by profession have also taken magic directly into their classrooms, not merely to amuse their pupils but to enrich their daily learning experiences.

John Pooley

John Pooley, who teaches at the Hyatt Elementary School in Riverside, California, has developed the educational uses of magic in his fourth-grade classroom and has also

John Pooley uses educational magic as a school teacher to help make the learning of science, social studies, math, and other subjects a lot more fun for his fourth-grade students. He also conducts university courses to teach other teachers how to use magic in their classrooms.

112

given courses at the University of California to show others how to teach with magic.

An aerospace engineer before he turned to a teaching career, Pooley spends his nights and weekends as a very busy magician, performing shows at clubs, parties, and shopping centers. In 1957, long before he became a schoolteacher, he began teaching magic by offering a "magician's workshop" course at Inglewood. Sponsored by a local dance studio, the two-hour magic classes every Friday night generated good newspaper publicity and attracted a lot of would-be magicians as students. Most of them continued their interest, and Pooley conducted the classes for many weeks.

That first workshop became the basis for courses he later taught at YMCAs and other places. Beginners were taught basic tricks with familiar objects. Each lesson included three or four tricks, starting with the simplest puzzle-like effects with strings and rubber bands and gradually progressing to magic with paper, ropes, coins, balls, cards, and so on. Lectures were kept short to allow adequate time for learning, and the number of students in each group was limited, to give individual help to those who needed it—and so that everybody had a chance to get up and perform.

Students were taught something about the history of magic, patter, and presentation, and Pooley emphasized the need to entertain rather than just "do tricks." He stressed presentation from the start of the lessons, with tables set up for student performances. Spotlights and recorded music were available. "I emphasized having the students stand up, speak up, and hold up the props so they could be seen," says Pooley. "My purpose was to teach and not to dominate the meetings with my own skill as a performer."

Each student was told to bring a small box or carrying case for props, together with a notebook. Students also supplied their own easily obtained materials, with Pooley providing any specially needed extras such as magician's wax or soft rope. Elaborate props were ruled out, as were complicated sleights and fancy manipulations.

Before each class session ended Pooley would perform the tricks that were to be taught the following week, without explaining how they were done. This helped to maintain a continuing interest in the course. "I found it imperative to have lesson plans worked out in advance," he says. "These were handed out weekly, so students would have an outline of what was to come and a list of the materials needed."

As Pooley's interest in educational magic grew, along with his interest in teaching in public schools, he worked with a local educational television station and produced a special show sponsored by the PTA. Called "A World of Magic," it was repeatedly televised by various stations and was still being shown six years after he made it.

Meanwhile he became a substitute schoolteacher, which led to a part-time teaching job, and he was presently put in charge of an "exploration school" for gifted children. In 1975, he moved to the Riverside school district, became a full-time teacher, and in addition to his public performing as a magician started to develop fully his concept of the uses of magic in classroom teaching. His university courses in teaching magic to other teachers evolved from that, and from his earlier experiences conducting the "magician's workshops" course.

In his classes at the Hyatt Elementary School, where he teaches fourth graders aged nine and ten, Pooley uses some tricks to demonstrate specific lessons in various schoolroom subjects, others to provoke eager curiosity and questioning, or just to provide an atmosphere that makes learning a lot more fun.

To teach his pupils about circles, squares, and straight lines in a way they will remember, he may hold up a large metal circle and visibly transform it into a metal square. The youngsters are also not likely to forget a science lesson that involves pumping a sudden flow of green water into a funnel from the arm of a classmate, or a math lesson taught by magically producing the aces from a pack of cards.

There are some tricks Pooley teaches them to do themselves, so as to get them to read and follow directions. "Learning magic means learning to read instructions carefully and follow them," he points out. "These are skills that children often lack today. In magic, if you don't follow directions, you don't get the desired effect."

Pooley has developed some sixty tricks, card-catalogued and adaptable to various instructional uses, that form the basis of the magic teaching. His classroom has a "magic center," with children's magic books, posters and art work depicting magic and magicians, recordings such as Mickey Mouse as "The Sorcerer's Apprentice," and other things of magical interest to children.

In the fall of 1976 the University of California Extension at Riverside offered Pooley's "magician's workshop" course, announcing that it would be "of value to elementary school teachers, recreation leaders, occupational therapists and other professional people working with children." Enrollment for the five-week course was filled two months before it began and it was very successful, but Pooley himself wasn't satisfied with it. Basically it was still a beginner's course in how to do magic, and what he was working toward was one more directly tied in with classroom teaching.

During the next summer he worked out a new course, approved by the university's education department, which he first called "Magic, A Teaching and Learning Tool." A three-unit credit course with nine weekly three-hour sessions from January to March, it was made a part of the 1978 winter program at Riverside, and renamed "Using Magic to Improve Children's Learning." Its purpose was to help the teacher create a good learning atmosphere through the use of magic and to show "how to set up instructional presentations and classroom projects."

The course was so popular and teachers so enthusiastic that it was given again during the summer of 1978 at a special one-week seminar. Pooley developed the seven-hour seminar meetings so that four hours were devoted to teaching the magic in his basic series of sixty tricks, and three hours were given to showing how to apply the tricks to specific teaching problems and projects various teachers had in mind. There were also brainstorming sessions that produced many new ways of applying magic to classroom teaching.

"I am firmly convinced that students are motivated wherever magic is used," says Pooley, "whether it be an academic subject, nonacademic subjects such as physical education, music, and art, or in the areas of classroom management and discipline."

Paul Klingler

Performing professionally as "Paulo the Magic Clown," Paul Klingler teaches a number of magic-hobby courses. Some are part of adult education programs; others are included in community projects for children at schools in various cities near Klingler's Belleville, New Jersey, home. He often teaches several different classes a week and has developed the teaching into a prof-

itable sideline to his public performing.

He has been a magician for more than twenty-five years since giving his first paid show when he was twelve, and has also become a successful children's entertainer. As "Paulo," with his magic clowning and making of toy balloon animals, he entertains children at popular family restaurants. He draws youngsters and their parents to store openings and special sales, stages five-a-day shopping-center shows, and presents Saturday matinee shows for children at area movie theaters.

"Strictly corny" is the way Paul Klingler laughingly describes his professional fun-making as "Paulo the Magic Clown," and laughing audiences of children agree. A successful children's entertainer, Klingler has also developed his school teaching of magic to adults as well as children into a profitable sideline to his public performing.

As an experienced teacher of magic, Klingler has planned a series of courses to fit into various educational programs, so that basically the same courses can be taught at different schools. He also combined teaching assignments, with two or more classes at one school the same evening.

Typical of the adult education classes Klingler has taught were those at the Nutley, New Jersey high school. The program was among a number of ten-week evening courses offered from September to December in subjects ranging from shorthand, typing, foreign languages, and automobile mechanics to career planning, photography, bridge, golf, dancing, and yoga. These courses were open to all adults or high school students at a fee of about twenty dollars per course, and at a minimum fee of only three dollars for senior citizens. There was an additional small cost for classroom materials, which in the magic course included such items as cards and rope. Klingler was paid on an hourly basis as the teacher.

Each Monday night he taught his two-hour beginner's course, "Magic Is Fun." Students learned such tricks as how to tie a knot in a pocket handkerchief without letting go of the ends, basic sleight of hand with cards and coins, rope and sponge ball effects—and how to present these entertainingly. The class was limited to twenty students.

The first year that Klingler taught in a somewhat similar adult education program at the nearby Pompton Lakes high school, he offered the "Magic Is Fun" course. In his second year of teaching there, he repeated the beginner's course for new students, and also held an advanced course for those who had already taken the beginning lessons. Both classes were taught, one right after the other, in the same classroom each Thursday night for ten weeks. Much of the time in the second course was devoted not only to learning more advanced tricks, but to perfecting performing skills and presentation.

In teaching children, Klingler adapts his beginner's course to various age groups. For the Glen Rock Community School's program of Saturday morning classes in a variety of hobbies and other subjects of special interest to children, class enrollment was according to school grades. Klingler taught third and fourth graders a "Magic for Moppets" course, to give them some appreciation of what magic is all about, and to show them how to do simple magic puzzles for the fun of fooling their friends. Older children, from the fifth and sixth grades, were taught his "Magic is Fun" course.

Sam Wishner

Sam Wishner, better known to his audiences as "Zovello," has been teaching magic and using magic to teach many other things for a good

116

Sam Wishner, known to audiences as "Zovello," has put a half-century of professional performing experience into his teaching of magic as a performing art. He is pictured here during the years he was NBC television's original magic clown.

part of the more than half a century that he has been a professional magician.

He teaches classes of adults and children at several New York schools, has been in charge of the magic instruction at a summer camp that trains young people in the theatrical arts, has created city parks department teaching and performing programs, is a lecturer on magic to magicians, and has conducted workshop sessions of the Parent Assembly of the Society of American Magicians.

As a performer, Zovello was the original magic clown of a long-running NBC children's television program, and was "The Sultan of Magic" on another New York television series. He has entertained hundreds of audiences in theaters, outdoor showplaces, and at trade shows. The U.S. Postal Service once employed him for three years as a "Magic Mailman" to present magic shows that would teach "good postal habits" to thousands of children in the public schools.

"There is more to magic than a trick to fool or puzzle," Wishner tells beginning students. "It is a medium for expressing personality in a dramatic or theatrical fashion. Magic is a creative tool to challenge the imagination."

His classes stress the *performing* of magic and the need always to keep in mind that it *is* a "performing art," not merely an acquiring of tricks, techniques, and apparatus. "Unlike other self-interest pursuits and hobbies," he points out, "magic to be enjoyed must be shared. The performer requires an audience, whether one-to-one or in an auditorium."

Wishner takes some of his students out on performing "field trips" after their fourth classroom lesson, when they have learned to present a few tricks and have put in some time rehearsing. He encourages them to volunteer for performances he arranges at senior citizen centers and in hospital wards. He goes with them, starts off the entertainment by performing himself, and then has them perform.

117

The free entertainment is welcomed and the students have practical experience giving their first public shows—within weeks after starting to learn magic.

Wishner believes that with the booming interest in magic as a hobby newcomers are often caught up in an enthusiasm to rush out and buy whatever dealers advertise as new and easy to do—gimmicks, gadgets, and flashy apparatus, all sorts of things that are impractical for a beginner. "Some of them wind up with trunks and closets full of stuff they will never present publicly," he says. "They ignore the classical and charming effects requiring practice because they assume they are too difficult to learn. But there are many fine things that can be learned with a minimum of practice, basic things that lead to the easier learning of other things. Just as in music, you must practice the scales before you can play."

That is where a good teacher can really help, he feels, by "teaching magic progressively," starting with a simple basic sleight or move, which when learned can be incorporated into a series of effects that lead to something more advanced. Wishner frequently teaches a series of coin tricks, for example, that gradually lead the student into performing a coin-catching routine for an entertaining version of the classic "miser's dream." There is no overwhelming complexity of sleights to learn and practice all at once. The student learns step by step, by doing each trick in the series, has fun presenting it, and also gains in self-con-fidence by performing it successfully. "It may be a cliché, but it is true," Wishner says, "that in learning to do magic nothing succeeds like success."

A teacher of magic in the New York City schools has to obtain a certificate of competency from the Board of Education, which requires an examination of his knowledge of magic and ability to teach it. Other big cities have somewhat similar requirements, but a certificate is not always necessary in some smaller communities, where a magician may arrange directly with a local school administrator to teach a magic-hobby course. After a course has been announced, it must attract a large enough enrollment to keep it in the program.

The continuing series of courses Wishner has taught each winter and spring at the Adult Education Center of New York's Stuyvesant High School are spaced out over eight-week periods, with each of the various classes meeting one evening a week for a two-hour session. The courses have always been over-subscribed, with a combined enroll-ment of some seventy-five students, and seldom a single dropout. Wishner also teaches younger students in the after-school program of the Cal-houn School.

His advice to a classroom teacher of magic, whether working with adults or children, is to begin the very first lesson with the *doing* of magic, not just talking about it—by entertainingly performing some good but simple trick the students can almost immediately learn. "The

118

instructor should be equipped at the start to teach an effect that stirs attention and surprise," he says. "One that requires nothing to buy, no previously learned skill, and a minimum of practice, if any. There are many such effects."

One of his favorite lesson-starters is showing two pieces of string and magically joining them together into a single length. He then shows how easily it was accomplished, but makes students realize they were entertained by the simple trick because it was amusingly routined and presented. Five minutes into the first class session, they are performing magic themselves.

Before the first lesson is over he will teach them tricks with dollar bills, cards and coins, rolled-up paper napkins, newspaper comic sheets, a pocket handkerchief that turns into a dancing girl. He also will have taught them something about the psychology of misdirection, and started them learning several moves and sleights on which many other tricks are based. Each student is given lesson lecture notes for home review.

"A sufficient variety of effects should be taught so students may make a choice to suit their individual preference," he says. "The purpose of the beginner's course is to teach the basic sleights for effective and easy-to-do routines with readily accessible articles, and with emphasis on presentation."

During the summers, Wishner has supervised the teaching of magic as a performing art to coeducational groups of young people from eight to eighteen at Stagedoor Manor, a summer camp at Loch Sheldrake, New York, which offers classes, workshops, and training in all branches of the theatrical arts. The camp, with luxury hotel accommodations and four theaters is fully equipped with modern stage facilities, and attracts young people aspiring toward careers in drama, music, dance, playwriting, directing, costuming, and scenic design. Those who major in magic get individual as well as class instruction.

The course includes stage and close-up magic, stage presence and movement, patter, mime, makeup. Each student is guided toward preparing a personal magic act, depending on age and ability. Students are required to perform weekly for the public and are encouraged to take part in the camp's other theatrical productions. Some of them also perform at nearby hotels and resorts.

Tannen's Magic Camp

Magic is taught at various summer camps as part of their craft and hobby programs. But a unique camping experience, devoted *entirely* to learning and performing magic, has drawn an enrollment of some two-hundred magic-minded boys of ages ten to twenty to a week-long magic camp held each August at the La Salle Military Academy at Oakdale, Long Island, about fifty miles from New York City.

119

Show time at magic camp gives young performers a chance to take center stage and demonstrate their skill and originality, as in these scenes from Tannen's camp. For a full week, several hundred boys from age ten to twenty do magic, practice magic, live magic, take lessons from magic instructors, listen to lectures, and see well-known magicians perform. PHOTOS BY HOWARD PALINSKY

Started in 1974 by William Camacho, an amateur magician and full-time director of La Salle's special activities, and sponsored by Louis Tannen, Inc., the New York magic company, the camp is conducted on the preparatory school's two-hundred-acre wooded campus, with the boys housed in its dorms.

There are outdoor playing fields, tennis and basketball courts, indoor gyms, a heated olympic-sized swimming pool, and a golf course. But what the boys come for, some from homes as far away as California, is magic. And they get that for a full week—morning, noon, and night.

The week's tuition includes room and board, and a kit of magic supplies and tricks for each camper, furnished by Tannen's, which rents the dormitory facilities from the academy and also provides the teachers, the performers, and the feast of magic. Camacho directs the camp and staff. "It's a good way for the kids to learn their real inclinations in magic," he says. "They have a chance to experiment with everything from cards and coins to illusions, an opportunity to exchange ideas, to be taught by top performers, and to watch them perform."

There are morning and afternoon class sessions, a full magic show every night, and a chance to meet, talk to, and collect the autographs of leading professionals. In between, there is personal tutoring. A "late room" is provided for the older boys, who are allowed to stay up later than the younger ones to practice and learn more on a personal basis from the visiting pros

and resident magicians. The magic camp week is climaxed with talent shows of both stage and close-up magic, with competition for prizes of magic books and equipment.

The camp usually has about twenty magicians who take part in the teaching and magic counseling. Two-thirds of the campers are returnees from previous years. The enrollment is limited and generally filled long before each August.

Using Magic in Public Lectures

Magic's teaching and lecturing activities have their public side in the "lecture show." Unlike a "magic lecture," which is what a magician gives when he explains tricks to an audience of other magicians, the "lecture show" is a term applied to the whole range of specialized presentations that combine an educational lecture on any subject with a magic show.

The successful lecture show requires an approach different from the usual magic show. Instead of using tricks for their effect as tricks alone, the magician-lecturer uses magic to illustrate or emphasize the ideas he wants to put across. The tricks *are* entertaining, amusing, puzzling, but their magical effect is secondary to their purpose in demonstrating or dramatizing the lecturer's principal subject. In a magic show, the "patter" is used to make the tricks more entertaining; in a lecture show the tricks are chosen to make the *talk* more entertaining.

A particularly active branch of lecture shows is gospel magic, in which magic is used by touring evangelists, ministers, and church and Sunday school workers to teach religion and Bible lessons. The gospel magicians, of whom there are several thousand, have their own magic associations, literature, and magazines. Some professional magician-evangelists tour the country, using their skill as entertainers to present gospel messages in hundreds of churches, for youth groups, and on local television programs, sometimes performing a different show each evening and twice on Sundays. Others are amateurs who devote their magic to church work. There are gospel supply companies in the business of providing complete scripts and all necessary magic equipment for the presentation of Bible lessons.

Another very popular field for magic lecture shows is safety and health. Columns on safety lecturing are regularly printed in magic magazines, and books for magicians have been written on the subject. Many tricks marketed by dealers have safety themes. Some of the safety lecturing is done by police officers who are magicians, and other touring magician-lecturers are sponsored by industrial corporations and insurance companies.

William Hyatt

Police officer William Hyatt of Lakeland, Florida, never expected to be a stage magician, but he combined his hobby with his occupation and created police magic shows that put him on school auditorium stages. The shows also led to his becoming a special crime-prevention officer, and helped bring about the formation of a new police department crime-prevention unit.

Hyatt joined his city's police force at the age of twenty-one, served first as a patrolman and then in the criminal investigation division; he had been a policeman for half a dozen years before he became interested in magic. As an enthusiastic amateur magician, he enjoyed entertaining his friends, but had no thought of performing in public. Magic was his sole hobby and because of his avid interest in it, two of his fellow policemen, Detective William Creamer and officer Terry Willoughby, also took it up as a hobby.

In the summer of 1976, Hyatt decided that it might be fun for them to put together a police magic show. They got involved to the extent that they felt the show was "almost professional," and they planned to present it that September for a group of children and adults at a community center. The policemen-magicians performed, included some safety-themed magic, and introduced as a character who helped them do their tricks an "in-

Happily reclining in space, which he seldom has time to do, is Lakeland, Florida policeman William Hyatt, whose hobby inspired a program of police magic shows. So successful were the shows in the public schools that they helped bring about the creation of a new police-department crime-prevention unit in which Hyatt became a special officer.

visible policeman" called "Officer Do-Right."

The first show was a hit, not only with the audience but with Herbert Straley, Jr., Lakeland's police chief. Straley encouraged Hyatt to develop the show as a means of promoting safety, crime prevention, and public goodwill for the police department. Shortly afterward, Hyatt and his fellow magicians were invited to city hall to appear before the city commission and present a demonstration of their police magic program. The city commissioners were enthusiastic about it too, and the show was taken into the schools throughout the Lakeland area.

Soon there were more requests for performances than they could fill.

Hyatt's show evolved into a series of programs covering various areas of safety and crime prevention. The "invisible policeman," after a year of being invisibly on foot, was modernized. Hyatt and his friends built a small motorized remote-control police car, complete with flashing blue lights, siren, and public address system. Still invisible himself, "Officer Do-Right" now drives the car onto the stage, talks to the students, and answers their questions about police work.

For his concept of the program and the hours of his own time that

A car with an invisible driver is no police problem in Lakeland, Florida, where the magic of Sergeant W.L. Creamer (left) and Officer William Hyatt (right) created this remote-controlled model car, which is driven on·stage by the never-seen but talkative character "Officer Do-Right" during their police magic shows.

he devoted to it, Hyatt was named Police Officer of the Year by a local civic organization. He also won national honors, in competition with 7,500 others, by being chosen as one of the nation's top police officers in a contest sponsored by *Parade* magazine and the International Association of Chiefs of Police.

Meanwhile Chief Straley created a new crime prevention unit of the police department, and in January 1977, assigned Hyatt to it. Hyatt completed a five-week course in crime prevention theory and practice at the National Crime Prevention Institute in Louisville, Kentucky. He was made a crime prevention specialist in the newly organized police unit, of which Sergeant Creamer became supervisor, and the two officers developed a number of related lecture programs and community projects.

Willoughby, one of the three original police magicians, later left the department, but Hyatt and Creamer have continued staging their magic shows as often as their tight schedule of other crime prevention work will allow.

"We feel our program has to give a good bit of credit to magic for its beginning and its present," Hyatt says. "Magic can keep an otherwise dry presentation from becoming boring. Not only are we able to make it interesting and enjoyable for the audience, but we are able to make it enjoyable for ourselves."

Irving Desfor

The world's best-known photographer of magicians, Irving Desfor is also the creator of what probably is magic's longest-running lecture show. It is a blend of photography and magic he put together as a "Photo-Magic" show back in 1948 and has been presenting ever since to audiences of photographers and others around the world.

Even before that, Desfor started photographing magicians in action and has taken thousands of pictures of them for more than forty years. Among magicians he is known as "the photographer" and among photographers as "the magician."

By profession Desfor is neither a photographer nor a magician. But both his hobbies have been directly tied in with his work as a photographic art director and writer of a nationally syndicated newspaper column for camera fans. He has been prominent in the photographic field as a judge of major national photo contests, as a member of panels and seminars, and as a lecturer at camera clubs and photographic conventions.

Magic began for Desfor, a native New Yorker, at the age of twenty-four, in 1931, when he met Dr. Joseph Fries, a New York physician

Irving Desfor, photographer of magicians for more than forty years, shown adjusting a panel of his photo collection for an exhibit at Manhattan Savings Bank in New York. IRVING DESFOR

and skilled amateur magician, at a vacation camp in the Berkshires. Fries got him interested in the hobby and later sponsored him for membership in the New York Parent Assembly of the Society of American Magicians, of which Desfor eventually was to become president.

With photography already a hobby, Desfor naturally was interested in photographing magicians, especially since their performances offered strikingly different and offbeat subject material. The first pictures he took during a magic show were at the Strand Theatre in Brooklyn, in December 1938, where the great Blackstone was appearing. Desfor took his pictures while seated in the audience. Restricted in his use of equipment, he wasn't sure how the pictures would turn out. But the success of his first attempt to photograph a magician on stage under those conditions inspired him to go on.

At about the same time, he began photographing other magicians at shows of the SAM Parent Assembly, then holding its meetings at New York's McAlpin Hotel. He had been wanting to do that since joining the society, but had put it off because he was uncertain how members would react. "Finally, somewhat timidly, I brought a camera to one of the meetings and started taking pictures," he recalls. "Instead of anyone objecting, I was encouraged. They saw to it that I got an unobstructed front seat."

He soon was named the Parent Assembly's official photographer, a

The first of the thousands of pictures that Irving Desfor was to take of magicians in action was this one of the late Harry Blackstone, giving a boy a rabbit during a performance of the Blackstone show at the Strand Theatre in Brooklyn, December 21, 1938. Desfor shot the picture while seated among other spectators in the audience. IRVING DESFOR

position he continued to hold for years to come. It was the beginning of his decades of photographing magic and magicians everywhere: at meetings, banquets, public shows, conventions, and informal gatherings. Countless Desfor pictures have been published in the pages and on

126

the covers of magic magazines, in books and photography journals.

As a performer Desfor's first interest was in sleight of hand, but he also became a clever platform entertainer with apparatus routines. During World War II he gave hundreds of shows at hospitals, canteens, and service centers as a volunteer member of the American Theatre Wing War Service.

In 1948 one of the editors at the Associated Press, where Desfor had become photo art director of AP Newsfeatures, suggested that he try his hand at writing a weekly column for the nation's growing number of camera fans. He took it on in addition to his regular job, at first without extra pay. It was immediately popular and became a regularly published feature in several hundred newspapers. Thirty years later, long after his official retirement from AP in 1972 at the age of sixty-

five, Desfor was still writing the column and newspapers were still publishing it every week.

Called "Camera Angles," the column was written in plain nontechnical language for the average camera fan, and broadly covered the whole photographic field. Desfor often used pictures of magical events and personalities to illustrate it. But for him personally, the column brought about an even closer tying-together of his hobbies. It was the springboard for his "Photo-Magic" lecture shows.

Several months after he first started writing the column, an editor of the *Perth Amboy Evening News* asked him to speak at that New Jersey city's camera club. Desfor couldn't make up his mind what to talk about, and while trying to decide on an interesting topic, he hit upon the idea of combining magic and photography. He built his first-ever lecture around the audience-tested tricks he had been performing as a magician, added a few other standard magic effects, and devised patter and presentations that would furnish a photographic angle.

But since the format was all new to him he didn't know how to time the length of the program. On the night of the lecture, he took to the platform at Perth Amboy's public library a little after nine in the evening. He was still performing at midnight, when the building's custodian interrupted to announce it was time to turn off the lights. But the camera club audience had been enthusiastic and the lecture show had made a successful debut.

Desfor as a young performer at Halloran Hospital on Staten Island in 1947, one of the hundreds of magic shows he gave during and after World War II for the Theater Wing War Service. IRVING DESFOR

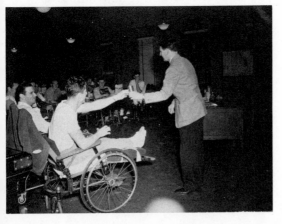

Over the years his "Photo-Magic" has taken him all over the world. He has presented it thousands of times, in cities from coast to coast, on national and local television, in Europe and Asia, at international photo fairs, photo industry conventions, gatherings of camera groups, press photographers and newspaper executives, at dinner meetings, banquets, and university forums. Audiences have seen him in Rome, Paris, Oslo, Casablanca, Helsinki, Vienna, Crete, and Singapore, to name only a few places.

"Photo-Magic" has been a feature attraction of the international travel tours Desfor has conducted for amateur photographers, and of picture-taking expeditions arranged by travel agencies, airlines, and photo equipment manufacturers. Acting as guide, giving photographic advice, and presenting his lecture show at one of the points visited along the way, Desfor has led camera groups on twenty-one-day air and bus tours of Germany, Austria, and Italy, and cruises to the Caribbean and South America.

He has gradually built the lecture show into a precisely planned and organized program, improving the magic and the presentations and discarding some things he previously performed because, even though they were effective with audiences, they required equipment too bulky to pack compactly and carry easily.

All the routines have been designed as "blocks" or "units," each complete in itself and exactly timed, but constructed so that the various

Desfor presenting his "Photo-Magic" in 1955, when the long-running lecture show was in its seventh year, but with decades yet to go. IRVING DESFOR

"blocks" can be shifted around and put together to fit any occasion or time requirement. The full lecture is a one-hour presentation, but Desfor can as easily present a half-hour show, or one that will run precisely twelve and a half minutes. There is no need for elaborate pre-planning of each program; it is simply a matter of choosing the "blocks" to fit that situation, and however he decides to put them together he is always working with routines he has constantly performed. If he is asked to do a segment of a television show, for instance, he has no trouble delivering one that will run to the prom-

128

ised time, not a minute over or under. Never since that years-ago first lecture at Perth Amboy has anybody threatened to turn off the lights because Desfor was "on" too long.

Basically the presentation centers around an illuminated easel, on which Desfor displays large blowups of various photographs, one at a time as the show goes along. Each of the pictures illustrates some point he is making about photography, and each picture also becomes part of a magic effect that helps to put that point across.

"Photography *is* magic, the magic of light and chemicals on film and paper," he tells his audiences as he introduces his lecture. "Photo-magic, however, is something special with me."

As an example, he displays a picture that is a symbolic representation of color photography, explaining that it is produced photographically by a combination of primary colors. That leads into his presentation of a "blendo effect," in which red, yellow, and blue handkerchiefs are magically blended together in his hands into a large multicolored silk picture.

During a discussion of realism in

Desfor's "Photo-Magic" at the Kodak pavilion at the New York World's Fair in 1965.
IRVING DESFOR

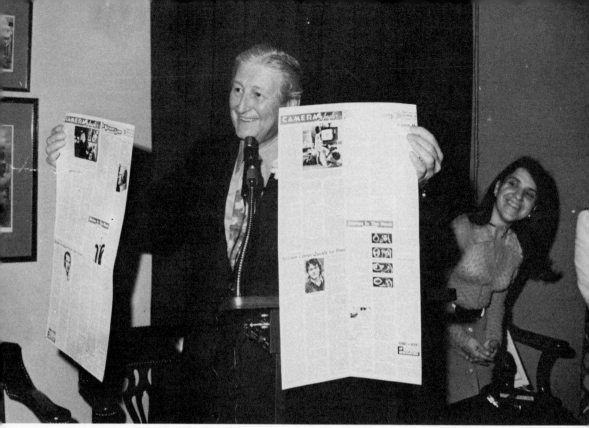

At his Associated Press retirement party in April, 1972, Irving Desfor demonstrated to top AP officials how he could magically crop page proofs to make his own "Camera Angles" newspaper column grow bigger while other columns disappeared from the sheet. Although he officially retired from his art director's job at the age of sixty-five, he went right on writing the column, photographing magicians, and performing his "Photo-Magic" lecture shows. A collection of more than 40,000 of his pictures of magicians is at the American Museum of Magic in Marshall, Michigan. IRVING DESFOR

photography, he shows a picture of rope in various stages of manufacture, then magically demonstrates how three-dimensional it is by producing from the picture two twenty-foot lengths of real rope, which are used in a trick. He may include other tricks: a pictured egg, for example, becomes a real egg, or a chosen card rises up out of a photograph. Or there may be "Photo-Magic" demonstrations of such subjects as portraiture, picture-cropping, or the instant processing of color film.

In Irving Desfor's lecture shows, his column, and his photographic activities, the combination of hobbies has benefitted both camera fans and magicians. Magic has enriched his knowledge, ability, and accomplishments as a photographer, and photography has enriched his enjoyment and performance of magic.

5

THE CREATIVE SIDE

Magicians invent new tricks for as many different reasons as there are individual magicians. They invent them to provide something different for their own acts, for ego satisfaction, to gain the respect and admiration of other magicians, to share ideas with those who share their hobby, for profit, or simply to enjoy the creative fun of it.

Magical invention is no different from other kinds of invention in that it starts with what is known and develops the new out of the old. There is no limit to the new tricks, or to new variations of old ones, that may be created from the basic effects and methods that have become the common heritage of all magicians. But the creation of a totally new effect or the discovery of an entirely original principle is rare.

Each trick has two parts: effect and method. The effect is how the trick looks to the audience and the method is how it is done. A basic effect, for example, is *penetration,* the magical passing of one object through another. But the penetration of a coin through a handkerchief looks quite different to an audience from the linking together of steel rings in the classic "linking rings," or from the illusion of walking through a brick wall. The three tricks have different effects, and each is done by a different method, but all of them are built on the same *basic* effect of penetration.

Obviously basic effects are adaptable to thousands of tricks, and basic methods can be applied in thousands of ways. It is sometimes said that everything in magic has been done before and that despite the constant invention of tricks there is nothing really new. But that is a little like saying that Edison's electric light bulb was not a new invention because the effect of lighting had been produced before with gaslight, oil lamps, and candles.

There is so much in magic that is new from year to year that it takes a very knowledgeable magician to keep up with all the developments, even within whatever branch of it may be his particular specialty. But the more a magician knows about what *has* been done the better equipped he is to explore the creative possibilities of what *can* be done.

Back in the early 1940s, which must be at least forty thousand tricks ago, the late Dariel Fitzkee, an acoustical engineer turned magician, made a comprehensive scientific study of the fundamentals of magic, which became the basis of his book *The Trick Brain*. He reduced tricks to their essential elements, systematically classified them, and found that all the tricks of every kind of magic, from sleight of hand to stage illusions, amounted to a total of only *nineteen* basic effects. According to Fitzkee, the possible effects any magician could present were these:

1. Production (an appearance, creation, or multiplication)
2. Vanish (disappearance, obliteration)
3. Transposition (change in location)
4. Transformation (change in appearance, character, or identity)
5. Penetration (one solid through another)
6. Restoration (making the destroyed whole)
7. Animation (movement imparted to the inanimate)
8. Anti-Gravity (levitation and change in weight)
9. Attraction (mysterious adhesion)
10. Sympathetic Reaction (sympathetic response)
11. Invulnerability (injury-proof)
12. Physical Anomaly (contradictions, abnormalities, freaks)
13. Spectator Failure (magician's challenge)
14. Control (mind over the inanimate)
15. Identification (specific discovery)
16. Thought Reading (mental perception, mind reading)
17. Thought Transmission (the projection and transference of thoughts)
18. Prediction (foretelling the future)
19. Extrasensory Perception (unusual perception, other than mind)

Other writers have compiled different lists of basic effects, ranging from a dozen to two dozen or more. Lists also have been made of fundamental effects in specialized fields of magic, such as basic card effects or basic mental effects. All such lists offer starting places for creating new tricks.

Fitzkee's book included a mechanical method to inspire creative thinking about tricks. The list of nineteen basic effects was numbered. There were also a list of essential factors for each basic effect, a list of basic methods to accomplish each effect, and a long numbered list of various objects that might be used in different tricks.

The Trick Brain device called for making up a set of numbered cards, shuffling them, choosing numbers entirely by chance, and matching the numbers against the lists to come up with an effect, method, and props for a trick. The idea was to start the magician-inventor thinking about all sorts of unusual possibilities suggested by the random association of basic ingredients. Whether it resulted in anything practical ultimately depended upon the user's imagination and knowledge of magic.

A somewhat similar approach to magical invention, but without any mechanical device, is the so-called "brainstorming" session. The magician sets aside an hour or two at a previously decided-upon time each week in a place where he won't be interrupted. He takes a pad and pencil and as rapidly as possible jots down every idea for a trick he can think of, no matter how wild or impracticable it may seem to be at first. His immediate purpose is simply to generate ideas, to include anything and everything without critical judgment or any attempt to work out any details. Then, at a later time, he can go through his accumulated notes, select one likely idea, and try to develop it into a practical trick. Brainstorming sometimes is done by a group, with three or four magician friends tossing ideas back and forth.

Many magicians have found old magic books, magazines, and dealers' catalogues good sources for ideas. Tricks that have been long-neglected are often rediscovered and given a new look by adapting them to do away with outdated props and bulky or complicated apparatus. The whole plot may be changed and streamlined, entirely different objects may be used, or the original effect may be retained but the method changed to meet present-day performing conditions.

Enlarging the size of the props that are used may convert what originally was a pocket trick into one that can be performed for a large audience; or reducing the size of the props may make it possible to present what was a stage illusion as an interesting close-up effect.

An old rope trick may be made to look new if it is done instead with a jeweled necklace, a necktie, or a live snake. Various inventors have substituted for the standard "Linking Rings" such things as pretzels, metal coat hangers, and big hula hoops. Instead of plucking coins or cards from the air, live goldfish have been caught at the fingertips; instead of producing a rabbit from a top hat, an assistant costumed as a big rabbit has produced a magician from a big hat.

Variety stores, stationery stores, toy counters, craft and hobby shops, and other places that display a wide range of new or unusual products have long been favorite stalking grounds of magical idea hunters. They look for things that might serve as props, or for novelties and odd gadgets that might be put to secret use in accomplishing some trick. A toy space ship, a bag of sea shells, or a plastic alligator may suggest a novel effect, magical plot, basis for a patter story or presentation, for which a method then has to be worked out. On the other hand, tiny magnets, an electronic or hobby device, or a new adhesive may suggest a method, which then means working out an effect to embody the method.

Instead of physical props, it may be some spoken conversation, or something read about, seen on television or in the theater, or some happening in daily life that sparks a new trick. Jokes, stories, puns, proverbs, catch-phrases, and popular songs have frequently been made into tricks. Current events, problems everybody is talking about, common concerns, annoyances, business or family relationships, all may be entertainingly illustrated with magic. Knowing the point of the joke, story, or situation that he wants to put across, the magician works out his effect, then devises the method.

Some magicians recommend starting up the imagination by thinking of things an average person would do if he were a magician himself. How would he magically deal with parking meters, taxes, government red tape, finding lost luggage, dieting? How would he magically repair a flat tire, stop a leaking faucet, please the boss, fill his pockets with money, win a lottery or a bet on a horse race?

Another way is to start with a theme or a characterization and to build magical effects around it. What magical things might happen along the way to a person pushing a food cart through the aisles of a supermarket, or to someone aboard a plane or stranded on an island? What magic could be performed by a magician playing the role of a cowboy, a senator, a monk, a door-to-door salesman, a radio disc jockey, a tennis player, baseball star, artist, fashion designer, bartender, construction worker, carpenter, king, or court jester?

Several well-known professionals have said that when they consider adding a new trick to those they perform, they make a habit of starting with all the published and marketed versions of similar effects. They work over this version and that, adding their own ideas and refinements, until they gradually develop a routine that can be tested with audiences.

Quite often the idea for a trick, method, or move begins more by accident than planning, from just playing around with props, magical gadgets, and apparatus, until something new is hit upon. Then, of course, it has to be planned out, to try to make something practical of it.

But successful magical inventors seem to agree that far more often the inspiration starts with the effect or magical plot, rather than with any initial consideration of equipment or methods. It is after they have the effect in mind that they begin to think of the simplest possible way to perform it convincingly.

Here are five of magic's more inventive personalities.

Al Baker

Al Baker, who left magicians a legacy of valuable advice as well as many clever inventions, once wrote: "It is an axiom in geometry that the shortest distance between two points is a straight line. In the same way it may be said that in magic the best way to present a trick is by the simplest and most direct methods. The effect or plot must be simple and easily understandable and the means for bringing it about must be covered by natural actions, direct and to the point and without any tedious divigations which tend to obscure the issue."

Baker, who began his professional performing in the late 1800s and actively continued it into the early 1950s, was a veteran of traveling medicine shows, chautauquas, and the vaudeville circuits, a long-successful New York club-date magician, and co-owner of a Broadway magic shop that was the informal meeting place of some of the most creative magicians of his time.

Many of the scores of tricks he invented have become standard effects in the programs of today's magicians, and have also inspired

The late Al Baker, shown here exercising his famed sense of humor as he puzzled over a "gag" gift presented to him by fellow magicians who expected him to create magic with almost anything. Magicians everywhere still perform many of the tricks invented years ago by Baker, who greatly influenced the modern trend toward simplicity in props and presentation. IRVING DESFOR

countless variations of them. Among them, to mention only a few, were the silk handkerchief that visibly unknots itself, the pack of cards that cuts itself, the mental addition slate, the first torn and restored newspaper that allowed showing the restored paper on both sides, the Baker dollar-bill switch, coins and purses, handkerchiefs through the wrist. Baker's mental magic and card tricks broke new paths, as did his many subtle uses of threads, human hairs, and false thumbtips and fingertips.

Famous for his wit, Baker was much admired by other magicians, not only for the cleverly practical tricks and routines he devised but for his own performing style—and for the commonsense advice in all his writing. He greatly influenced the modern trend in magic toward simplicity in props and equipment, methods, techniques, and presentation.

"Start out in magic by being yourself," he advised beginners. "Don't try to be the other fellow, and remember: knowing a thousand tricks does not make an entertainer; doing a few tricks entertainingly does. . . . After all, the trick isn't the important thing. It's the way you do it that makes the entertainment. . . . Take a trick, any trick, the simpler the better. Think about it. Look for possibilities for emphasizing the mystery in it. Don't just *do* the trick and say to yourself, 'I've fooled them.' . . . . Every time you do this sort of thing, a flop is on its way to happen. Don't do a trick until you have thought out its simplest presentation."

Theodore Annemann

Recognized by magicians during his lifetime as a creative genius, Theodore Annemann has become a legend in the years since his death in 1942. Called the "father" of modern mental magic, his tricks and his writing set patterns that have inspired the creation of hundreds of effects in the Annemann tradition of strong presentation combined with simple and cleverly subtle methods.

Theodore Annemann, the "father" of modern mentalism, whose clever concepts and approach to magic as entertainment in terms of "what a real magician or mind reader would do" have long outlived him. Since his tragic death at the age of thirty-five in 1942, the man who sometimes billed himself as "Annemann the Enigma" has become a legend in the world of magic, with an ever-growing appreciation for his creative genius.

Annemann's magic was designed to fool the mind by seeming to do "what a genuine magician or mind reader would do." He believed that as far as the method was concerned "anything goes" as long as it produced an effect that would entertain and hold the interest of an audience.

"The effect is the thing and don't forget it for a moment," he wrote. "The end justifies the means." Saying that "usually tricks become greater as they become simpler," he advised, "Don't be silly about things in some tricks being too simple. The simpler, the better."

But Annemann's effects, while they often depended on simple secret devices, setups, or prearrangements, were brilliantly conceived, and perhaps his greatest genius was in his painstaking attention to details. "Why don't magical enthusiasts realize," he asked, "that it is a little detail or two which makes one performer better than another?"

Born in East Waverly, New York, in 1907, he was christened Theodore Squires, but after his mother remarried he took his stepfather's last name of Anneman, and added another "n" to give himself his professional name. He was about ten when a schoolmate showed him a trick with a ball and a vase that intrigued him and led to his spending the money he earned as a newsboy on magic books and a boxed set of tricks. He saw the big Thurston show, soon discovered the magic magazines, and while still in his teens began writing up tricks of his own to contribute to them.

Annemann broke into show business as a helper with a trained-bird act, but did his first professional performing as a magician and mentalist at the age of nineteen with a medicine show that toured New York and Pennsylvania. He moved to New York City, and by 1928, at the age of twenty-one, was playing club dates as "Annemann the Enigma."

At first he wore the turbaned costume of a Hindu mystic, but abandoned that for conventional evening attire as he began to develop his modern style of presentation. He lifted his mental magic out of the realm of old-fashioned vaudeville crystal gazers and circus carnival soothsayers, did away with the phony mumbo-jumbo, elaborate equipment, and flashy theatrical trappings.

What he wanted to put across was his personality, his personal ability as an entertainer and mentalist, and he made the props he used seem unimportant: paper and pencil, envelopes, cards, a few other simple and apparently ordinary articles that could be carried in a briefcase. With such things, he could do a forty-five-minute performance. Although the mental magic was his specialty, Annemann at times did other kinds of magic, but again with the simplest of props.

"Study to be entertaining first, and make your trick incidental," he wrote. "Impress the audience at the outset with your personality. . . . Keep well in mind that if you please the ladies, half the battle is won." He also emphasized: "The art of magic does not end with the ability to perform a certain effect well, nor in rattling off a line of patter. Give attention to every angle of the presentation, and don't forget there are such things as dramatic import, atmosphere, grace, style, continuity and proper routining."

Much of Annemann's performing was as a society entertainer at fashionable private parties. Although the fees were good, the bookings were spotty, and he had a never-ending struggle to get by financially. He appeared in clubs and theaters, and later in his career toured with a promotional show sponsored by a liquor manufacturer. But he never really made it into the big time as a public performer.

His lasting fame eventually rested almost entirely upon his reputation among magicians. From the time he first arrived in New York, they were impressed with his ability as a card expert, as well as with his originality in mental magic. To make ends meet he began advertising and marketing tricks and routines, and quickly became recognized as a brilliant creator of unusual effects—clever and practical magic others could use.

Annemann's first book for magicians, *The Book Without a Name*, which included many fine effects—some that were to become classics of mental magic—was published in 1931. Al Baker wrote the introduction. Over the years this book was followed by nearly a dozen other books of Annemann creations, several of them made up of collected material and published posthu-

mously. Annemann also continued his prolific output of individual tricks and manuscripts.

Most of the effects he created bore the indelible stamp of his unique approach to magic, his ability to simplify the working of a trick to greatly enhance its effect, and the creative faculty he had for dramatizing the simplest of tricks and making them into small miracles. His contribution to mentalism was immense, and he brought much that was new, in principle as well as in presentation, to other fields of magic.

In October 1934, he began a project that was to become probably his greatest contribution, and his monument: the editing and publishing of a magazine called *The Jinx*. It started as a four-page publication that sold for a quarter a copy and was conceived, as he put it, "with a single thought in mind, that of supplying magicians and mystery entertainers at large with practical effects and useful knowledge."

He kept it going for more than seven years—through 151 issues, putting it together himself from the writing to the production—and the consistent excellence of the material it contained has seldom been matched by other conjuring publications. It was filled with his own creations, ideas, suggestions, hints, tips, and advice, and with many contributed effects from some of the best minds in magic. *The Jinx* became his beloved brainchild and firmly established his enduring reputation among magicians.

But Annemann's private life had

become increasingly tragic, a torture of complex emotional and personal problems, self-doubt and financial worries, and on January 12, 1942, at the age of thirty-five, he took his own life in his New York apartment. Nonetheless, his inventions, books, and writings in *The Jinx* have long outlived him, and the Annemann legend has continued to grow—and to inspire other creators of magic.

Dai Vernon

Famous among magicians who have long honored him as one of the greatest, Dai Vernon has remained little known to the public—partly because of his lifelong prefer-

---

Dai Vernon, affectionately known as "The Professor," a teacher of three generations of magicians, dean of Hollywood's famed Magic Castle, and credited with having "revolutionized" close-up magic and the modern performance of sleight of hand classics.

ence for close-up magic rather than prominence as a stage performer.

Few close-up magicians in the world have not at one time or another made use of the magic that Vernon created. Leading professionals have featured his magic in stage and television shows that helped make them famous. Three generations of magicians have grown up learning moves, methods, principles, techniques, and routines Vernon devised, and he has influenced a whole school of followers who have at least attempted to create their own magic in the Vernon style.

The "brain wave deck" he conceived in 1930, and first fully explained eight years later in the pages of Annemann's *The Jinx*, has since been sold by the thousands of packs and has inspired a score of other versions. In addition to his originations, his routines for some of magic's classic old effects have become accepted standards.

Born in Ottawa, Canada, in 1894 and named David Verner, he took to using the name "Dai Vernon" while in high school, the "Dai" being a Welsh nickname for "David" and the "Vernon" being the way a newspaper misprinted his last name in a story about his winning a swimming contest. He decided the combination sounded appropriately "tricky" for a young amateur magician, and he kept it.

His father, a government official, had started him in the hobby by showing him some tricks, and as Vernon later said, "Since I was a boy of five I have been almost pas-

139

sionately interested in magic, particularly that branch utilizing cards and coins." His passion led to a study of magic books and to the buying of equipment, but he gradually put aside "the type of apparatus that could only have been constructed for trickery," and concentrated on sleight of hand.

He enjoyed practicing magic almost as much as performing it, and found real pleasure in the hours he put in trying to make whatever he did seem entirely natural and suited to his own personality. For Vernon, there was a sense of accomplishment and delight in working over things he had already learned, striving to improve them by incorporating his own ideas. "If people cannot derive pleasure and satisfaction from practice and are not prepared to spend time and thought and energy required because they find it irksome," he once wrote, "then magic is not for them—they should find another hobby."

He was an accomplished young performer by the time he was in his early teens, an entertainer at charity-sponsored shows and social affairs, and frequently at Government House in Ottawa, Canada's capital. In addition to his magic, he had become skilled at making silhouettes, having taught himself the art of scissor-cutting people's profiles from black paper. Vernon made his first vacation trip to New York in 1913, when he was nineteen, and earned a summer's living cutting silhouettes at Coney Island while spending his free time doing magic.

After his World War I service as a Canadian air force officer, he returned to New York in 1917. Soon he was amazing some of the big city's expert magicians with his tricks, and was accepted among the best of them. In the magic shops he met and formed close friendships with many of the "greats" of magic, constantly sought magical knowledge, and practiced and created. But he didn't make much money from magic and for quite a few years he performed in New York only during the winter months, and in the summers traveled about the country profitably cutting silhouettes.

His first booklet of twenty-five card tricks, published in 1924, sold well at novelty-shop trick and joke counters, but Vernon collected a total of only twenty dollars for all rights to it. By the early 1930s, however, he had gained such a reputation among magicians that a manuscript of some of his other secrets was sold in a limited edition for twenty dollars a copy.

With his wife, who had been Jeanne Hayes, an assistant to illusionist Horace Goldin before Vernon married her in 1924, he toured an act of stage magic, ending it at times masked as an old Chinese magician presenting the classic "linking rings." Over the years he gradually developed a routine with the rings that became a Vernon classic, eventually featured by leading magicians around the world.

In his most elaborate stage act, which briefly played the Radio City Music Hall and the Rainbow Room, he appeared as a satin-costumed Harlequin, combining dance and classical music with dramatically colorful and exquisitely performed magic. It was an artistic but not a financial success, and Vernon felt relieved to turn from it again to the intimate close-up magic at which he excelled and which he much preferred to perform.

Under the long-time personal management of a top theatrical agent who specialized in providing "class" entertainers for private parties, Vernon also presented his close-up magic at some of New York's most popular nightclubs, entertaining guests at their tables. One of his featured table-to-table routines was with the most ancient of all feats of magic, the "cups and balls." It became another of the Vernon-modernized classics he afterwards shared in print with the magic fraternity. But much of the close-up he did was with cards.

"Vernon knows cards better than a mother knows her baby," the *New York Daily Mirror* said of him in 1938. "He practices the most difficult 'over the table work,' where his audiences can get as close to him as they like. The work is the cream of the business; only the best get it. Unlike most magicians, he doesn't want publicity, because he doesn't need it."

Need it or not, he got publicity, not only in the public press but in the magic magazines, and when magic dealer Max Holden published Vernon's *Select Secrets* in 1941 the little forty-two-page book was eagerly received. Vernon released some of his other secrets for publication, personally taught sleight of hand to a few selected pupils, and during World War II spent most of the war years in the Pacific doing USO camp shows.

In the early 1950s he was lecturing on magic to magicians, between performances on cruise ships to South America. By then famous throughout the world of magic, he made a highly successful European lecture tour in 1955. He received ovations from groups of magicians who assembled in such cities as London and Amsterdam to watch his magic and listen to his advice. During the trip, Vernon also performed for members of British royalty and for the Queen of Sweden.

While in London he began the close collaboration, with British magic writer and editor Lewis Ganson, that resulted in the publication in 1957 of *The Dai Vernon Book of Magic*. Vernon spent hours with Ganson, demonstrating and explaining his effects, in photographic and tape-recording sessions. And during months of correspondence, he also carefully checked out each detail of the manuscript as Ganson wrote it. Hailed by many as a landmark in conjuring literature, the book was followed during the 1960s by a long series of other Ganson-Vernon collaborations—providing magicians with Vernon's *Inner Secrets of Card Magic, More Inner Secrets of Card Magic, Further Inner Secrets of Card Magic, Ultimate Card Secrets*, his *Cups and Balls Routine, Symphony of the Rings*. Also written at this time were detailed recollections of the

141

magic of two of the legendary "greats" Vernon had known, his *Tribute to Nate Leipzig* and *Malini & His Magic.*

Through the years that followed Vernon became America's most popular and celebrated magic lecturer, drawing such eager attendance on his lecture tours that admission often had to be limited to those who had bought tickets long in advance. At national conventions, he sometimes held special lecture sessions that began at midnight and went on for hours as he talked of his experiences, demonstrated his sleights and techniques, and explained the detailed psychological reasoning that had gone into each move and gesture to create the effects he achieved.

In Hollywood, where he eventually made his home, Vernon became the dean of magicians at the famed Magic Castle. Here he was surrounded by his magician friends and by the film and television celebrities to whom he was the Castle's main celebrity, and where the intimate close-up room was named the Vernon Lounge in his honor. His monthly column of reminiscences and advice, "The Vernon Touch," became a feature of *Genii, The Conjurors' Magazine.*

Spoken of as a "living legend" and credited by many with having revolutionized close-up magic, Vernon was awarded nearly all the honors the world's magic societies could bestow. When the Society of American Magicians, meeting at New York's Waldorf Astoria in 1978, dedicated its fiftieth anniversary convention to him, that dedication was made by one of his star pupils, Doug Henning. The eighty-four-year-old Vernon also rewarded the convention by delivering a midnight-starting four-hour lecture.

Sid Lorraine

Sid Lorraine is a leading creator of novel magic built around humorous patter presentations, unusual themes, unexpected props, and simple but ingenious methods. For well over half a century other magicians have been entertaining audiences— as Lorraine has entertained his own—with close-up and platform tricks he has invented.

His recent creations have involved magic with such things as a house fly, a horse fly, and a bar fly, with tiny shoes that appear, vanish, and change color; and with a "moon rock" that changes into a wedge of green cheese. He has devised tricks about pollution, international espionage, thumbprints, the missing section of an ancient Egyptian wall, the discovery of a spectator's chosen drink by the imaginary tasting of a bottle cork. His props have included jigsaw cards, snakes, a giant watch, and the ABC's.

Born in 1905 in St. Neots, Huntingonshire, England, Lorraine grew up in Canada and has spent most of his life in Toronto. He was christened Sidney Richard Johnson, but in 1915, at the age of ten,

When America's space men reached the moon, did they discover it was really made of green cheese? Some magicians can entertainingly "prove" that's what happened, thanks to the creative talents of Sid Lorraine (above), who has been supplying fellow performers for years with many such novel tricks and routines, built around unusual magical themes and funny patter presentations.

He studied art in school and college, started work in 1924 with an engraving and publishing firm and stayed with the company fifty-one years, as a commercial artist and then its art director, until his retirement in 1970—having meanwhile not let the job interfere with his magic hobby.

In 1920—at the age of fifteen—Lorraine started writing for magic magazines and over the years has written for eighteen of them, freely giving tricks, ideas and information for no reward except the satisfaction of richly contributing to the hobby. Many of his tricks reflect his skill as an artist in cleverly designed cards illustrated for various magical plots, and in paper-folding novelties, such as one imprinted with Chinese lettering that can be folded to reveal the names of five different playing cards, one at a time. Since 1927 he has marketed some of his other tricks and routines, selling them directly or through the dealers, and forty-six of his creations have been commercially produced. Quite a few are standard items in dealers' catalogues, and long-popular with magicians around the world.

Lorraine's friendship with the late Percy Abbott, founder of Abbott's Magic Manufacturing Company, resulted in Abbott's marketing of many of his tricks. His cartoon illustrations for hundreds of other tricks filled the pages of Abbott catalogues, and the close relationship has continued with the company's present owners.

When Abbott's decided to publish

already casting about for a name to suit the magician he hoped to be, he decided to call himself "Sid Lorraine." He took the name from headlines about the French province of Alsace-Lorraine, then being fought over in World War I. "I checked the phone book," he recalls, "and found a lot of Johnsons but not many Lorraines."

143

Sid Lorraine, in one of the funny character roles he plays as a performer, shown here stringing along an audience of magicians with a gadget designed to demonstrate that the end result is hilarious entertainment, at a magic convention in Colon, Michigan, 1972. PETE BIRO

its own magic magazine, called *Tops,* Lorraine began writing a column that started with the first issue in January, 1936. He wrote it every month for more than twenty years, until *Tops* ceased publication in 1957. When it was revived by Abbott's as *The New Tops* in 1961, he resumed his columning, and "Sid Lorraine's Chatter" has continued ever since as probably the most widely read feature of the magazine.

He reviews books, magazines, and other publications, gives his opinions about new tricks and various things being offered to magicians, passes along news of happenings in the world of magic, and informally comments about its various related hobbies. He answers queries, helps magicians and collectors get in touch with each other about specific interests, provides name-and-address sources of information.

Lorraine gets so many requests for information that as a separate project he has compiled and published *Sid Lorraine's Reference File,* a listing of 495 names and addresses of magazines, club journals, magic dealers, manufacturers, and specialist suppliers. He has also published four sets of lecture notes, detailing the tricks and routines he demonstrates during his lectures to magic clubs and conventions.

His first book, simply titled *Patter,* was published by Abbott's in 1938. It was followed a year later by *A Magician in the House,* then in 1950 by *More Patter,* and in 1962 by *Gags, Routines and Patter.* In addition to funny patter, jokes to tell with tricks, sight gags, and other humorous material, the books contain many of Lorraine's novel tricks and routines, as well as his presentations for standard and classic tricks. All the books have remained popular over the years and have gone through several printings.

"Patter for magic is not really a completely separate item," Lorraine has written. "It is an important part of the whole. With me, in many instances, the trick and patter develop together."

Phil Goldstein

In hardly more than a dozen years since he first began devising tricks and routines for fellow magicians, Phil Goldstein has become recognized as an outstanding young creator of mental magic and card effects in the Annemann tradition.

Goldstein's first contributions to magic magazines were in 1964. Since then, dozens of his tricks have appeared in some sixteen different publications, in magic anthologies, and in books he himself has written. He has lectured to magic clubs and conventions in the United States and Europe. And he has had as many as fifteen marketed effects in current release at the same time, sold to magicians through the dealers.

Born in 1950, Goldstein grew up in Boston. When he was seven, an older cousin introduced him to magic by teaching him two simple card tricks. By the time he was twelve he had taught himself enough tricks to begin performing for children's birthday parties, which he continued to do until he started college. He graduated from Brandeis University in 1972 with departmental honors in American Civilization, after writing a thesis on the development of postwar American youth culture. At various times he worked as a disc jockey, singer-pianist, graphic designer, and chef, before reaching the point where he was earning his living entirely from magic.

Goldstein enjoys all forms of magic and his inventions include various types of tricks, but the kind he publicly performs for money is mental magic. He is a professional mentalist, and happily enough he works frequently, mostly in nightclubs. But while building his public reputation as a performer he has earned the bulk of his income from a combination of sources. His lecturing, together with sales of lecture notes and related materials, has been quite lucrative. He is a paid consultant for other magicians. His

Now you see him and now you don't. But behind the clever hands is Phil Goldstein, definitely keeping an eye on things as he peeks into people's minds as a performing mentalist, when not putting his own mind to work on the prolific invention of scores of tricks and routines for other mentalists and magicians.

books bring in royalties. He will sometimes sell all rights to an invention to a single dealer; at other times he takes charge of all production, jobbing, and wholesaling. He has written and illustrated the advertising and the catalogues for Hank Lee's Magic Factory in Boston, as well as most of that company's instruction sheets. Sometimes he acts as the company's convention booth demonstrator. Often he is hired to lecture to the same convention and to perform as one of the convention acts.

"My career as a performer is, of course, important to me, and I am working hard to build it," he says. "But sometimes I joke that my performance work is merely field research for my *real* job of sitting up in bed in the middle of the night, inventing magic tricks. Actually that statement is not entirely a joke."

He is so prolific an inventor that he sometimes creates more than a dozen effects in a single week, with a weekly average of at least four or five. In that same week, he is likely to write up to fifty letters, and also reads what works out to about one hundred and thirty magazines and books each month. Asked how he can find the time to do it, he says:

"The answer is simple: this is precisely what I *do* with my *life*. I do not have a job, rather I have sporadic, interrelated sources of income. My work is that of analyzing, theorizing, learning, creating, writing, reading, teaching, exploring magic."

In his *Blue Book of Mentalism*, published in 1976 as the first of a series of small books, each containing a dozen or more of his tricks and routines, Goldstein pointed out that mentalism is even more limited in its basic effects and methods than other forms of magic. Mentalists, according to his analysis, have only four basic effects to work with: *telepathy*, communication between two minds; *clairvoyance*, the reception of information that is unknown to everyone present; *precognition*, knowledge of future events before they happen; *psychokinesis*, physical manifestations of mental energy.

In his discussion of the fundamentals of mental magic, Goldstein explains in his book something of his own approach to inventing routines built on the basic elements. "The only way to rise above the limitations of our field is by developing unusual and interesting presentational approaches. It is my intention whenever I set out to create a new routine to try to develop a theme which will hold an audience's interest."

For Further Reading

These are generally available in magic shops, from specialized dealers in magic books; or they may be obtained directly from the publishers.

Annemann, Theodore. *The Jinx.* 3 vols. 1963-64. Louis Tannen, Inc., 1540 Broadway, New York, N.Y. 10036. A complete file of Annemann's magazine, reprinted in three bound volumes from the original that he published 1934-42, includes his advice, suggestions, tips, comments, many of his tricks and routines, and a wealth of other magic from the *Jinx*'s contributors.

Fitzkee, Dariel. *The Trick Brain.* New edition of original published by author, 1944. Magic Limited, Lloyd E. Jones, 4064 39th Ave., Oakland, CA. 94619. A comprehensive, detailed analysis of basic effects, methods, and fundamentals of magic and the invention of new tricks. For the serious student, whether or not he is creatively inspired by Fitzkee's mechanical plotting device, it provides a thorough exploration of the underlying principles of magic.

Ganson, Lewis. *The Dai Vernon Book of Magic.* London: Stanley, 1957. 1971: The Supreme Magic Co., 64 High Street, Bideford, Devon, England. In the second chapter, Vernon's views about the creative side of magic are set forth: his methods for the evolution and performance of his magic, his thought process when studying a new trick, his approach to original presentation, advice on naturalness of action, adapting a trick to suit one's style and personality, and other observations. The book also details many of Vernon's routines, including those for the classic "linking rings" and "cups and balls."

Goldstein, Phil. *The Blue Book of Mentalism.* 1976. Philip T. Goldstein, 121 Charles St., Boston, MA. 02114. A good sampling of Goldstein's clever mental tricks and routines, plus his brief but interesting analysis of the basic effects and methods of mentalism, this was the first in a series that also includes *The Red Book of Mentalism, The Green Book of Mentalism,* etc.

Hades, Micky. *The New Make-Up of Magic.* 1974. Micky Hades International. Box 476, Calgary, Alberta, Canada, T2P 2J1. A practical how-to-do manual on the creation, design, construction, and decoration of magical apparatus for the home workshop builder. This also contains much information on the invention of tricks, suggestions on how to create them and to plot new effects and presentations, and an analysis of the basics generally incorporated into apparatus to perform various secret functions.

Lorraine, Sid. *Gags, Routines and Patter.* 1962. Abbott's Magic Manufacturing Co., Colon, MI. 49040. Lorraine's fourth book of novel tricks and ideas, plus humorous patter routines for a score of standard effects, each typically original in theme and presentation.

6

BOOKS AND MAGAZINES

Books, booklets and pamphlets are all called "books" by magicians. The term includes publications of a few dozen pages as well as what are generally thought of as full-length hardcover or paperback books. Regardless of length, size, or format, they are listed and advertised as "books."

Each year there are sixty to eighty new magic books published in the English language. Ten or so come from general book publishers. The rest are published by magic dealers, by small publishers who specialize in magic books, by the authors themselves, or, occasionally, by magic clubs.

There are books of history, biography, showmanship, business methods, and other specialized subjects, but the great majority are books of tricks. In the new books, and in the several thousands already published, are nearly all the "secrets" of magic, with countless variations. They are available to anybody interested enough to buy them, whether from magic dealers, by mail, or from a public bookshop or paperback rack.

But, in fact, their circulation is pretty much limited to magic hobbyists. Nobody is likely to pay money for a magic book, or to spend the time and effort borrowing one from a public library, without some interest in the hobby, even if it is only the beginner's curiosity out of which new magicians are born. Magic books never sell by the millions, even as paperbacks. In hardcover editions, best sellers among them rarely reach a total sale of twenty-five-thousand copies, and some books and booklets have only a few thousand readers, or a few hundred. But many popular magic books go through several printings and sell steadily for years.

With the number of American magic hobbyists said to be doubling every ten years, there is a constantly increasing demand for new books, and there is an ever-new readership for older books that have become standard. Most readers are looking for tricks or routines they may be able to use, for originality in effects and presentations, for improved methods, techniques, better ways to present the classics, for information and advice to broaden their general knowledge of magic. But magic books also are read simply for the pleasure of reading about magic.

Somewhat like the sports fan who enjoys watching television football games for the spectator sport of vicariously imagining himself part of the game, the magic hobbyist often imagines himself performing the magic he reads about. He becomes, at least for the time, an armchair magician, mentally seeing himself up on a stage or at a close-up table with his friends, out there performing. He follows the plot of the trick, the action, the thinking behind the moves, the way the trick is played out. He may dismiss it as not practical, not for him, or he may tuck the idea away in his mind as one he might use some day. The reading may even inspire him to put together the necessary props and give the thing a test run. But whether he actually ever tries a par-ticular trick or not, he has the fun of reading about it. And from such reading he gradually acquires a learning that deepens his total enjoyment of magic.

There have been at least a thousand different English-language magic magazines published at one time or another since one called *The Conjuror's Magazine* first appeared in London in 1791. The first American magazine, *The Magician,* published in 1893, quickly disappeared; the first one of real influence and significance was *Mahatma,* started in New York in 1895 and continued until 1906. By that time there had been quite a few others.

Houdini became editor and publisher of his own *Conjurer's Monthly Magazine* in 1906 and kept it going until 1908. But before him, what was to become an institution in conjuring literature, *The Sphinx,* began in Chicago in 1902. It was published for more than half a century, until its final issue in March, 1953, and under the latter-day editorship of the erudite John Mulholland it grew into what was possibly the best magic magazine ever printed in the United States.

Every year, there are new magazines. Some last only a few issues and others survive considerably longer. In addition to general magic magazines, there are many smaller publications that specialize in close-up magic, card techniques, mentalism, gospel magic, escapes, or various collecting interests. There are also innumerable newsletters and journals issued by local magic clubs. The large and well-established general magic magazines fall into three categories: those published by magic societies; independent publications; and magazines published by magic dealers. Magic-society magazines are intended for members only and are not sold by subscription or single copy to nonmembers. Subscription is included in the membership dues. Back issues, however, are available from dealers in used magic books and magazines.

Anybody can subscribe to the dealer-published and independent magazines, and single copies can be bought in magic shops, although not every shop stocks all magazines. Most of the magazines probably have at least twice as many readers as their declared circulation because magic hobbyists do a lot of swapping, borrowing, buying and selling, and browsing through friends' magazines.

The Linking Ring, official publication of The International Brotherhood of Magicians, has the largest circulation of all magic magazines, and is mailed each month to more than ten thousand members throughout the world, including some behind the iron curtain in Poland, Hungary, and Czechoslovakia. It began in 1922 as a little multigraphed newsletter, devoted mainly to brief personal notes about members of the then small but rapidly growing new magic brotherhood. The editors announced that it would be published "now and then," perhaps eventually even monthly "if at all possible," but they predicted it would be "a long time before we could afford to get out a printed magazine." By the third year, it was being printed in the format it was to keep.

The Linking Ring has grown over half a century into a magazine that averages 150 pages a month, and it has had to restrict the advertising it can accept because of limited space. Editor Howard Bamman fills each issue with a rich blend of historical, biographical, and "how to" articles, along with humor, editorial comment, news and pictures of the world's magic and magicians, of the international organization, and of its affiliated "rings."

A feature of *The Linking Ring,* which is almost a small book within the magazine, is the monthly "Parade" of twenty or so pages of fully illustrated tricks and routines, contributed by an individual magician or compiled by a group. For mentalists there is Syd Bergson's column; for close-up workers Rick Johnson presents a column of entertainingly original effects; and card experts can turn to Charles Hudson's "The Card Corner." Consistently excellent reviews and previews of new books, periodicals, other conjuring literature, and marketed tricks are provided by the informed and highly respected former editor of *The Linking Ring* and present feature editor, John Braun. The magazine's stellar writers include Frances Marshall and John Booth.

M-U-M, the official magazine of the Society of American Magicians, is sent out monthly to its six thousand members in the United States and foreign countries. The name comes from the initials of the society's slogan, "Magic-Unity-Might." It was first published in 1911, issued irregularly at the start, and then monthly until 1927, when it took the form of an SAM supplement to *The Sphinx* and much later to *Genii* magazine. In 1951 it again resumed separate publication and is now a big and attractive magazine that averages sixty large-sized pages an issue.

M-U-M's editor, David Goodsell, a young educator by profession and headmaster of the Heritage Hall private school in Oklahoma City, refers to his editing of the magazine as "my hobby," but it is one he pursues with a professional approach and to which he devotes hours of his time. He collects, selects, and edits the material, prepares it for the printer, lays out and pastes up the pages, reads proof, and plans new features and special issues.

Goodsell manages to maintain a good editorial balance, satisfying the varied magical interests of *M-U-M*'s readers. There is a biography of a cover-featured "magician of the month," often a well-known performer who also contributes explanations of some of his pet effects and routines. Throughout the pages, there are many fine tricks, in addition to those in such specialized columns as Tom Ogden's "Card Stuff," David Ginn's "Entertaining Children with Magic," Jon Racherbaumer's "At the Table," and Bev Bergeron's "Notebook."

Among the long-popular features is "Ask the Doctor" by noted collector and magic authority Dr. John Henry Grossman, who answers readers' queries about magic problems and collectors' questions about magic literature. Current books, marketed tricks, and other things available to magicians are reviewed by Tom Zoss, and Goodsell reviews what is being published in other magic magazines.

M-U-M also has a "Playbill" of magical news from around the world in capsule form, reports of the official business of the SAM and its affiliated assemblies. There is news of the interesting happenings around the New York Magic Table, and of the new museum acquisitions, development projects, and programs presented by the SAM's Magic Hall of Fame in Los Angeles.

The oldest of magic-society magazines, and the longest continuously published periodical in magic history, is *The Magic Circular*. For more than seventy years, since 1906, it has been published "for private circulation only" among the two-thousand-odd worldwide members of London's prestigious Magic Circle.

Outside its British membership, the Magic Circle probably has more Americans among its members than from any other country. *The Magic Circular* keeps them well informed on the Circle's activities between what for most American members are infrequent visits to the London headquarters. Published eleven times a year, it is also among the most literate of magic magazines, with well-researched articles on magic history, literature, biographical accounts and descriptions of per-

151

formances of the past, and discussions of the principles and techniques of the art.

Editor Alan Snowden's "Backstage" column gives a lively and informal view of the present-day magic scene and the shows, events, and happenings in which members are prominently involved. In his "Americana" column, Dr. John Henry Grossman regularly tells of what is happening magically in the United States. John Holland's reviews of books and magazines are detailed in their analysis of what is being offered and whether it is worthwhile.

The Magic Circular's reports of shows and lectures at the club also are more informative than most such reports. In the case of lectures, brief explanations are often given of the working methods and devices of tricks and routines that were discussed. The reviews of the shows detail not only the effects but the appearance, dress style, personality, and presentation of the performer.

Among the independently published magic magazines, the most prominent in the United States is *Genii, The International Conjurors' Magazine*. Started in 1936 by California attorney William Larsen, Sr., who combined his law career with performances as a professional magician and illusionist, lecturer and writer, *Genii* was left by him to his family when he died in 1953. It was part of a magic legacy that inspired his sons, William Larsen, Jr., and Milton, to create the famous Magic Castle in Hollywood, and to undertake many other enterprises for the advancement and prestige of magic. (See: *Showplaces of Magic.*)

Larsen's widow Geraldine, who was also a performing magician, continued publication of *Genii* for several years, until William Larsen, Jr. became its editor in 1957. He has built it into one of the world's largest, most popular, and most respected of magic magazines, doubled its size to a monthly average of sixty to eighty pages, and tripled its circulation to nearly nine thousand worldwide subscribers. *Genii* is unique in having been published by a whole family of magicians; its masthead legend reads, "in loving memory of William Larsen, Sr."

Genii has done much to further the understanding and friendships of the international magic community with many special issues, each devoted to the magic and magicians of some particular foreign country. Other special issues explore in depth the life, personality, philosophy, tricks, and creations of some American or world-prominent performer or magic celebrity.

Genii's regular features include William Larsen, Jr.'s informal personal comments in "The Genii Speaks"; Dai Vernon's column, "The Vernon Touch"; Mickey O'Malley's "Workshop" of easily made-at-home equipment and tricks; Larsen's "Bagdad" pages of pictures and capsuled news stories about magicians around the world; book reviews by veteran magic editor and publisher Lloyd Jones; and the knowledgeable Ed Mishell's "Tricks of the Trade," in which he evaluates new products in the magic marketplace by awarding them from one to four stars. There are also detailed word-and-picture convention reports, a monthly column about activities at the Magic Castle, articles on nearly every aspect of magic and its varied hobby specialties, and a goodly assortment of explained tricks and routines. Editor emeritus Geraldine Larsen Jaffe turns back the pages to give readers a monthly account of what was being published "Twenty-five Years Ago in Genii."

The world's only weekly magic magazine, *Abracadabra,* has been independently published in England every week since February, 1946, by Goodliffe the Magician (C. Goodliffe Neale). In a magic world where magazines are apt to appear and disappear more quickly than a manipulated playing card, Goodliffe's publication of now well over seventeen hundred consecutive issues is in itself a rather magical feat.

Almost everybody in magic calls it "Abra," and it has a large circulation on both sides of the Atlantic. Readers are kept informed on the international magic scene, on who is performing what and where, on conventions, clubs, magic society gatherings, and on new magic books and equipment. Although *Abracadabra* naturally deals mainly with magic in Britain, there is much in it of interest to U.S. readers.

Tightly edited to include a lot of material in its average twenty or so comparatively small-size pages, each issue presents several above-average tricks and routines, quick reports of late-breaking news, a "What's New"

column of the latest dealer offerings, and brief reviews that frankly appraise books, shows, television programs, and other events that involve magicians. There are series articles in which prominent performers explain some of the tricks they use in their shows, historical and biographical pieces, and other concisely written features.

Goodliffe's lead editorials, a blend of news comment, practical advice and outspoken personal opinion, tell it as he sees it, but with grace and good humor. He gives readers a fair chance to talk back to the editor or to sound off on other sometimes controversial subjects in their published letters, which frequently add good spice to *Abracadabra*'s weekly feast of information and education.

Magigram, the largest of the dealer-published magazines, also is English, and was started only a little more than a dozen years ago, in 1966, by the Supreme Magic Company. Since then it has grown into a monthly magic book that averages eighty or more large pages, mostly filled with explanations of tricks and routines of every variety. It has a circulation of eight thousand, with probably half its readers in the United States.

Edited by Ken de Courcy, a professional performer, inventor of many marketed tricks, and author of more than thirty books, *Magigram* regularly contains an array of practical magic, novel presentations, and columns of instruction and advice by some of magic's best writers. While there are also interesting personality pieces and news of magic activities and events, the editorial accent is on material the reader can use in doing magic.

Lewis Ganson, who collaborated with Dai Vernon on his landmark books—and who has also written and edited a number of other works that have become standard reference volumes in the working libraries of magicians—conducts a monthly "Teach-In" column of clearly explained and photographically illustrated routines, detailed with step-by-step instructions. George Blake, whose books also are "standards," writes a *Magigram* column that creatively gives new dimensions to old principles and methods, cleverly twisting them to new uses. Billy McComb, much admired by the magic fraternity as a long-prominent working professional who has entertained worldwide audiences under every sort of performing condition, shares his experiences and down-to-earth advice in "At Home With McComb." There is a "Dove Column" by Supreme Magic's Ian Adair, author of *The Encyclopedia of Dove Magic* and prolific innovator of tricks and equipment. Mental magic is the province of Arthur Carter in his column. Alan Kennaugh deals with the show-business scene. A U.S. view of what is right or wrong with magic, typically peppered with his humorous asides, is presented in "News and Views from The Colonies" by George Johnstone.

Throughout *Magigram* there are other features of special appeal to children's performers, card workers, stage magicians, make-it-yourselfers. During the year there are special issues, some running to more than a hundred pages, that furnish a "book within the magazine" featuring the creations of an individual magician or magic society group, or built around a particular type of magic or presentation theme.

The leading American dealer-published magazine is *The New Tops*, published monthly by Abbott's Magic Manufacturing Company since 1961, but much older than that as the successor to *Tops*, which was started by Abbott's back in 1936. Edited by Neil Foster, an exceptionally talented professional performer long experienced in the magic business, *The New Tops* averages forty-eight large pages an issue.

Its popularity is due not only to its broad coverage of the whole spectrum of magic interests, including some specialties not regularly covered by other magazines, but to its many featured columnists and frequent well-known contributors. Sid Lorraine's "Chatter" has a large and loyal following of those who depend on him not only for help in solving their magic problems but as a source of information and for his reviews of new tricks, books, magazines, club publications, catalogues and lists, and whatever else is new or old and good. As a separate feature, Lorraine also provides a "Tip of the Month"—his own discovery or one passed along by a reader, of some gadget or product originally intended for non-magical purposes that can be put to good use by magicians.

Frances Marshall views magic

from the woman's viewpoint, and keeps *The New Tops'* readers aware that there are two sexes involved in the hobby in her "For Women Only" column. Micky Hades looks into things mental and psychic in "Out of My Mind." Dale Salwak writes of magic "For That Special Occasion," explaining tricks and routines patterned for Christmas, Thanksgiving, other holiday seasons, or for special audiences and events. George Johnstone writes about whatever he pleases in "Johnstone's Column by George," out of his long experience as a professional entertainer, and deals by turn with subjects anecdotal, humorous, historical, ironic, or controversial—always interestingly. For card tricksters there is Nick Trost's "Conjuring with Cards," for children's entertainers, Bruce Postgate's "Kid Show Forum." Magic clowns get special attention in Daren Dundee's "Clownin' Aroun'," and ventriloquists in "Vent Views" by Colonel Bill Boley. Ralph Mills furnishes "Magic for the Gospel Magician." The business problems of publicity, promotion, advertising, career-building, and obtaining bookings are taken up in "This Business of Magic" by Thomas Zoss.

Young wizards have "Just for Us Young Guys" by John Sherwood and old wizards are reminded in another Frances Marshall column that "It's Never Too Late." Circuses, carnivals, sideshows, road shows, and outdoor magic show business are the "Magical Whirlgig" Walt Hudson writes about. "Magic Update" by Richard Greeno is a time-and-place listing of upcoming conventions, magical happenings, and show-date schedules of touring magicians.

The New Tops has a monthly cover feature biography, and surrounding the columns are featured tricks and special articles. Although it is Abbott's house organ, its advertising pages are open to other dealers. The magazine has the comfortably informal editorial style of a friendly big get-together in print of magicians sharing their hobby fun and knowledge.

For those who would rather listen to a magazine than read one, England's *Abracadabra* publisher Goodliffe started the first monthly magic magazine on audiotape in 1978. Recorded on cassettes for home playback by subscribers and called "Abracassetta," it presents "in person" talks and interviews with magic-world personalities. Creators of tricks explain how to do them, others discuss their particular specialties, and there are news items, tips, advice, and brief voiced advertisements.

What amount to magic books on tape for home listening have also gained recent popularity. Craige M. Snader, Jr., of Mexico City, pioneered in the organized collecting and location of recordings of magicians, and in the commercial production of "Magic Sounds" releases, starting in 1975.

The Sound of Magic studio in London, a project of well-known professional magician Patrick Page and his partner Vic Pinto, has produced a series of in-depth interviews with famous magicians, including among others Dai Vernon, close-up star Albert Goshman, and mentalist Maurice Fogel. The cassettes are studio recorded, boxed in attractive lucite cases with spine-printed titles for bookshelf storage, and include biographical booklets illustrated with photographs.

Martin Breese, also in London, has produced a series of excellent and reasonably priced "Magicassettes" featuring audiotaped interviews, talks, and instruction by prominent performers. Sets range from one to four or more "volumes," with each cassette in a set running an hour or longer. Breese also has an "Archive Series" of voices of famous magicians of the past, with accompanying recorded biographical and historical information. He offers a Magicassette of samplings from the various tapes as a sort of sound catalogue of his products.

Here are seven of magic's prominent authors, editors, and publishers.

Walter Gibson

Magic's most prolific author, by far, is Walter B. Gibson. As a professional writer for nearly sixty years—whose creations include the famed mystery fiction character The Shadow—his published output has totalled a staggering 29 million words, quite a few million of which have been about magic and magicians.

He has written fifty full-length magic books for hobbyists and the general public, under his own name and as a ghost writer for some of the world's most famous magicians, including Houdini, Thurston, and Blackstone. His other magic writings have spread out into national magazines, newspaper columns, syndicated features, how-to-do-it courses, booklets and lessons, the

---

Walter B. Gibson (left), magic's most prolific writer, shown here with Mark Wilson while they were working on The Mark Wilson Course in Magic. *Gibson has written more than fifty full-length magic books, including some he "ghosted" for such famous magicians as Thurston, Blackstone, and Houdini. He has also written millions of published words of magazine and newspaper articles. And as a novelist, he created the mystery fiction character "The Shadow."*

editing of several magic magazines, the creation of magic comic books, and novels in which magicians have been his fictional chief characters.

A native of Philadelphia, born in 1897, Gibson started toward a writing career at the age of seven when he invented a puzzle, wrote it up, and had it published in *Saint Nicholas* magazine for children. At about the same age he saw magic performed for the first time when his parents took him to a theater where the celebrated actor Henry E. Dixey, costumed as an angel for his role in a play, came out between the acts to do a card trick.

Watching an "angel" baffle the audience with a pack of cards was an impressive sight for a young boy and Gibson soon acquired a toy magic set. A little later he discovered a Philadelphia magic shop, bought more tricks and books, subscribed to the magic magazine *The Sphinx,* and was actively performing and writing about magic before he was in high school.

During a trip to New York, he met and began a lifelong friendship with the soon-to-be-famous magician and mentalist Dunninger, for whom he later became a ghost writer of books and magazine articles. Another of the early close friendships Gibson made, after meeting him backstage in Philadelphia, was with magician Harry Bouton, who was about to adopt the stage name of Harry Blackstone and become the great traveling big-show illusionist.

Gibson was a writer of mystery stories and of more than two hundred published articles on magic and other subjects by the time he graduated from Colgate University and became a Philadelphia newspaper reporter in 1922. Through the newspaper, he was commissioned to write a nationally syndicated series of columns explaining simple magic tricks and puzzles. They caught the attention of no less a magician than Howard Thurston, who asked Gibson to write some booklets on magic to be sold at the Thurston shows.

He wrote not only the booklets for Thurston but more than fifty tabloid-page newspaper features on magic published under Thurston's name, as well as several series of articles "by Thurston" for *The Saturday Evening Post, Collier's,* and other national magazines. The magazine articles were the basis for Thurston's autobiography, *My Life of Magic.* Gibson's full-length books for Thurston included two that became best sellers for beginning magic hobbyists, *200 Tricks You Can Do* and *200 More Tricks You Can Do.*

Meanwhile, for his old friend Blackstone, then building a big show to rival Thurston's, Gibson also wrote magic booklets, newspaper features, and several full-length magic books. Two of those became standards on the shelves of American bookstores, reprinted in many editions and still popular: *Blackstone's Secrets of Magic* and *Blackstone's Modern Card Tricks.*

Houdini, who had been collecting notes for three magic books he wanted to write, called in Gibson to do the writing and editing. But only one of the volumes was completed before Houdini's death in 1926. Houdini's widow and attorney later turned over to Gibson the great mass of unpublished notes that Houdini had left, and with the cooperation of the Houdini estate Gibson used them for two books published under his own name, *Houdini's Escapes* and *Houdini's Magic*.

In addition to all his other professional writing, including mystery fiction and daily features for a newspaper syndicate, Gibson had produced ten important magic books in about ten years, under his and other names. But in 1931 his magic writing took second place to turning out fiction for a time. He had created the character of Lamont Cranston who doubled as the mysterious crime fighter soon familiar to millions of Americans as The Shadow.

Gibson had contracted to write four novel-length stories of his character's adventures for a quarterly publication called *The Shadow Magazine* under the pen name of Maxwell Grant. The first issue was such a sellout that the magazine quickly went monthly, then jumped to two issues a month. During a single year, from 1932 to 1933, to meet the demand, Gibson wrote an all-time record of 1,680,000 words about The Shadow. Eventually the magazine settled down to a monthly schedule again, but before it finally ceased publication in 1949 Gibson had written a total of 272 Shadow novels.

Their popularity was boosted during radio's golden years by the broadcast series based on The Shadow, which had listeners hugged close to their loudspeakers to hear the latest episode as the announcer solemnly warned evildoers, in what became a national catchphrase, that "The Shadow knows!"

The old magazine novels have become prized collectors' items, but a new generation has now rediscovered The Shadow and formed a fan club, and a score of the novels have been reprinted in paperback for new readers.

During the late 1940s, as the pressures of writing The Shadow began to ease, Gibson turned more of his attention to magic books again, to add another few dozen to those he had already written. Their continuing quantity was matched by their quality. Among the outstanding ones in more recent years have been *The Master Magicians*, *The Complete Illustrated Book of Card Magic*, and *The Original Houdini Scrapbook*. With Mark Wilson, he was co-author of *The Mark Wilson Course in Magic*.

Robert Orben

Robert Orben, who was chief of the White House speechwriters for President Gerald Ford, started as a magician writing comedy patter for other magicians to use with their tricks. For years he has been putting funny words into the mouths of

Robert Orben started as a magician writing comedy patter for other magicians. He built a career out of helping people make other people laugh. Then he became a speech-writing expert and chief of the White House speech writers for President Gerald Ford.

pattering magicians around the world.

He is a top comedy writer, an author of more than forty books of comic material, head of a company whose sole business is constantly supplying a flow of topical jokes to all kinds of public speakers and entertainers. He has built a career out of helping people make other people laugh.

"I was ten years old when I fell in love with magic," he says, "and now in my forties I am still fascinated." He also began to develop his comedy talent as a boy growing up on the streets of New York. "I was a terrible ballplayer and a non-leader type," he recalls. "But I discovered I had a knack for saying things that were funny."

He remembers his early attempts at becoming a magician as "disastrous" because "I suffered stage fright and shook so bad I couldn't do the dirty work. As a teenager," he says, "I read my way through every book on magic in the public library and perhaps it was inevitable that my first job was as an assistant in Stuart Robson's New York magic shop."

Orben was eighteen when he went to work in Robson's shop on West 42nd Street, demonstrating tricks across the counter for other magicians. He soon came to feel that what magicians needed as much as new tricks were new comedy presentations to appeal to modern audiences, fresh jokes to replace the tired old wheezes that had been used since the early days of vaudeville. Convinced that there was a crying need for a book of up-to-date laugh material written specially for performing, Orben wrote one.

Published in 1946, his small paperbound, *The Encyclopedia of Patter,* priced at one dollar, packed a lot into its forty pages: fifteen complete comedy routines, plus monologues, classified patter, puns, jokes, comic song titles heckler-stoppers, and advice on the effective delivery of comedy. It was eagerly bought not only by magicians but by comedians,

159

and disc jockeys, ventriloquists, and also by public speakers, advertising copy writers, and clergymen. Eventually it went through more than twenty printings and was the first in a long series that sold a total of well over a million copies.

It set the format for some forty more Orben comedy books he continued to produce over the years; they became for many a basic library of vocal humor, containing over thirty thousand jokes. Orben quit performing as a magician and comedian and became probably the nation's most prolific writer of comedy for others, specializing in quick-gag "one-liners."

As television viewers grew into the millions, Orben became a writer for some of its leading comedians and talk-show hosts. For six years, he was a writer for comedian Dick Gregory, for whom he also edited two books. During the early 1960s he was a writer for the Jack Paar television show in New York. He was in Hollywood from 1964 to 1970, where he wrote for Red Skelton.

Concurrently, Orben established his own "laugh manufacturing company," The Comedy Center, which operates out of offices in Wilmington, Delaware. It publishes two four-page newsletters, each filled with topical jokes and one-liners as fast-breaking as whatever happens to be making news. One is *Orben's Current Comedy*, published twenty-four times a year. The other, issued twelve times yearly, is *Orben's Comedy Fillers*.

Orben writes eighty per cent of the material himself, buys the rest from other joke writers and edits it to his style. For inspiration, he regularly scans the headlines and top news in eight daily newspapers and forty magazines. He sets himself a quota of twenty-five original jokes every day, seven days a week. However he feels, in a good or grumpy mood, he faces the typewriter each morning and makes jokes that will set people laughing around the world as they hear others tell them.

"If it takes two hours to turn out twenty-five jokes, fine," he says. "If it takes twelve hours, that's okay. But I won't get up from the typewriter until I have twenty-five workable jokes."

The Comedy Center started as a show-business service, and the jokes they supply are quickly put to use by comedians and other performers in Las Vegas, Hollywood, London. But Orben discovered that the entertainers among his more than two thousand subscribers were all but outnumbered by corporation executives, government officials, politicians, and heads of organizations of every kind, who were eager to inject humor into their public speeches. Accordingly, Orben quit Hollywood and writing for television shows and moved to the Washington area, close to the nation's capital, where in addition to his joke manufacturing he could serve as a speechwriting consultant to those in need of his personal services to brighten a corporate image or a political career. He gradually developed a knowledge that went beyond the jokes into the expert business of researching, writing, and editing speeches.

His new clients included politicians of both political parties, although he was careful not to work for both sides at the same time. One who used his services was then Republican leader of the House, Congressman Gerald Ford, who sought Orben's help with a humorous speech he was to make to the Gridiron Club of Washington's newspaper correspondents.

That led to a relationship that made Orben a speech consultant to Vice-President Ford in early 1974. By August of the same year, Orben found himself a speechwriter for President Ford. In January 1976, he was appointed a special assistant to the president and director of the White House speechwriting department.

After his work in the White House, Orben resumed his consulting, continued his Comedy Center services, and became an active speaker himself on the cross-country lecture circuits. The talk he delivers to business and college audiences is entitled "Laugh While It's Still Free," and provides a peek into the backstage world of the professional comedy writer. He also lectures occasionally to conventions of magicians, who for more than thirty years have been using Orben patter.

Among his more recent books (large hardcover encyclopedia-like volumes that have already gone through several printings) are: *The Joke-Teller's Handbook, The Ad-Libber's Handbook,* and *The Encyclopedia of One-Liner Comedy.*

Jay Marshall

Jay Marshall is in every sense a magic bookman. He is a publisher, writer, editor, printer, discoverer and creator of magic books, a wholesaler, distributor and retail bookseller, and an avid collector of old magic books whose worldwide book hunting has filled his rooms to overflowing with them.

With his wife Frances, his partner in the literary creativity that has produced nearly three hundred books for magicians under their imprint, Marshall operates the Chicago-based magic company Magic, Incorporated. In the building that is

Magic bookman Jay Marshall with his celebrated friend "Lefty," the glove that became a talking rabbit as the climax to his magic act and delighted theater and television audiences around the world.

also their home, store, magic factory, print shop and publishing house, books fill two former bedrooms from floor to ceiling and spread out in towering stacks over their entire living quarters, except perhaps for the top of the kitchen stove. Storage rooms shelve more stacks of books they have printed, and there are almost always two or three new ones in the process of production. (See Chapter 3, "Women in Magic.")

For all of that, there is nothing of the reclusive bookworm in Marshall's genial, fun-loving and fun-making personality. Books may be his love and publishing them his business, but to many magicians throughout the world he is a clown prince of convention pranks and shows, a favorite master of ceremonies, and the stager of and actor in hilarious convention show sketches and satires.

He is also a long-experienced top professional entertainer: magician, comedian, ventriloquist, puppeteer, Punch and Judy man, Broadway legitimate musical comedy actor, television star, nightclub performer. He began as a trouper of the vaudeville circuits and has played some of the best and biggest theaters of the world, modestly advertising himself as "one of the better cheaper acts."

Marshall made up his mind to become a professional magician while he was still a schoolboy giving his first neighborhood magic shows in his home town of Abington, Massachusetts. It was also while he was in school that he first saw a ventriloquist perform, and became so fasci-

nated that he constructed a wooden dummy at home and taught himself ventriloquism to add to his magic shows.

His ability as an entertainer took him to New York and won him success touring in vaudeville. But when World War II found him in military service, he himself found that he couldn't carry bulky magic equipment and a wooden dummy with him into the army. He had an established act and the troops needed entertainment, so he rebuilt the act around the kind of magic using props that were easy to pack and carry. While he was riding on a troop train, the idea came to him of using an ordinary glove for ventriloquism instead of the traditional dummy.

That was the origin of the glove transformed into a talking and singing rabbit that Marshall was to make world-famous as "Lefty." Using a standard army glove at first, he added a pair of shoe buttons for eyes, two scraps of cloth for ears, formed a mouth with the thumb and finger of his fisted hand, and with a lot of talent and his ventriloquial voice seemed to bring it alive. It wasn't a mitten-type glove puppet, but obviously just a plain glove that became a comic little rabbit sophisticatedly joking about the affairs of the day.

It went over so well with the soldiers that Marshall brought the glove novelty back with him into show business when the war ended. His first important postwar booking was at a New York nightclub, where he was engaged as a magician, wearing top hat and tails and with white gloves as part of his costume. The gloves suggested creating a "talking glove" that would have a distinct personality, and the full character of Lefty finally developed.

Lefty was such a hit as the climax to his magic act that before long Marshall was putting the glove through its routine at the world's biggest theater and at one of New York's most intimate nightclub rooms during the same week. By day and evening, huge audiences at the Radio City Music Hall watched his magic and the animated white glove, and then Marshall hurried down to Greenwich Village for late shows at a smart nightclub where audiences were as close to him as in a home living room.

He and his magic and Lefty toured the nightclubs and theaters of the world, the Palladium in London, the Palace and Loew's State, and Paramount on Broadway, and in other big movie and stage-show presentation houses. Marshall's best-known magical presentations were with the "linking rings," with the silk handkerchief that mysteriously unknots itself, and with "Troublewit," an accordion-like folded paper formed into dozens of amusing objects.

Marshall carries boxes of gloves with him when he travels so he will always have a fresh one, since he has found that a glove is no good for making Lefty once the sizing has been washed out of it. A cheaper grade of white cotton seems to be better than more expensive ones, which won't stretch enough to allow

full freedom for working his thumb. Having to hold his thumb-down left hand shoulder-high with his wrist bent at a sharp angle for a full six minutes during four or five performances a day sometimes cramps the muscles in his arm. But the character he has created with a glove often becomes so real that even Marshall himself is carried away. "Sometimes Lefty speaks out of turn," he says, "and it isn't always easy to answer him."

As an actor playing the role of a magician, he appeared with Nanette Fabray in the Alan Jay Lerner–Kurt Weil long-running Broadway musical comedy *Love Life,* and his own act has been part of other musical comedies and revues. He was one of the pioneer entertainers on television, starting in 1940, when a TV booking was "something to pick up" between what were then more important theater and nightclub shows. Except during the war years, he has been on television ever since.

Marshall set a record of nineteen repeat engagements on the Ed Sullivan network variety shows, has appeared on just about every other big-name TV show that ever presented a magician, and also on more interview and talk shows than he can count. Among the books he has written and published, his *TV, Magic and You* has become a standard reference for magicians. Others cover many specialties, including *Parakeet Magic.*

Each year, in Chicago, Marshall and Magic, Inc. play host to an annual get-together of collectors of magic. Aside from books, he also has an outstanding collection of magic coins, posters, advertising material of famous magicians, photos, memorabilia, and apparatus.

Once, when he was asked what single book he would save out of his entire collection if he could preserve only one from destruction, Marshall said his choice would be *The Modern Conjuror* by C. Lang Neil. Published by Lippincott, Philadelphia, in 1902 and about the same time in England, it is not extremely rare as magic books go. Reprint editions sometimes are available from dealers in used magic books. It was from *The Modern Conjurer* that Marshall learned some of his tricks, including Troublewit and others that got him his early television shows. "The items in this book can make one a living as an entertainer," he says. "I know."

Micky Hades

A self-made publisher of magic books, Micky Hades built a small mail-order magic company into the biggest in Canada and made it into an international operation that supplies more than two hundred Hades publications, plus other books new and old, to magicians and mentalists everywhere.

When he was a boy of ten, living on a remote farm in Alberta, Hades walked five miles over a dirt road to see his first magic show, carrying a lard pail filled with three dozen fresh eggs he sold to a village storekeeper for the quarter that paid his admission into the community hall. The performer was John C. Green, a flamboyant white-haired old-timer who toured the hick towns of western Canada with a full-evening show. Dazzled by Green's production of yards and yards of colorful silks, young Michael P. Hades decided right then that someday he would be a magician.

He taught himself magic from books, made his own equipment, and soon advertised himself as "Micky the Magician." In 1941, while still in his early teens, he was distracted into taking a job as an office boy with a wholesale food merchandising company in Edmonton. But his heart was with magic and he spent most of his time studying a pamphlet explaining the secrets of escapes that he kept hidden under a blotter on his office desk. He finally announced to the staff that if they locked him up in the office safe he could escape from it.

The office manager reluctantly agreed to let him try. Hades was locked up and the event drew a crowd out of all the offices and practically disrupted the company's business for the day. Within minutes, Hades made the escape, to the resounding applause of his fellow workers. But the next day the company's owner called him in and told him he would have to make a choice between this "magic nonsense" and a future career in the food business. Hades told the boss, "I guess I'll be a magician."

Jobless and with few paying magic

engagements available, he decided to join a traveling carnival. From another itinerant magician, he bought a small tent-show outfit that included a painted banner showing magical feats and fire eating. He was able to paint over the name and to banner himself as "Professor Hades—The Man of Wonders," but he couldn't paint out the fire-eating picture. Ignorant of the possible painful dangers, he taught himself to eat fire from a flaming torch, and added that to his repertoire. He ended the carnival season with a fistful of money—and with the confidence that he could earn a living from magic.

In later years, Hades landed a full-time job as a city fireman in a suburb of Calgary, and used magic to lecture on fire safety. But meanwhile, for eight years he was associated with a well-known Canadian touring-show group known as The Clifford Entertainers, and with their shows he traveled across western Canada doing magic. Between tours, he worked carnivals and club dates and presented his own touring full-evening show, which was quite a theatrical task since at first he used no assistants and staged two hours of magic all by himself.

He became a popular club-date performer in the Calgary area, presented a weekly children's magic program on television, and also established a reputation as a mentalist who could predict the headlines newspapers were about to print. Prominent in magic societies, he helped organize large regional magic conventions. He also set up a

studio magic shop and began what grew into a successful mail-order business of supplying books and equipment to magicians in Canada and the United States.

In 1957 Hades began publishing a magazine, which two years later became Canada's only monthly magic magazine, the *Hade-E-Gram Magizette*. It was mostly a labor of love, a project in which his wife and whole family took part, with twenty or more full pages an issue to be edited, illustrated, home-typed, mimeographed, assembled, and mailed. Along with news and explanations of tricks and routines, it reflected Hades's views about magic and his personal interests in magic literature and book collecting.

Among *Hade-E-Gram's* regular monthly features was a column for teenage magicians, conducted by one who was then a teenage Toronto performer himself, Doug Henning. Hades continued the magazine as a monthly through 1965, and published occasional issues after that. But it was mainly a hobby and had become too time consuming. His business had grown and he turned to the publication of books.

He wrote, illustrated and home-published his first book, *The Make-Up of Magic*, in 1962. It became a best seller among books for magicians and launched him fully into the publishing business. Books by other authors quickly followed, mimeographed at first and later offset printed, with the editing and production as well as the marketing and distribution done by Hades. He

165

afterwards wrote half a dozen more books himself, but the list by other writers grew to include all the specialties of magic.

In 1972 he bought out Nelson Enterprises, which had specialized in books and manuscripts on mentalism, and incorporated those into his list. The next year he acquired the rights to a popular line of card books by Nick Trost, and in 1974 purchased rights to two more established series of books, by George Blake and Burling Hull. Combined with the increasing publication of Hades's books, the company had 204 titles to offer magicians. He also expanded his service of selling magic books by other publishers, as well as used books, and soon claimed to carry the largest stock of ready-to-ship magic books in the world.

Deciding to go international in 1974, he opened a studio and supply center in Seattle to give faster and more direct service to customers in the United States and to help solve the problems of customs delays in book shipments. In addition to the Seattle branch and the headquarters in Calgary, Alberta, agents were established to distribute the books in Europe, England, and Australia, and the company was renamed Micky Hades International.

New books now come from his presses as rapidly as those strings of colorful silk handkerchiefs he saw his first magician produce years ago.

Lloyd Jones

There is hardly anything to do with magic books that Lloyd Jones hasn't done. He has been prominent in magic for half a century and during most of those years has been involved with the literature of magic, as a publisher of books and magazines, as author, editor, and book reviewer, and as a collector who has put together one of the world's best libraries of rare magic books.

Out of his home in Oakland, California, Jones operates Magic Limited, one of the oldest established magic-bookselling services. Over the years he has published more than fifty books, and has also reprinted and kept in circulation many good older books and a number of magic classics.

For years Jones owned an Oakland drugstore and until his retirement was chief pharmacist of a busy big city hospital—occupations which seldom seemed to limit his literary activities, organizing of magic clubs, or performing of close-up and platform magic. He has won magic society trophies for original magic, card magic, and comedy magic. But as a performer he is probably best known for his comic bartender act, built around the hilarious production of constantly multiplying bottles of liquor.

Jones was one of the founders in 1933 of the Pacific Coast Association of Magicians, and was elected its president in 1955. The following year he was elected national president of the Society of American Magicians and is a member of its national council. He was the prime organizer of two SAM-affiliated assemblies and also of several independent clubs and lecture groups in the San Francisco–Oakland area.

He wrote his first magic book in 1934—a compilation of tricks by West Coast magicians entitled *Meet The Boys of The Pacific Coast*. His book-reviewing career began with a short-lived magazine, *The Die Box* (1933–34), but soon he was reviewing books for two other magazines at the same time, *Tops* and *Genii*. His reviews for *Genii* started with its first issue in 1936 and his "Light From The Lamp" book-review column is still a regular monthly feature.

Jones began publishing his own monthly magazine, *The Bat*, in 1943, and ran it for eight years; it was filled with tricks and routines by contributors whose prominence amounted to a Who's Who of magic. *The Bat* was succeeded by another publication, *The Bat, Jr.*, published at intervals until 1955.

Meanwhile, Jones had launched his bookselling and publishing business and for several years in the 1940s ran a magic-book club called TAB, which was *Bat* spelled backwards and stood for "keeping tab on the new books." It offered a monthly selection and bonus books and resulted in the printing of some fifteen magic paperbacks. He was also publishing hard-cover books, some of them the first works of now well-known magic writers.

It wasn't until 1970 that Jones took up publishing a monthly magazine again, calling the new one *S.O.B., Jr.,* meaning "Son of The Bat, Junior," although some took the initials to have another meaning. In the format of a twelve-page newsletter, filled with unusual features, pictures, cartoons, and reprinted newspaper clippings of magic interest, it often brought news of events and personalities weeks or months ahead of other magic periodicals. Without being aggressively critical, Jones commented plainly and frankly on what he considered good or bad. Columnists included the inventive Phil Goldstein and Gerald Kosky. There was an entire section by Jon Racherbaumer, and a monthly supplement, "Pete's Leaflet," by the knowledgeable and creative performer Pete Biro, a peripatetic world traveler among magicians, who was given full freedom to say what he felt about the national and international magic scene. (Biro's writing later was to become the centerfold feature of *Genii*.)

Subscribers not only got the magazine but monthly "surprise" mailings in the same envelope—a free trick, specially printed playing cards, an out-of-print booklet, printed gag cards, stunts, show programs, brochures, collectors' items. Special discounts were given on new books and remaindered old books.

But as the magazine's circulation and popularity grew, the constant deadline pressure of getting it out as a one-man operation took far too much of the time and energy Jones wanted to devote to his book business and new book publishing projects. In 1978, after nine years, he brought *S.O.B., Jr.* to an end, announcing that instead there would be a publication called *Bat Droppings,* put together as time would allow.

Determined to concentrate on publishing new books, Jones had reduced his book collecting activities by selling his personal library, considered among the world's best and housed in a special room at the rear of his home. It included a collection started in the late 1800s by a prominent magic dealer and writer who subsequently sold it to two other collectors, under whose ownership it expanded further. Jones acquired it in 1943 and built on it for more than three decades. He finally decided that instead of presenting the collection to his alma mater, the University of California, he would entrust its future growth to a collector named Byron Walker, whom he had known since he was a teenager with a passion for magic books. In 1976, Jones sold the great collection to Walker and his wife Barbara, an equally dedicated collector, and they have reassembled it with their own collections in their San Leandro, California, home. "It is now getting the attention it deserves," Jones says. "Byron and Barbi are eagerly improving and adding to it, and making me quite proud."

Lee Jacobs

The full-color reproductions of posters of famous magicians produced by Lee Jacobs decorate the walls of many of the world's magic dens and libraries. Jacobs, a publisher and bookseller, operates a mail-order magic-supply business out of his home in Pomeroy, an Ohio River community with a population of less than three thousand, where his one-man industry is the most unusual in town.

Jacobs's interest in magic started when he was so young he doesn't remember exactly how it began, but he was performing for family and friends at the age of five. By the time he was eight he had given school shows and was advertising his

Lee Jacobs was a part-time magic dealer at fifteen, quit teaching literature at Ohio University to become a full-time dealer and performer, publisher, and bookseller, specializing in full-color reproductions of posters of famous magicians.

availability as a magician for parties and other entertainments.

Like most young magicians, Jacobs accumulated a lot of "extra stuff"—props and things he found he had no use for. But instead of stashing them away, he began selling them to other hobbyists. He was a part-time magic dealer at the age of fifteen, and soon was advertising in the magic magazines and renting counter space to display his wares at magic conventions.

Pomeroy's nearest "big city" was Marietta, forty miles away. It was the home of the late Tommy Windsor, who became Jacobs's close friend while he was in his teens. A veteran river showboat, tent-show and theatrical entertainer, Windsor settled down into a successful home-based career as a club-date magician and creator of popular tricks and routines sold to other magicians. He greatly influenced Jacobs, who still publishes and markets many of Windsor's effects.

"Practically everything good I learned about selling magic I learned from Tommy Windsor," Jacobs says. "And I learned more about performing just from arguing with him than I did from anyone else."

When he finished school, Jacobs's interest in writing and literature led him for a time into a teaching career. But he continued performing magic and dealing in it. As a magician and comedian, and sometimes as an illusionist or mentalist, he played clubs, civic affairs, department stores, and shopping centers. He also performed for business cor-porations and on television, in nightclubs, and resort hotels. He gave lecture shows on magic, hypnotism and the occult.

Meanwhile, as his publishing and magic-supply business grew, Jacobs made a choice and left the classrooms behind him to become a full-time dealer and performer. One lesson he learned well from Tommy Windsor was to keep his operations home based in a small town; this would limit costs and overhead expenses and thus allow him to keep his prices reasonable.

He writes some of the books and booklets he publishes, and markets selected books and tricks by others, together with used books and some collectors' material. Included in his publishing output are a series on publicity and promotion for magicians, a directory of theatrical agencies, and a detailed manual entitled *The Real Methods and Secrets of the Challenge Escape from 75 Feet of Rope* —a feat he performs himself to generate headline-making publicity.

But the most popular specialty of Lee Jacobs Productions is the reprinting in large size and full rich colors of posters of famous magicians, including Houdini; Thurston; Blackstone; Dante; Kellar; Chung Ling Soo; Le Roy, Talma, and Bosco; and many others. They are excellent reproductions, on fine quality paper, sold at a fraction of the cost of the rare originals.

Anthony Vander Linden

Anthony Vander Linden started as a collector of magic books and magazines. As he bought other collections to add to his own, he found himself with duplicates and gradually began selling or trading those. "One day I acquired a single lot of over five thousand," he recalls. "I suddenly found that my collecting hobby had become a business."

A scholar of magical literature, he became one of the leading dealers in it, supplying magicians, collectors, other dealers, and serious newcomers to the hobby with long-sought books or specific issues of magazines to fill their needs. His first list, in the early 1960s, was only two pages long. His recent listings have run to two-part catalogues, totaling forty-six pages, offering 1,586 different magic books, and many issues of 169 different magic magazines, plus lecture notes, magicians' programs, photos, old dealer catalogues, and various other items.

Born in Bayside, Long Island in 1924, Vander Linden was taken as a boy to Africa and Europe and spent his early life in Belgium, where an uncle who was a parish priest at Ghent showed him his first magic tricks. While there he also saw his first magic show, performed by a professional magician who entertained the Sunday school. By the time he returned to the United States he had been well-bitten by the magic bug.

As a teenager, he studied the magic books in his high school library in Brooklyn and dreamed of owning the wonders advertised in magic catalogues, but like most young hobbyists on a limited allowance he had little to spend for equipment and mostly made do with the tricks he put together from books. While studying magic, he also completed his academic studies, graduating from Brooklyn College. He studied law for two years at Fordham before turning to a business career and eventually becoming divisional manager of a large food company.

It was during those years that his hobby of collecting magical literature turned into the business of dealing in it. Meanwhile, in 1970, he was elected village clerk and treasurer of Mill Neck, Long Island, where he and his family had long made their home. "As chief fiscal officer for my village, responsible for large sums of money, I underplay my prowess as a magician," he jokes.

But under the stage name of Tony Presti, billed as "The Continental Magician," he has been an active semiprofessional club-date performer in the New York area, entertaining children and adults with comedy magic, which has also won him magic society awards. A popular master of ceremonies of magic-club shows, prominent in several magic organizations, he is past president of his local assembly of the Society of American Magicians, and the founder of its library.

For his personal library, he has kept some three hundred carefully selected magic books, in addition to countless files of magazines. He combines his vacations with searches for books in Europe and elsewhere. Every day's mail brings him not only orders for books and want lists to fill, but offers of surplus books and entire collections. His stock of magic books and magazines is housed in 150 feet of bookcases and metal shelving, plus large filing cabinets and half a dozen big storage boxes. It has remained a highly personalized business.

For Further Reading

Bibliographies

Gill, Robert. *Magic as a Performing Art: A Bibliography of Conjuring.* London and New York: Bowker Publishing, 1976. A fully annotated listing, evaluation and description of the scope and content of 1,066 magic books and booklets of "practical value to the modern performer," chosen from among those published in the English language during the forty years between 1935 and 1975. Gill, a professional British librarian and performing magician, received the Bowker Bibliography Prize for this book. There are several other fine bibliographies of older books, mostly of interest to collectors, but this is the first extensive appraisal of recent books for their magic content. Some of the listed books are out of print, but may be available through used-book dealers.

Potter, Jack. *The Master Index to Magic in Print.* 14 vols. and supplements. Calgary, Alta.: Micky Hades International, 1967–77. These fourteen large volumes, each of which runs to some five hundred pages, contain more than 100,000 cross-indexed references to specific tricks, routines and various categories of magic in books and magazines published in the English language up to the end of 1964. The index is mainly of value to those having access to a large library of magic books and periodicals. Available as separate volumes or as a set.

Book Lists and Catalogues

Many magic booksellers and publishers issue separate book catalogues and lists, while other magic companies include book listings in their general catalogues of equipment and supplies. (See: Chapter 10, "The Dealers.") When inquiring about current prices of book catalogues, enclose a stamped self-addressed envelope, or for foreign inquiries an international postal reply coupon.

Magic, Inc. 5082 N. Lincoln Ave., Chicago, IL. 60625, has three big illustrated book catalogues that amount to descriptive bibliographies of more than 1,000 books. *Book Catalogue One* covers all their own publications. *Book Catalogue Two* covers books by other publishers around the world, which the company stocks and sells. *Book Catalogue Three* describes their own and other titles published since 1976.

Micky Hades International, Box 476, Calgary, Alberta, Canada, T2P 2J1, offers a large illustrated catalogue of its own publications, frequent updated now-book announcements, a *Book-A-Log* catalogue of other books, manuscripts, lecture notes, and limited and special editions in stock, a used-book list, and a catalogue that pictures and describes plans sold for constructing stage illusions.

Lee Jacobs Productions, Box 362, Pomeroy, Ohio 45769, issues illustrated catalogues of its poster reproductions, books, manuscripts, and other publications, frequent announcements of new books and products, lists of illusion plans, and used books and equipment.

Magic Limited, Lloyd E. Jones, 4064 39th Ave., Oakland, CA. 94619, has lists and announcements of books Jones publishes, and keeps customers advised of other books in stock and various special offers.

Anthony Vander Linden, R.F.D. 2, Oyster Bay, N.Y. 11771, periodically issues catalogues of used books, magazines, and other magic literature. As is customary, it is assumed that those seeking such publications are acquainted with them. Thus, used books are listed simply by title and author, magazines by their issue dates or serial numbers.

Magazines

The Linking Ring, The Magic Circu- lar and *M-U-M* are available only to the members of the magic societies that publish them. For address listings to inquire about possible membership see Chapter 9, "Clubs and Conventions."

Abracadabra. Goodliffe the Magician. Arden Forest Industrial Estate, Alcester, Warwickshire, England.

Genii, the International Conjurors' Magazine. Box 36068, Los Angeles, CA 90036.

Magigram. The Supreme Magic Co., Ltd., 64 High Street, Bideford, Devon, England.

The New Tops. Abbott's Magic Manufacturing Co., Colon, MI 49040.

Tape Cassettes

Abracassetta. Monthly magic magazine on tape. Produced by Goodliffe, Arden Forest Industrial Estate, Alcester, Warwickshire, England.

Magicassettes. Recorded volumes made by Martin Breese, 77 Bolingbroke Road, Hammersmith, London W14 OAA, England.

Sound of Magic studio. 8 Herbal Hill, London E.C. 1, England.

Sounds Unlimited. Craige Snader, Jr., Apartado 12-655, Mexico 12, D.F., Mexico.

7

COLLECTING MAGIC

The collectors of magic are the keepers of its archives, history, and knowledge. They are the preservers of its literature and artifacts, the explorers of its past and recorders of its present. Their collections and research provide a heritage of information and tradition for magicians of the future to build upon.

Collectors are also the happy magical junkmen of the world, whose enjoyment is in the constant search for treasure in what others have discarded, ignored, or may be willing to sell or trade. For most, there is as much fun in the quest as in the finding, in the sleuthing and deductions, the seeking of information, the following of trails that may lead to discoveries, and in acquiring further knowledge of what they have in their collections and what they hope to get.

Obviously there are many rare things the average collector can hardly hope to obtain, but there are also many good collectibles to be had: literature, apparatus and other items that originally were produced in fairly large quantity. And the lure of collecting always holds out the possibility that even the newcomer may turn up something scarce.

Without much expense, but with some patient and knowledgeable searching, many have followed their personal interests and formed unusual specialized collections of magic's artifacts that are sometimes overlooked by other collectors. Even a small, well-assembled and carefully researched collection in some

Magicians' bookplates are popular collectibles, for their unusual designs and because they are available in great variety and take up little space. Meant to be pasted inside the covers of books to identify the owner, they are widely traded among magic collectors, and some collections run to several hundred. COURTESY F. WILLIAM KUETHE, JR.

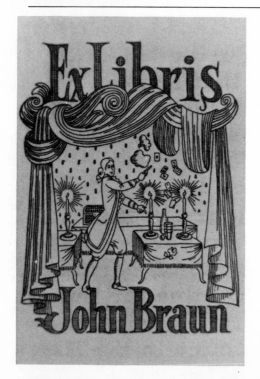

particular area of magic's past or present frequently brings the collector recognition from his peers as an authority on that subject.

The average magician buys tricks to use in performing, and buys books for their practical content as he gradually builds a working library. Over the years he may acquire quite an accumulation of magical articles, but he seldom thinks of himself as a collector. The true collector is interested in books not only for their content but for their intrinsic value, and in apparatus as objects to be collected.

An accumulation becomes a collection when it is organized. The collector sorts out by category, identifies and classifies, keeps a card-file index or other record to which he may add pertinent notes from time to time. He plans proper shelving and housing, how best to protect and preserve the collection, and how to display his most important prizes for the admiration of other magicians or collectors.

Some specialized collections, such as those of magic coins, tricked cards, or magicians' bookplates, take up little space, while a collection of big stage illusions may require renting room in a storage warehouse. Despite that, there are collections of illusions, but not many; it is more usual for those interested to collect blueprints, construction plans, sketches and diagrams, or miniature working models.

Posters are among the more difficult items to store properly and display, especially large ones with several sheets that were designed to be matched together when pasted up for billboarding. But old original posters of famous magicians, hard to obtain in good condition, are among the most wanted by collectors. When available they are often high priced, and some have soared in value in recent years.

There are collectors of apparatus once used by famous magicians, and of their personal effects such as watches, combs, cufflinks, or cigarette cases. Other collectors seek anything and everything related to a single performer, or perhaps all the apparatus illustrated and described in some classic book of magic. Still others collect varieties of a single trick as it developed through the ages—many different versions of the Cups and Balls, for instance, or the Linking Rings.

This is not a bookplate but a rubber stamping, which served the same purpose in the books once owned by Chung Ling Soo. Acclaimed by the world's audiences as a famous Chinese magician, Soo was really an occidental New Yorker, William Robinson. Successful for years with his skilled Chinese impersonation and superb magic, he was tragically shot to death on stage in London in 1918 while performing the bullet-catching feat. COURTESY F. WILLIAM KUETHE, JR.

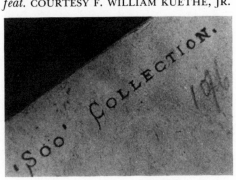

This small cannon originally belonged to the great Alexander Herrmann. He would borrow a gentleman's pocket watch, smash it up, and fling the pieces down into the mouth of the cannon. Then he would fire the cannon at a box that had hung suspended from the theater ceiling from the start of the show. When the hanging box was lowered to the stage, the missing watch—restored and unharmed—would be found inside it. After the magician's death, his widow, Adelaide Herrmann, used it in her shows for years. Much of her other equipment was destroyed in a fire in the 1920s, and the famed Harry Blackstone came to her rescue by lending her apparatus so she could continue appearances until she rebuilt her show. In gratitude, she presented him with the Herrmann cannon. Blackstone had a special crate built for it and carried the cannon around the country with his shows for forty years, always intending to use it, but he never did. Picture, with Robert Lund, shows relative size of cannon, now in his collection at the American Museum of Magic. ROBERT LUND COLLECTION—AMERICAN MUSEUM OF MAGIC

Specialist collectors search out the magic of circuses and sideshows, spook and ghost shows, the apparatus of celebrated vaudeville performers, the trappings of old-timers who toured the Wild West in stagecoach days, the crystal balls and secret electronic or mechanical devices of mentalists, and the spirit-message slates or floating trumpets of pseudo-spiritualists.

They collect the handcuffs, chains, locks, straitjackets and other restraints of escape artists, the up-the-sleeve holdouts and varied gaffs of crooked gamblers, magicians' costumes, old and newer magic sets of every country, magical toys and

Houdini was in hot water, but deliberately so, when he performed his celebrated Chinese Water Torture Escape. This brass pail, one of a matching set of four, weighing 27½ pounds each, was used to bail water into the glass-fronted cell in which he was suspended head-down after his feet had been securely shackled. He defied death at each performance, but had no desire to be immersed in icy water. Houdini's written instructions to the stage crew specified that the pails were to be filled before the show with "boiling water—must be boiling." What his prop sheet listed as the "four brass tubs" are in the Lund collections at the American Museum of Magic. ROBERT LUND COLLECTION— AMERICAN MUSEUM OF MAGIC

poses: balancing wands that defy gravity; rising, jumping, and floating wands; vanishing, appearing, diminishing, expanding, and color-changing wands; wands that fall limp, break apart, spin in half, fire blank shots, bursts of flame, or geysers of water; wands that serve as secret aids in the production or disappearance of handkerchiefs, cards, coins, billiard balls, or flowers.

False hands fascinate some collectors. There are wooden replicas of hands, which, when rested on a sheet of glass, magically come alive to tap out answers to questions or to reveal chosen cards. There are hollow fake palms, backhand knuckles, extra fingers, fingertips and thumb-tips made of metal or rubber to conceal small objects while covering the performer's own digits.

Extensive collections have also been made of gadgets and gimmicks, including hidden devices audiences normally never see, such as spring-hinged tabletop trapdoors and hidden shelves. There are also mechanical trays, craftily designed glasses, mirror-partitioned vases, and glass tubes, most of them more frequently used by old-time magicians than those of today. Such collections may also include smaller aids, hand-held or concealed about the person to hold, drop or deliver coins, balls, lighted cigarettes, or handkerchiefs into the hands—or to pull them away and make them disappear. Some long-ago discarded gadgets are puzzles to their collectors and provide the fun of searching through the literature of magic

mechanical toy banks with miniature magicians performing, and the magic premiums and giveaway tricks enclosed in breakfast cereal boxes or bagged potato chips.

Wands are among popular collectibles. Some have been used personally by great magicians. Others were designed for magical purto try to find out what they originally were intended for. Especially intriguing are gimmicks that were one of a kind, made to the specifications of an individual performer, or home-made and kept secret even from other magicians.

Identifying and authenticating apparatus of every kind, discovering the time period of its manufacture and use, its probable maker, and the detailed original effect and routine for performing with it, are pursuits that often require considerable study and much correspondence among collector friends who share reasoned guesses and theories.

Old catalogues of magic dealers are primary sources of information about apparatus. Since these old catalogues are collectors' items in themselves, they become doubly wanted. Old instruction sheets, dealer advertisements in old magic magazines, well-illustrated old magic books with detailed descriptions, and photographs and drawings showing magicians with their equipment may help with identification.

Collections of playing cards that have been tricked for magical uses include those with specially printed faces or backs; narrow, wide, long, and short cards; marked cards; single cards; sets of these; entire packs; card cases that have been faked or altered in various ways. There are collections of trick cards produced by one inventor or manufacturer, collections of the many varieties designed for one particular trick such as "the four aces" or the "rising cards," collections of antiquarian trick cards, collections of animated cards in which the pips visibly move around or a King of Diamonds tips his crown.

Throw-out cards are another popular field for card collectors. These are the thicker-than-usual cards—with a magician's picture on the face and a "Good Luck" message on the back—that were scaled out into the audience as souvenirs. Thurston and many other performers used to toss them from the stage and send them flying over the heads of spectators to the very last rows of a theater—even high into the balconies. There are also specially printed playing cards, widely used business cards by various magicians, with regulation playing card designs on the backs and pictures, slogans, or self-advertisements on the face. Collectors also seek the more usual types of business cards, personal calling cards, letterheads and other stationery, brochures, announcements, and every sort of printed material issued by well-known magicians, as well as correspondence, diaries, scrapbooks, notebooks, working scripts, scribbled notes, bills, bank statements, and cancelled checks. To the autograph-hunting collector, a cancelled check is proof positive of the authenticity of a signature.

Photography fills collectors' files with pictures of magicians performing, relaxing with others, attending magic gatherings and conventions, standing in front of theater marquees that spell out their names in lights. Pictures that are auto-

Frederick Eugene Powell memorabilia. Powell, who first gained fame in the 1890s, recreated his old-time magic at a special performance, for which this theater ticket was issued in 1929, a testimonial in his honor by the Society of American Magicians. His autograph is on the back (not shown). The playing card with his picture has a standard card design on the back and is similar to advertising cards once used by many magicians, now sought by collectors.

graphed, with interesting or informative personal comments, usually are the most valued.

Some collectors specialize in the visual treasures of magic in the fine arts: century-old prints and lithographs, etchings and oil paintings, sculpture, busts and ceramics, fine antique magical cabinetry, and unique apparatus that reflects in its beautiful woods and metals the hand artistry of master craftsmen or the ingenuity of concealed clockwork and mechanisms.

Collectors' files also bulge with clippings from newspapers and magazines about magic and magicians. Such material requires careful sorting, indexing, and notation of places and dates, to transform the clippings from a bewildering accumulation into valuable reference sources of information.

Magic used as a theme of printed advertisements has produced specialized collections of a thousand or more examples—in which stores, companies, and corporations have used magic to promote products and services of every kind, from industrial insurance to steel pipes to bread and butter, with eye-catching illustrations and text. Also collected are innumerable little illustrated advertising booklets explaining how to do magic tricks. These were once published by makers of patent medicines, soaps, cereals, beverages, cigarettes, motor oil, rope, toothpaste, and other products; some date from the 1800s. Given away or used as write-in premiums to advertise the products, they were often written by well-known magicians—who usually were careful not to explain any of their own tricks.

Souvenir programs and "pitch books," sold in theaters where magicians appeared, have long been collectors' items. These were hawked in theater lobbies or up and down the aisles between acts after a "pitchman" or the performer himself had delivered a spiel from the stage urging the audience to buy the books and learn the "secrets" revealed. Usually they explained some simple parlor tricks and included the illustrated life story of the magician and his world triumphs. Houdini, Thurston, Blackstone, and others sold thousands of them.

Collectors of political and satirical cartoons depicting magic have found that theatrical wizards have been inspiring cartoonists at least since the French Revolution. Those who collect comic books featuring the adventures of fictional supermagicians or illustrated tales about famous real-life magicians find themselves competing with other general comic-book collectors to acquire them.

Harder to track down are the published predecessors of the comic books, the dime novels. About the same size as comic books, and with equally gaudy color-splashed covers, dime novels entranced young readers of the 1890s with fictional derring-do in such classics as *Frank Merriwell Magician, or For Fun, Fame and Fortune,* and *Getting To The Top, or Zig-Zag the Boy Conjuror.* Among other dime-novel favorites were

Souvenir programs and "pitch books" were sold in theaters where great magicians presented their touring shows. Houdini's Life, History and Handcuff Secrets, *early 1900s, explained some escapes and tricks, and advertised his* Conjurers' Monthly Magazine *as something that should be bought by "anyone desiring to know all about handcuff secrets and how to open all the handcuffs in the world." The other* Houdini Souvenir Program *was printed for his last tour in 1926.*

Thurston's Fooling the World *booklet, 1928, went for a quarter a copy, claimed a first edition of one million, and offered not only explanations of* Magic YOU Can Do *but also advice about dreams, numerology, astrology, and fortune telling. His next year's booklet,* Thurston The Great Magician, *priced at fifty cents, cover-promised "love, luck, money, fate," and contained an ad for a mail-order course in magic for one dollar.*

The Great Blackstone's Secrets, Easy Magic for Everyone sold for a dollar, with photos of him showing how to do some tricks. There was also a listing of other tricks for sale by his mail-order magic company. Dante, another of the big show magicians, published his Tricks for Everybody *as his 1941 "pitch book."* ROBERT LUND COLLECTION— AMERICAN MUSEUM OF MAGIC

Stanley's Boy Magician Lost in Africa
and *Herman the Boy Magician on the
Road with a Variety Show.*

There are collections of sheet music written by or inspired by magicians, early cylinder-type recordings of magicians' voices, later records and albums, recordings of radio broadcasts, and more recent tape recordings. Collected visual images of magicians in action include slide projections, silent and sound movies, and videotape recordings. Showings of collected films and videotapes are often featured at magic conventions, and some collectors and magic societies provide film rental services for magic clubs. Collectors are interested not only in movies about magicians but in magicians who acted in films or contributed to the advancement of motion pictures. Related material, such as magic-movie posters, lobby cards,

Sheet music featuring magic and magicians, now sought by collectors, was a popular form of publicity. "The Amateur Conjurer" apparently was one of the hit songs of a late 19th-century "burlesque fairy drama" called Ariel *presented at London's Gaiety Theatre. "La Malle des Indes," with its picture suggesting the trunk escape illusion, was a galop for the piano, dedicated by composer Georges Lamothe to his friend, France's famous Robert-Houdin. The "Polka D'Illusion Magique" was inspired by its cover-pictured floating-head illusion, performed by magician and New York magic dealer Michael Hartz, for whom it was composed by Juliet Levy in the 1860s.*
ROBERT LUND COLLECTION—AMERICAN
MUSEUM OF MAGIC

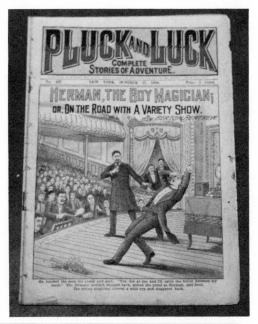

Before there were comic books, dime novels such as these, featuring adventures of fictional magicians, thrilled young readers. One of the heroes of Tip Top Weekly "an ideal publication for American youth," which sold for a nickel in 1898, was "Frank Merriwell Magician." The 1906 Pluck and Luck shows "Herman the Boy Magician" doing the bullet-catching trick. Another Pluck and Luck, 1915, offered "Stanley's Boy Magician or Lost in Africa," while Brave and Bold, published every Wednesday in 1910, had "The Young Magician or Conjuring to Fame and Fortune." That cover picture shows him producing white ribbon and the caption says "he kept on pulling until he had a strip a dozen yards in length."

ROBERT LUND COLLECTION—AMERICAN MUSEUM OF MAGIC

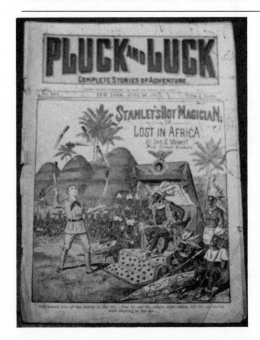

and movie publicity photos of actor-magicians, is further grist for the collector's mill.

Postage stamps have not offered magic collectors much to go on, since stamps honoring magicians have been issued by only three or four countries—not including the United States despite a long campaign to have Houdini pictured on a stamp. But coin collecting offers a far broader field, not only in the many varieties of trick coins and the apparatus and gimmicks used in coin magic, but in the highly specialized collecting of tokens and medals issued by or for magicians. They include those made for advertising and publicity, medals commemorating magical events and personalities, and so called "palming coins" manufactured as stage-money substitutes for real money. Magic numismatists, like other coin collectors, are concerned with dates, sizes, design variations, types of metals, and historic identification.

From the sixteenth century to the present, magicians of many countries have had medals, tokens, and "good luck" pieces made, for presentation to admirers, public circulation, distribution to theater audiences, or sometimes admission to performances. The first in America to publicize himself that way was the visiting German magician Herr Alexander (Heimburgher), who had a medal struck to honor his performances in New York in 1847. Other magicians of about the same period adopted the practice of having their names counterstamped into the metal of real coins then being used as legal tender. When spent and passed from hand to hand, the name-stamped money provided effective and inexpensive advertising, until "mutilating the currency" finally was outlawed.

Among those who had their names stamped on real coins, which were to become collectors' prizes, was Young the Magician, who also got himself into serious trouble by somewhat innocently counterfeiting half-dollars to use in his shows. Magically producing a great number of genuine silver coins from the air meant a heavy investment for a performer, so Professor Young decided to make lead-alloy reproductions of 1858 half-dollars. Arrested and brought to trial, Young testified that the counterfeits were used only in his act and that he had taken great precautions to see that they were never circulated. The coins were confiscated, but he was let off with a suspended sentence after he promised to make no more.

By the late nineteenth century Martinka & Co., New York magic dealers, began to issue coins specially designed for sleight of hand. The first Martinka "palming coins" had the firm's name on one side, while the other side pictured a magician astride the world producing objects at the touch of his wand. Worded around the coin's edge was the legend: MUNDUS VULT DECIPI: DECIPIATUR (The world wishes to be deceived: let it be deceived). Later Martinka coins were produced in varying sizes for different magical uses. Other magic dealers soon were making them,

This 1847 Herr Alexander (Heimburgher) medal probably was the first of many circulated in America to publicize a magician. Herr Alexander, a German magician, came to the United States for a successful tour, appeared before President James Polk, and scored a theatrical triumph at Niblo's Garden in New York.

The medal to honor him was presented at a testimonial dinner, and he had copies made to give to friends and spread his fame. Some accounts say the original was minted in gold, others that it was die-struck by a New York engraver. The inscription reads: "Presented to Herr Alexander as a testimony of esteem from his friends in New York 1847." COURTESY F. WILLIAM KUETHE, JR.

Until it finally was declared illegal to deface the currency, early American magicians sometimes had their names counterstamped into the metal of United States and Spanish coins that people were using at the time as money. When the coins were spent, the advertising also passed from hand to hand. Coin at left advertises John Wyman, prominent magician in the mid-1800s, who frequently entertained Abraham Lincoln and White House guests and toured the country for nearly fifty years. Professor Young, counterstamped coin at right, played mostly in New England around the same time. COURTESY F. WILLIAM KUETHE, JR.

each with its own design and specifications to facilitate "improved" handling.

Palming coins remained popular with magicians for years and some are still sold by dealers, but inflation has pushed up their cost to nearly that of real half-dollars, and since most coin magic is now performed close-up the real ones are preferred. But meanwhile collectors have been provided with scores of different issues and variants—as well as tricked palming coins, faked in many ways, as genuine coins are for magicians.

Noted for his fabulous collection of magic coins and tokens is F. William Kuethe, Jr., a recognized authority who has done much original research and published guides and articles on the subject. Kuethe, a Maryland real estate and banking executive, has more than 750 pieces—including many rarities—in his personal collection. Since 1966 he has been publishing a unique periodical, the *Journal of Necromantic Numismatics,* of which only fifteen to twenty copies of each issue are circulated; so specialized is the *Journal* that only those who contribute to it receive a copy. Strictly a "reciprocal" publication, it is Kuethe's hobby within a hobby, and few complete files of it exist, which makes it rare in itself for magazine collectors.

But for general circulation among magic collectors of every kind, Kuethe also published, from 1964 to 1976, what many consider one of the best collectors' journals ever issued, *The Magic Cauldron.* It ran through sixty-four quarterly or annual issues, with supplements, and contained contributions from noted collectors around the world; much new information first appeared in its pages. After he suspended the *Cauldron,* Kuethe began a new series, printed in miniature size, which collector friends who correspond with him regularly receive.

Kuethe has himself struck and minted several magic-related tokens, including one he generously gave copies of to all members of the Magic Collectors Association on its twenty-fifth anniversary. Although best known for his interest in coins, like most specialists he also collects other things. He has an extensive collection of magic books and magazines, another of magicians' bookplates, and perhaps the world's largest collection of "forcing books"—volumes specially printed for use in mind-reading tricks.

Whatever specialties magic collectors may have, most of them also collect books, magazines, and the literature of magic. There are far more collectors of magic in print than of anything else. In addition to the great multivolumed general book collections, some of which contain scarce antiquarian treasures, book collecting itself has many specialized categories. Old and new magic books are collected in English, in foreign languages, in translations from original languages, by editions, printings, bindings, and title variations. There are collections of autographed copies, collections of all published material by a particular author in all languages and editions, collections of limited, special, and numbered editions, collections of books whose pages are scribbled over with handwritten notes and comments by some famous previous owner, collections of original manuscripts, original rough sketches for book illustrations, printers' proofs, book jackets, related author correspondence, and reviews.

Category collections include patter books, those about specific types of tricks or styles of performing, pseudopsychic phenomena, exposés of fraudulent spiritualists, magic history and biography, books largely copied from earlier books, and books ghost-written for famous magicians. There are collectors of plays about magic, of magic in poetry, of various non-magic books that include material about magicians, of novels in which magicians are fictional characters, of children's storybooks, of coloring books, activity books, cutout and punch-out books of magic tricks, and of "flip books" whose illustrations seem to become animated when pages are quickly riffled by thumb and fingers.

Among the world's great library collections of magic books are those in the British Museum and in the library of The Magic Circle in London. In the United States, Houdini's book and periodical collections, and the notable collections of Dr. Morris Young and John McManus are in the Rare Book Division of the Library of Congress; while Houdini's theater programs, playbills, posters, and memorabilia can be seen at the Theater Library of the University of Texas. John Mulholland's collection is housed in the Walter Hampton Memorial Library at The Players in Manhattan. At the Library of the Performing Arts in New York's Lincoln Center, there is a Society of American Magicians collection, and also much magic-related material in the library's other theatrical collections.

Outstanding private collections of magic in print include those of Milbourne Christopher in New York, Byron and Barbara Walker in California, Jay Marshall in Chicago, and J. Gary Bontjes of Illinois, who also has one of the world's best collections of magic lecture notes.

Robert Lund created the American Museum of Magic in Marshall, Michigan, to house and display his enormous collection of more than a quarter of a million items, with books and every sort of printed material in nearly every collecting field and specialization. (See: Chapter 8. Showplaces of Magic.)

Here are some of the other leading personalities among collectors of magic literature.

H. Adrian Smith

H. Adrian Smith, whose great library in his Massachusetts home covers conjuring and closely allied subjects in all languages with a breadth and depth probably unequaled, is not only a world-recognized authority on the literature of magic but also is America's foremost private collector of early magic books in their best-preserved rare editions. As a boy, Smith first became acquainted with magic books in the public library of his native city of Providence, Rhode Island, and later helped to put himself through Brown University by presenting magic shows. While in college, he also acquired a collection of three hundred magic books, which became a beginning for the library he would gradually spend much of his life building.

During subsequent tours with his full-evening magic show, he also gained a reputation as a performer of mental magic and concurrently added two more large collections of magic books to his own: the Peter Graef collection of fifteen hundred titles and the famous Dr. Milton Bridges library of six thousand. Smith continued to build on those additional foundations, and to devote himself to the pursuit of books and scholarly bibliographical research. Few other magic bibliophiles have spent as much time as he has exploring the great magic-book collections of the English-speaking world.

A past president of both the International Brotherhood of Magicians and the Society of American Magicians, Smith has written extensively for magazines on conjuring literature and its history, has lectured, and displayed some of his rare volumes, at special magic convention exhibits. After his semi-retirement, in his late sixties, from his job as general manager of a Boston manufacturing company, he became more active than ever as his own full-time librarian, reorganizing and card-cataloging hundreds of recently acquired books, and adding new bookcases to the more than three hundred feet of shelving covered by his collection.

Among the thousands of books in Smith's library, the German-language section alone fills seventeen feet of shelves and perhaps holds as many volumes as any of the collections in Germany. In other categories, there are complete runs of magic magazines, including rare ones, of dealers' catalogues, and a big collection of playbills, letters, photos, and memorabilia. "It is a lot of work but it is also a lot of fun," he says, "and even I am beginning to be surprised at what I own."

John Henry Grossman

Dr. John Henry Grossman, whose research, writing, and many activities on behalf of magic have earned him a place in magic's Hall of Fame, has for years specialized in collecting dealers' catalogues. This collection—although only part of the rare treasures of literature and apparatus Grossman preserved in his New England home—is generally recognized as the world's finest.

The collection includes some of the few existing copies of early catalogues, among them what may have been the first published in the English language, issued by London magic dealer W. H. Crambrook in 1843. Compared with later lavishly illustrated catalogues from other dealers, which were to grow to the size of telephone directories, Crambrook's was a mere listing of tricks for sale, without illustration. The first dealer in America known to have published a catalogue was Joseph Michael Hartz, a famed English performer who came to the United States to star in vaudeville. Between tours, Hartz opened Manhattan's first magic shop on Broadway, and in 1873 issued a fine and well-illustrated 116-page catalogue. A copy now belongs to Dr. Grossman.

Cloth-bound on Dr. Grossman's shelves are copies of most of the important dealer catalogues ever published. His other books start with several editions of Reginald Scot's *Discoveries of Witchcraft*, including the 1584 first edition, and extend through early English and American scarcities and classic volumes. There are handsomely bound magic magazines—including the first of them, *The Conjuror's Magazine* of 1791—albums, folders of letters, bookplates, and sheet music. On the stairway walls leading to Dr. Grossman's magic den are framed lithographs and playbills. Antique apparatus, old magic sets, tables and stage properties used by famous past performers add to making his home a collection of collections.

Professionally a well-known gynecologist, Dr. Grossman has also performed stage magic and is an entertaining close-up performer. A founder-member of the Magic Collectors Association, he serves by unanimous election as its honorary lifetime president. Magicians know him, too, as an international magic magazine columnist, lecturer, and historian. His world-famous library and collections may be only less celebrated than his generosity in sharing his in-depth knowledge with other magicians and collectors.

James B. Alfredson

James B. Alfredson, of Lansing, Michigan, editor of *Magicol*, the quarterly journal of the Magic Collectors Association, is convinced there are two kinds of people in the world: those who collect and those who don't. "I'm sure you're born with it, either the inclination or the lack thereof," he says. "If I didn't collect magazines, I'd likely collect stamps, coins, barbed-wire, or whatever."

Specializing since his youth in collecting magic magazines, Alfredson is an authority on the subject, and has some four hundred separate files of periodicals, some complete and in many volumes, some lacking only a single issue, some containing only a single copy. How many thousands of individual magazines that adds up to, even he doesn't know, but says, "I'd know it if one were missing."

As a youngster interested in performing magic, Alfredson accumu-

Whatever their specialties, most magic collectors also collect books and magazines. Houdini once advertised that bound 404-page volumes of the Conjurer's Monthly Magazine *he edited and published (1906–8) were for sale at one dollar a volume. Today's magazine collectors wish it were still so.*

lated all the books, magazines, news clippings, magicians' photos, and whatever else came his way. The second-hand magazines were rather plentiful because, as he puts it, "magicians' wives generally get after their husbands to keep them from cluttering up the house, and the magazines find their way into the hands of little boys." That is a fact he has since come to deplore as a collector, but not as a boy, when the

magazines that got into his hands provided him with the names of other magicians with whom he began to exchange letters.

He gained the friendship of several magic collectors who advised him that instead of trying to accumulate everything, he would find more enjoyment in specializing and in trying to have the best possible collection in some rather narrow field. He says that since he had some magazines and found them appealing, "I seemed to be propelled in that direction"—although he now wonders at times why he didn't decide to collect "something less troublesome and more compact."

Alfredson's really serious pursuit of magazines began about the time he entered college in 1954. "A short purse somewhat limited my acquisitions," he recalls. On the other hand, there weren't so many other magazine collectors keenly competing for them: "I would hate to try today to obtain some of the material I have." He was helped in his specialized collecting by two pioneers in the field who then had the largest American collections, Paul Koch and Albert Blackman. "I started corresponding with them and both men were kind and generous with their descriptions of magazines and most helpful in steering me to sources."

The Blackman collection was broken up after his death, with parts of it eventually going to the Library of Congress, although much was sold to the public through Manhattan bookstores. After Koch died in 1966, his widow kept his collection intact until it was purchased in 1974 by collector George Daily of York, Pennsylvania. Daily added it to his already large collection and has continued to build upon what is now undoubtedly the largest privately held magic-magazine collection in the United States. Because of the many duplicates in his various purchases, Daily also became a dealer in magic literature, catering to other collectors.

Alfredson and Daily are co-authors of *A Short Title Checklist of Conjuring Periodicals in English.* Privately printed in 1976 in a very limited edition of two hundred copies, this manual is based on their own collections and indexed catalogue files; it gives basic information on nearly a thousand magazines, to help other specialist collectors solve some of the problems Alfredson and Daily encountered in their earlier collecting days.

"I would come across two or three issues of some magazine that I'd never heard of and there was no way to find out when it started or ended or what made up a complete file," Alfredson explains. "The *Checklist* is still full of gaps which we're continually trying to fill in, but at least provides some guidelines for the would-be periodical collector."

Most collectors of anything in magic also collect some magazines. Many have files of the standard magazines, old and new, and some of the great general collections include very rare magazines that are found in none of the specialized collections. The real specialists are relatively few—those who seek out tattered little local magic-club publications of long ago, or the obscure one-shot magazine issued by some enthusiastic teenager with a home duplicating machine.

Alfredson points out that collecting magazines has its problems as well as its pleasures. "They're bulky to store, expensive to bind, and it takes long hours of correspondence to all parts of the world just to find, if you're lucky, that last missing issue or two necessary to complete a file." But on the plus side is the fact that they include a lot of really good magic. "More important," he says, "they contain the 'raw material' of magical history, the accounts of performers as seen by their contemporaries, the gossip, dealer advertisements showing which tricks were popular at the time, and much else, all complete with dates. The magazines provide a rich lode of information available nowhere else. Thus it is in the interest of magic in general, and up to the collectors in particular, to preserve them."

Todd Karr

In 1977, at the age of twelve, Todd Karr of Southfield, Michigan was already a serious magic collector when he began to publish a bimonthly magazine for other collectors.

Karr's interest in magic began when his grandmother gave him a magic trick. That led to his visiting a magic shop to buy more tricks. He took some lessons in magic at another shop and soon worked up an act he performed at children's birthday parties, mostly at their homes, but sometimes at a country club.

It was a used copy of the great old magic magazine, *The Sphinx,* that started him collecting magic. "As they say, one good thing leads to another," he explains, "and I began buying up all the magazines and literature I could find." By 1977 he had become publisher of the *Periodical for Collecting Conjurors,* with a circulation limited to fifty copies per issue. He also began writing a regular column for *Top Hat,* the long-established magazine of the Magical Youths International. He has had articles in *Mystics Quarterly* and in the Magic Collectors Association journal, *Magicol,* and has researched and compiled checklists, indexes and other material of interest to collectors. Karr's own collecting interests range from literature to bookplates, magic rubber stampings, and coins and tokens.

At the 1978 Collectors' Weekend in Chicago, he delivered a showstopping talk: "On Being a Young Collector." Karr entertainingly described the devious approaches young collectors may be forced to take to get adults to part with potential collector's items.

By then the assembled oldsters were quite ready to take Karr seriously. His small but excellently written and well-edited *Periodical for Collecting Conjurors* was into its second year of regular publication every other month, with contrib-

uted articles by well-known specialist collectors. That summer, when he attended a collectors' gathering in New York at the national convention of the Society of American Magicians, and had a chance to meet in person a lot of the collectors with whom he had been corresponding, little notice was taken of the fact that he was the youngest of them. They were more interested in discussing with Todd Karr their shared collecting enthusiasms.

The Magic Collectors Association, founded in 1950, has a U.S. and world membership of general and specialist collectors, as well as people interested in the history and literature of magic. Organized to promote closer friendship and mutual assistance among "those with a unity of interest in the collecting of items and historical data pertaining to magic and its allied arts," the association includes among its two hundred members many of the more prominent and active collectors.

Its quarterly journal, *Magicol*—so named by combining the words "magic" and "collectors"—provides a means of exchanging news, research notes, and information on all kinds of magic collecting. Biographical and historical features are also included. A membership roster, listing members' names and addresses and indicating their special interests, is published to aid in correspondence.

Each spring since 1969 there has been what amounts to a small and informal convention of collectors, the annual Magic Collectors' Week-

Medal specially struck to commemorate the 25th anniversary of the Magic Collectors Association in 1975. Coin collector F. William Kuethe, Jr., issued them and provided each member with one in nickel-silver as a supplement to the anniversary issue of Magicol. *The obverse, picturing Robert-Houdin, was made from the actual die once used by Philadelphia magic dealers Yost & Co., for magicians' palming coins.*

end, held in Chicago and jointly sponsored by the Magic Collectors Association and Magic, Inc. The magic company serves as its headquarters on a non-profit basis, with Jay and Frances Marshall hosting, and with lectures and other events held in a nearby building and church basement. There are collector-dealer stands for selling and swapping; lectures and discussions; showings of special films; an old-time magic program in which tricks and apparatus of the past are demonstrated; displays; exhibits; door prizes; an envelope for each person, filled with souvenirs of interest to collectors; and a dinner.

The Magic Collectors Association also sponsors meetings of collectors at annual conventions of the Inter-national Brotherhood of Magicians or the Society of American Magicians, and cooperates with The Magic Circle in the annual Collector's Day held at its London headquarters. The British Ring of the International Brotherhood of Magicians holds its own collectors' gathering in connection with its annual convention. Magic societies in other countries, as well as some regional societies in the United States, have active collector groups.

There are occasional public auctions of notable collections of books or apparatus at prestigious New York and London auction galleries, with rare items sold at high prices. More frequent, and more within reach of the average collector, are the regular auctions of used books and equipment that are a part of the one-day magic conventions held at intervals throughout the year in New York and some other cities. Quite a few local magic clubs also have "auction nights."

Antique shows, antiquarian book shows, used-book stores, second-hand shops, and flea markets are frequent hunting grounds of magic collectors. They also make it a point to contact and keep in touch with book and antique dealers, to remind them of the things in which they are interested. Some collectors advertise their wants in magic magazines, collector journals, antique and hobby magazines. By corresponding with other magic collectors, they keep alert to whatever may come on the market, learn who has what and whether he may be willing to sell or trade.

At every magic convention there are dealers with tables stacked with old magic books for sale, as well as magazines, posters, old apparatus, other collectibles. Many general magic dealers and booksellers offer items of interest to collectors. There are also those who specialize in selling to collectors. Often they are collectors themselves, and make their dealing with collector friends a part-time hobby business.

For Further Reading

Findlay, James B. *How's Your Library?* 1958. Magic, Inc., 5082 N. Lincoln Ave., Chicago, IL 60625. A collectors' collector and author of many guides on magic collecting gives advice on the building of a personal magic library, indexing, care and preservation of printed material, etc.

Heyl, Edgar. *Cues for Collectors.* 1964. Magic, Inc., 5082 N. Lincoln Ave., Chicago, IL 60625. Heyl, a bibliophile and former dealer in magic literature, discusses old and rare magic books, catalogues, trick cards, tokens and medals, and many other things of collector interest in this compilation of his articles originally published in the *M-U-M* magazine.

Marshall, Frances, ed. *Magic Bookman,* 1974. Magic, Inc., 5082 N. Lincoln Ave., Chicago, IL 60625. Brief but informative articles by prominent magic collectors, dealers in magic literature, editors, writers, and others, who discuss their special interests and give experienced advice.

Scot, Reginald. *The Discoverie of Witchcraft,* New York, Dover Publications, Inc., 1972. Paperback. This is a reprint of the first book in the English language to explain conjuring tricks, originally published in 1584, which was written by Scot primarily to expose the charlatans who traded on the superstitions of the time. In this version, the average magic-minded reader is provided with an opportunity to browse through at least a reproduction of one of the rarest of magic books. Unabridged, it includes interesting old drawings of early tricks, many of which are still being performed.

Stott, Raymond Toole. *A Bibliography of English Conjuring 1581–1876.* 1976. Harpur & Sons of Derby, Rowditch Printing Works, Derby DE1 1LZ, England. The most complete currently available bibliography of early conjuring books in the English language, based on those in the world's great libraries and private collections, with copious notes by an experienced bibliographer. Volume two, published in 1978, deals with five hundred books not included in the first volume. Both published in limited editions.

Young, Morris N. *Hobby Magic.* New York: Trilon Press, 1950. A detailed and entertainingly informative introduction to all forms of magic collecting, with emphasis on books, by an expert whose collection is in the Library of Congress and who helped to found the Magic Collectors Association. Out of print, but worth looking for by anyone interested in starting a magic collection.

Information

Those sincerely interested in collecting magic and in magic history can obtain information about membership in the Magic Collectors Association by enclosing a stamped self-addressed envelope with an inquiry to:

Walter J. Gydesen, Executive Secretary, Magic Collectors Association, 5013 N. Lincoln Ave., Chicago, IL 60625.

Collector-Dealers

These are some of the dealers who specialize in things for collectors. There may be a small charge for lists, when available, of items currently offered for sale. Inquiries should be accompanied by a stamped self-addressed envelope. (See also listings in Chapter 6, "Books and Magazines.")

Mario Carrandi, Jr., 23 Virginia St., Kendall Park, NJ 08824. Rare and used apparatus, books, magazines, catalogues, posters, memorabilia.

George Daily, Jr., 3320 Spondin Dr., York, PA 17402. Magazines, books, magic comic books, catalogues, programs, manuscripts, palming coins and tokens.

Lewis Kohrs, 3876 Belmont Ave., San Diego, CA 92116. Antiquarian and classic magic books, magic literature.

Magic Art Studio, 137 Spring St., Watertown, MA 02172. Used apparatus and books.

Meyerbooks, P.O. Box 427, 235 West Main St., Glenwood, IL 60425. Books on magic and related subjects of special collector interest.

Michael O'Dowd, Rt. 2, Box 42, Ridge Dr., Barnhart, MO 63012. Magic books and magazines for collectors.

Stevens Magic Emporium, 3238 E. Douglas, Wichita, KA 67208. Used apparatus and books.

Tigner Magic Supply, P.O. Box 7149, Toledo, OH 43615. Books, apparatus, collectors' specialties.

Byron Walker, P.O. Box 3186, San Leandro, CA 94578. Magic books and magazines for collectors.

Tad Ware, Mystic Hill, P.O. Box 380, Excelsior, MN 55331. Apparatus, books, posters, instruction sheets.

SHOWPLACES OF MAGIC

American Museum of Magic

The American Museum of Magic in Marshall, Michigan, the nation's only general magic museum open to the public, houses 250,000 things of magic in a beautifully restored 130-year-old building that provides a showplace setting for the exhibits of magic's past. Included in the collection is much of almost everything about magic that it is possible to collect: 2,700 original posters; 9,000 books on magic and related subjects; 25,000 magic magazines; apparatus used by famous magicians; prints, portraits, statuary, mechanical magic toys; 350 old and new magic sets. There are letters, photos, advertisements, news clippings, programs, playbills, dime novels, comic books, premium giveaways, sheet music, record albums, coins, stamps, figurines, original book manuscripts, and rows of cabinets filled with carefully indexed files of biographical and historical material.

Created by Robert Lund and his wife Elaine, the museum is a long-held dream that the couple brought to reality, by their own work and largely with their own hands. Located midway between Detroit and Chicago in a town of historic old homes and buildings, which has taken community pride in having the museum of magic there, it attracts not only those interested in magic, but in Americana, theatrical history, posters, and the graphic arts. Antique buffs, seekers of

The American Museum of Magic at Marshall, Michigan, in a restored 19th-century building, has exhibits selected from a collection of a quarter of a million things of magic. Created by Robert and Elaine Lund, it is the only general magic museum open daily (except Mondays) to the public.

nostalgia, and tourists are simply drawn to see something that cannot be seen anywhere else.

Lund frankly admits he was not destined to become a great magician, a fact that has never lessened his lifelong love of magic. First interested at the age of seven, and with a later ambition to make a career of it, he realized when he was about eighteen that he wasn't going to make it as a professional.

"Success in magic depends ninety per cent on showmanship and ten per cent on technique," he explains. "With me, it was the other way around. I practiced and I had the technique, but I didn't have the showmanship. But I still loved magic and kept it as a hobby, became a collector instead of a performer, and looked for something else to do for a living."

Starting as a copy boy on a Detroit newspaper, he became a reporter and successful writer for magazines specializing in automobiles, and for many years has been Detroit editor of *Motor* magazine and other Hearst publications. But he himself didn't own a car until he was in his thirties, because rather than buy one he preferred to spend his money buying magic. He bought anything and everything he could find that was related to magic, wherever he could find it—from dealers, collectors, mail-order houses, second-hand stores, Salvation Army and Goodwill shops, estate sales.

Among the things he acquired as a young collector were dozens of letters written by Houdini. "I bought many of them for fifty cents apiece and they're worth at least fifty dollars now. But that's placing a false value on them. I didn't buy them to resell. I bought them because I coveted them, because I loved them."

Thirty years of insatiably collecting thousands of things of magic finally filled Lund's home to the point where he decided he had to do something: either buy a warehouse or open a museum. He and his wife Elaine, a commercial artist, had been considering the possibilities of a magic museum for a long time. They began looking around in various Michigan towns for an old building that might be a proper site.

The search took a couple of years before they finally found what they wanted in Marshall: an impressive-looking two-story 1850s storefront building, once a bakery, on the town's main street and only minutes from a convenient interchange of two main freeways. They bought the building, optimistically estimating at first that it would take six months to set up the displays.

It took four years. Once into the project, the Lunds not only renovated the old building but restored it to its original style and charm, faithfully preserving as much as they could. Grime and thick layers of bakery grease were cleared away. Eighty truckloads of trash and debris were removed. Old linoleum and ugly red paint were stripped from floorboards. False ceilings and partitions were torn down. Ten interior doors were remade. Broken glass was replaced, walls plastered

199

and painted, new wiring, plumbing, heating, and air-conditioning installed. Old-fashioned store display cases were rounded up to hold some of the magic exhibits, and discarded church pews were found to serve as benches for museum visitors.

The Lunds did much of it themselves, weekends and whenever they could, hiring local craftsmen for jobs they couldn't do, and relying on the help of friends who volunteered. Countless hours of work went into it, constant two-hour drives back and forth from their own home—until they finally sold that and bought a house in Marshall to live there, closer to the museum.

Converting a private collection into a public museum—which would depend for support on admission fees paid by those who visited it—involved time-taking decisions in choosing what to display, how best to show it, arrange it, and make it informative and interesting to the average person who knew little about magic and magicians. Three hundred and fifty of the collection's twenty-seven hundred posters were chosen for the display that filled the museum's first-floor walls. Apparatus had to be displayed so none of its working secrets were revealed. Additional hours of work went into the hand-refinishing of display showcases and the careful mounting of each exhibit.

The Lunds intended to staff the museum themselves, with the help of their grown daughter Susan, so someone always would be there who could provide a real tour of the place—not merely a quick look around—for those interested. As it later developed, some casual visitors saw all they wanted to see in fifteen minutes; others lingered for five hours, or came back a second day.

Among the museum's featured exhibits is the equipment used by Houdini in some of the sensational feats that brought him enduring fame. When Houdini died, he left the equipment to his magician brother Hardeen, who sold some of it to another magician, the late Martin Sunshine. He carted the Houdini props to Wisconsin and stored them for years in an old circus popcorn wagon behind his home. Lund eventually learned of their existence and persuaded Sunshine to sell them to him.

The Houdini exhibit includes the "milk-can escape," regularly performed by Houdini in his shows for several years, until other magicians began to copy it. The oversized metal milk can, about three feet high and seventy-eight inches around its widest part, was filled with water to the brim. After telling the audience to hold its breath and count the minutes, Houdini would squeeze himself down inside the water-filled can. The lid would be securely fastened with examined padlocks, and a small screen would be placed in front of the can. Houdini would emerge, dripping wet, having escaped despite the fact that the can still remained tightly locked.

Also on display is Houdini's "overboard packing box," which was used for some of the magician's

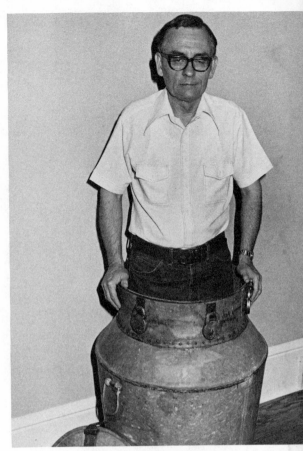

The milk can from which Houdini escaped after it was filled to the top with water and he was imprisoned inside, locked into it with six examined padlocks fastened to the lid. Houdini thrilled his 1908–12 audiences with his performance, mysteriously getting out of the can and leaving the locks still locked. The can, now at the American Museum of Magic, looked hardly big enough to hold a person. But as Robert Lund demonstrates, Houdini could just about squeeze down into it, which added to the illusion that he had no space to maneuver his escape.

The heavy wooden box, now much scarred from use and age, that Houdini used for some of his Overboard Packing Box Escapes, called that because the box was put overboard, into the river, with a handcuffed and leg-shackled Houdini nailed inside it. Thick-planked, forty-one inches high, and wide enough to allow some movement inside it, the box now at the American Museum of Magic had a part in the spectacular underwater escapes that helped make Houdini famous. He had to get free, he claimed, within the three minutes he could hold his breath, or suffer death by drowning.

even more spectacular underwater escapes. Handcuffed and shackled with leg irons, he would be imprisoned inside the big wooden crate by a committee that nailed the lid shut. The box would be slowly lowered overboard into the deep water of a river or lake. As the dooming seconds were counted, Houdini would splash into view, having won his struggle to escape from the box and death by drowning.

Usually the box was forgotten in the excitement, but if anybody asked what had happened to it, the answer was that it had been lost in the river. Actually an assistant was waiting to fish it out later so it could be used again. The equipment Lund acquired includes a metal-reinforced cardboard cover that Houdini had made to fit over the box's lid for shipping. Houdini's name is at the top of the cover in big letters and there is space beneath for chalking in the name of the next theater to which the box was to be shipped.

On April 1, 1978, hundreds of people crowded Marshall's main street, with traffic temporarily blocked off by town officials, for the grand opening of The American Museum of Magic. Present were many magicians, some who had come from as far away as California to see the assembled treasures. High above the crowd, suspended by his feet from the aerial ladder of a fire truck, magician Don Kill, "The Amazing Kildon," made a Houdini-like escape from a straitjacket.

Mayor George Brown performed the ribbon-cutting ceremony, and the only museum of its kind was ready to welcome the public. A committee of town officials and the historical society later presented Robert and Elaine Lund with an engraved silver cup: Marshall's first Community Preservation Award.

A museum poster, fashioned after those of a century ago, invites "come-who-may" to enjoy the entertainment and enlightenment of a "Colossal Colossus of Conjuring Culture," a "Temple of Thaumaturgy, Legerdemain, Hocus-Pocus & Abracadabra, consisting of Mementoes, Relics, Memorabilia, Souvenirs & Apparatus of all the Prominent Professors of Prestidigitation of All Time, dating from 1584 to the Present." Free smelling salts are promised to any "ladies who may be overcome" and a sign at the door warns: "No admission to persons of mean disposition, chronic tosspots and despoilers of public tranquility."

Information. The American Museum of Magic, P.O. Box 5, 107 E. Michigan Ave., Marshall, MI 49068. Open daily except Mondays.

Egyptian Hall Museum

The largest private museum, David Price's Egyptian Hall Museum of Magical History at Brentwood, Tennessee, near Nashville, exhibits one of the world's richest and most extensive collections of magic memorabilia—in a building specially constructed for it.

Egyptian Hall is not a commercial enterprise but "a permanent repository for relics of magic over which we exercise a relationship of stewardship," as Price describes it. "We collect, preserve and display such relics with a view to passing them on to future generations of magicians. Egyptian Hall is open at all times by appointment to magicians and other interested persons, subject of course to the convenience of the proprietor."

Price's museum traces its magical ancestry back to Kenton, Ohio, in 1895, when magician–politician– business executive W. W. Durbin

David Price, who transformed an Egyptian Hall in Ohio into a museum in Nashville and then expanded it into the Egyptian Hall Museum of Magical History at Brentwood, Tennessee.

erected a small white frame building equipped with a stage for rehearsing his magic act. Durbin named it Egyptian Hall after the exhibition hall in London that was the first theatrical home of the Maskelynes, who through several generations continuously operated a celebrated theater of magic.

Durbin's Egyptian Hall was the site of the world's first magic convention in 1926, and Durbin himself became the driving spirit behind the growth of the International Brotherhood of Magicians. (See Chapter 9: "Clubs and Conventions.") As a collector, Durbin covered every inch of the Egyptian Hall's walls with pictures, and when he ran out of wall space he papered the ceiling with them. Before he died in 1937, he had the largest collection in the United States of magicians' photographs. Thomas Dowd, now treasurer of the IBM, acquired Egyptian Hall from Durbin's estate, and moved it, building and all, to a nearby farm. In 1953, David Price bought the collection, the name, and everything but the old building, and transferred them to his home city of Nashville, Tennessee, where he was inspired to create a museum.

Price had been a popular professional magician for years until the Second World War left him with foot injuries that ended his career as a professional performer. He turned his interest in magic to collecting memorabilia and gradually built an impressive collection, which he exhibited at a 1951 convention. His home was already bulging with the collected things of magic when he bought Durbin's massive Egyptian Hall accumulation from Dowd.

He built a new Egyptian Hall in Nashville, a small separate museum that it took a year and a half to complete. Continuing his search for material, Price added not only scores of individual items, but also whole collections, including scrapbooks of Houdini, Laurant, and Dante, and the famed A. A. George Newmann poster collection, the first of a number of extensive poster collections that were to come to the museum. Also displayed were apparatus and stage equipment, wands, mementoes, the coin ladder of T. Nelson Downs, the King of Koins, and the prop case Downs carried throughout his career (including a performance at Buckingham Palace). Prominent magicians and collectors began to choose the Egyptian Hall as the repository for long-cherished treasures they sent there to be preserved.

After twelve years in the museum building in Nashville, it became necessary to move the Egyptian Hall again, to its present location at Brentwood. There Price built a combination of private home and museum under one roof, but with the museum in a separate wing of the building. In addition to the principal museum hall, it has two archives rooms, a library, and an office. The filing space covers every size of magical memorabilia, from small cases for magicians' business cards to a container for eight-sheet posters that needs a nine-and-a-half-foot ceiling to accommodate it. Still larger posters must be rolled, but even the largest is mounted full size and everything is available for almost immediate display.

There are two categories of wall exhibits, one of colorful lithographs from the era of Alexander Herrmann to recent years, and the other of pre-Herrmann playbills, dating back to early conjurors of the English outdoor fairs. One long photograph album holds pictures of fifteen hundred magicians and another photo exhibit takes the form of a giant book, with pages as tall as a person. Glass cases are used to display three-dimensional mementoes.

Almost every era of magic and every well-known performer of that era is represented in the collections, which also cover specialized fields such as lyceum and chautauqua magicians. The original Durbin collection that inspired the museum now accounts for less than five per cent of the material in the present Egyptian Hall.

Information. Egyptian Hall Museum of Magical History, 1954 Old Hickory Blvd., Brentwood, TN 27027. David Price, Archivist. Magicians and other interested persons may write for an appointment to visit.

Society of American Magicians Hall of Fame

Located in the heart of Hollywood, California, the Society of American Magicians Hall of Fame and Magic Museum spreads through eight rooms and additional galleries filled with historic displays and exhibits, stage and auditorium, library and office. But when it was founded in 1967, it wasn't located anywhere except on paper. There was no "hall" at all in a physical sense, no museum, and only a hope that somehow there might be one.

The society's national council had established the Hall of Fame as an institution to be created through a Hall of Fame Committee, which was made permanent by a special provision written into the constitution. John Zweers, a prominent California magician and the society's president in 1967, brought it into being by appointing the first Hall of Fame Committee, and the first magicians chosen for a place in the Hall of Fame were nominated and elected to it.

After years of discussion and crusading efforts by many supporters of the idea, the Hall of Fame was a working organization, but there were no funds available to build a hall of magic and a museum, and for several years the committee made a frustrating search for a site. Then early in 1970 the Los Angeles Home Savings and Loan Association became interested in the project and generously offered to provide permanent quarters for the Hall of Fame in its Hollywood branch building. At no expense, with no strings attached, the savings and loan association would reconstruct an entire basement area for the Hall of Fame to use as its own.

At the corner of Sunset and Vine in the center of Hollywood and only blocks from the meeting hall of the SAM's Southern California Assembly, the location couldn't have been better. Zweers presented the offer to the national council at the 1970 SAM convention, and it was unanimously accepted. He was appointed chairman of the Hall of Fame Committee, and later became director of the Hall's management board, a position he still holds.

After consulting with magic historians and collectors about what was needed to provide ideal museum conditions, Zweers prepared a detailed floor plan. Blueprints were drawn, and a fourteen-man work crew began converting the dream of the museum to reality. All construction costs, materials, and labor were paid for by Home Savings as an outright gift to the Society of American Magicians. The keys were turned over to Chairman Zweers in April 1971, and the management board took possession.

There was an initial generous flow of money donations and articles to be exhibited. Board members rolled up their sleeves, and with their spouses and a few volunteers began long nights of work, designing and constructing displays. After six months of feverish toil, the Hall of Fame had its grand opening, to

Performers' view from the stage, auditorium of the Society of American Magicians Hall of Fame. The gallery of Hall-of-Famers' portraits is at the left, pictures of past presidents of the SAM on the back wall. The museum fills eight rooms and additional galleries, but this is the actual Hall of Fame, with its "Wall of the Hall." COURTESY SAM HALL OF FAME coincide with National Magic Week, in October 1971.

But once a week "work nights" continued as the museum's acquisitions increased: apparatus, costumes, personal mementos, posters and memorabilia of Hall-of-Famers, willed or donated for exhibit. All gifts become the property of the SAM's national council forever, to insure their preservation. While not everything offered is accepted, no accepted gift can ever be sold or traded without the owner's authorization.

The Hall of Fame is financed almost entirely by monetary gifts from individual members or affiliated assemblies of the society, by a small annual appropriation from the society's national council, and by fund-raising events such as the annual public full-evening magic show with top professional talent staged by the hall's management board at a Pasadena high school. Some assemblies also have staged public shows to donate the proceeds to the hall. Assemblies and various individuals sponsor particular museum exhibits in which they have some special interest.

Members of the Hall of Fame Committee, now called the National Historians Committee, are selected on the basis of their knowledge and scholarship, to carry on research projects for the hall, to locate items of historical significance that need to be preserved, and to propose candidates for nomination to the Hall of Fame itself.

During its first few years, relatively large groups of magicians were elected to the Hall of Fame, which had a backlog of many centuries of magic history to catch up with. Now nominees are limited, and are elected by the SAM national council according to established criteria.

Although the whole place is called the Hall of Fame, the actual "hall" is the auditorium. Here, on a wall thirty-five feet long and ten feet high are the framed pictures of the great magicians who have been elected. Because the pictures come from many sources, all of them have been reprocessed for uniformity, with copies of old engravings used in the cases of performers who lived in the years before photography. On the auditorium's rear wall, facing the stage, are pictures of past presidents of the Society of American Magicians.

Since the hall opened, regular "program nights" have been held at least once each month in the auditorium. The general public is welcomed to these events, which feature not only an entertaining talk about the history of magic and the Hall of Fame but an actual magic show. Refreshments are served, and laymen as well as magicians can tour the museum and exhibits for an evening of fun and education. No admission fee is charged, but because of the limited seating capacity invitations must be sought in advance and reservations confirmed. There is usually a full house.

Many other entertainment and educational programs are presented throughout the year for civic organizations, various visiting groups,

Checking the pictures of the famed magicians in the Hall of Fame is José Vilardell of the Board of Management. Members of the Hall of Fame are nominated by a committee of magic historians and elected by the National Council of the SAM. JOHN ZWEERS

and magic clubs. Special events are staged whenever a magic convention is being held in the area. During Magic Week each October, Hall of Fame anniversary shows have become a tradition, with the show playing for two nights to overflow audiences. Each year there is a coronation of a Queen of Magic, who assists at hall functions during her reign. The hall plays host at an annual Christmas party for employees of the Home Savings and Loan Association.

A magic club for young people of both sexes from fourteen to eighteen—Explorers Post 1313E of the Boy Scouts of America—holds its meetings in the auditorium. In return for a meeting place, the young

magicians clean. up the Hall and keep it in order, and many of them also eagerly volunteer to work on exhibits, to help backstage during Program Night, and do other jobs.

The museum's main display area is divided into alcoves and sections featuring Hall of Fame magicians. Life-size mannequins, specially built to the size and height of the performers, with portrait-sculptured heads and historically accurate costumes, are shown in period settings. There is Dedi, the Egyptian magician of nearly five thousand years ago, Xenophon of ancient Greece. Scenes of medieval conjuring are prominent, as is Joseph Pinetti entertaining King Louis XVI of France and Marie Antoinette.

209

More cards than even most magicians have ever seen. One of the Ruth and Ronald Haines card rooms at the Hall of Fame, showing part of the collection of playing cards. On the center table is a "house of cards" of the kind magicians often magically produce. JOSÉ VILARDELL

A "chamber of illusions" features displays dedicated to Alexander Herrmann, Harry Kellar, Howard Thurston, Harry Blackstone. Other highlights include a Houdini-style spirit medium cabinet. A Houdini area has his personal collection of restraints and keys, as well as a die box he used in his early years. In glass cases are the complete equipment of the acts of famous vaudeville magicians. The Ruth and Ronald Haines Memorial Gallery houses what is considered among the finest of playing card collections,

as well as unique apparatus, historic wands, and a century-old John Rogers group statue, *The Travelling Magician.*

Information. The Society of American Magicians Hall of Fame and Magic Museum, 1500 North Vine Street, Hollywood, CA 90001. John U. Zweers, Director. Magicians wishing to visit should contact: Associate Director John Engman, 3731 Wilshire Blvd., 10th Floor, Los Angeles, CA 90010.

The Magic Castle

The most famous showplace of the world of magic, the Magic Castle, stands on a hillside above the center of Hollywood. It is a turreted old mansion built in 1909 and restored to its early-century elegance as the luxurious private clubhouse of the Academy of Magical Arts.

Within it are half a dozen intimate theaters and close-up performing areas, fine dining rooms, informal bars and clubrooms, and facilities for all the Academy's activities devoted to the advancement of the art of magic.

The Academy, a nonprofit organization, has more than a thousand magicians as members, professionals and amateurs being accepted after approval by a board of examiners. Some three thousand more associate members are not magicians but magic enthusiasts. They include businessmen, doctors, lawyers, advertising and communications executives, famous television and film stars, and other entertainment world personalities. Hollywood celebrities are frequent visitors and regularly take part in special academy shows and other events. Cary Grant, who enjoys performing magic as "The Great Carini," is one of the academy's directors.

The academy also sponsors a junior magicians' program for young people twelve and over who may become members when they are twenty-one; they use the Castle facilities during specified daytime hours. But the only time younger children of members are admitted is during family brunches on Sundays. Anyone attending the Castle at night must be over twenty-one and able to prove it. On Sundays "kid show" performers entertain the youngsters, but otherwise the magic at the Castle is for adults.

Members and guests must wear jackets and ties, and although informal fun and relaxation are encouraged, the magic is surrounded with a dignity that is part of the academy's purpose in promoting greater recognition of it as a performing art. The entire Castle is a showcase for the appreciation of magic at its best.

It began in 1952 when William Larsen, Sr., then editor and publisher of *Genii* magazine, announced a plan for a magic society, the Academy of Magical Arts and Sciences, and expressed the hope that some day it might have its own clubhouse and showplace. Larsen, who had combined an outstanding career in magic with the practice of law, died the following year at the age of forty-eight, and the idea temporarily died with him, but not in the minds of his two sons, William, Jr., and Milton.

Bill, Jr., and Milt had been in magic from childhood, as young assistants in the touring full-evening magic shows presented by their parents at theaters, clubs, and resort hotels. For a time their father owned the Thayer Magic Company, and Bill was active in its mail-order business. He also ran the retail shop,

The Magic Castle, famed private club of the Academy of Magical Arts, the restored 1909 mansion towering on the hillside above Hollywood, where magicians and magic enthusiasts gather nightly with film and television celebrities to watch the stars of magic perform.

Where the Larsen magic all began, in the years when young Milt (left) and Bill, Jr., (right) were assistants in the family's touring magic shows. Before his death in 1953, William Larsen, magician and attorney, announced plans for a society of magicians that later inspired his sons to create the Magic Castle and the Academy of Magical Arts. He is shown (center) with their mother Geraldine Larsen, who performed as "The Magic Lady."

demonstrated magic across the counter, and had his own illusion act. The Larsen home was a meeting place of prominent magicians, filled with the talk of magic and the doing of it, and the discussions there of the need for a permanent magic clubhouse left a deep impression on the boys.

After his father's death, Bill helped his mother carry on the publication of *Genii*, then became and

continues to be its editor. (See Chapter 6: "Books and Magazines.") Meanwhile he had graduated from college with a political science degree, studied law for a year, and after deciding that his true love was show business, had turned to a television production career. For fifteen years he was an associate producer at CBS of major network television shows.

Milt Larsen became a television

The Larsen brothers, Milt (left) who built the Magic Castle and Bill, Jr., (right) who built up the Academy of Magical Arts and is president of its governing board of directors.

comedy writer, for years the chief writer of the Ralph Edwards' "Truth or Consequences" shows. He has also created a number of other theater and show-business projects of his own, including a record company and the restoration of old-time variety theaters. He has what is considered one of the finest private collections of show-business memorabilia.

In the mid-1950s his love of magic and desire to do something to boost its prestige with the public started him producing a series of big-theater magical revues that presented star magic acts from all over the world in professionally staged shows surrounded with the glamor and excitement that would attract modern theater-going audiences. After some twenty-five years, his *It's Magic* revues have become an annual Los Angeles theater-going event, drawing both overflow audiences and high critical praise, which have extended their two-week runs to holdover performances for a full month.

Milt's inspiration for the creation of the Magic Castle came one day in 1962 while he was in his tenth-floor Hollywood office working on "Truth or Consequences." "Instead of writing, I was daydreaming," he recalls, "looking out the window at an old derelict mansion on the hill a couple of blocks away." He began thinking what a great place it would be for the magic club his father used to talk about. Two weeks later, he shook hands with Tom Glover, the owner of the property, on a deal to lease the old mansion.

Milt started the mansion's renovation, doing much of the carpentering himself, and also searching for its unusual antique furnishings. While he and NBC art director John Shrum were working on the decor and refurbishing, Bill Larsen resurrected the old Academy of Magical Arts idea, rallied the support of magicians and magic lovers, and started a membership drive. He built the foundations for the present academy on the guidelines his father had suggested ten years before.

When the Magic Castle opened its doors in 1963, it had only 150 members. Bill continued to build the membership and the academy, and kept his CBS television production job until his magic activities eventually demanded his full time. Milt also went on writing for television for a while, until the Castle and his other creative projects became full-time occupations. Gradually the Magic Castle underwent many renovations as the Academy of Magical Arts grew to a membership of nearly four thousand.

The Magic Castle is open seven nights a week from 5 P.M. to 2 A.M., on Friday for lunch, and on Sunday for family brunch. Friday and Saturday night guests are admitted only when accompanied by members. On other nights a guest can come in if he has a guest card given to him by a member.

As a visitor turns into the driveway from Franklin Avenue, two blocks up the hill from the famous Grauman's Chinese Theater in downtown Hollywood, the towering Castle looms ahead with its grand fountain and spouting statuary lions, its facade of stained glass and cut-crystal windows. In the reception hall, the guest faces a blinking owl and whispers the magic words, "Open Sesame." A hidden door opens and he enters into another world of magic and Victorian elegance.

There is the grand salon, with a long and glitteringly ornate old-fashioned bar. In the "Invisible Irma" room, a ghost by that name plays request numbers on a piano, her spectral hands invisibly running over the keys while she sips from time to time from a visible drink until her glass is empty. Nearby is a close-up room that seats thirty-five spectators and "stands" more. At four scheduled times each night, a performer sits behind a half-round table and entertains for fifteen minutes with expert close-up magic.

A few feet away, an unmarked entrance with a speakeasy-type door leads to the lower floor and the Hat and Hare Pub area where members and guests can relax and enjoy drinks while watching impromptu table magic. More exclusive is the Dai Vernon Lounge, where the superstars of close-up magic give unannounced performances for small groups of members and guests holding special admission tickets.

Up on the Castle's second floor, reached from the Grand Salon by a carved wooden staircase with brass handrails, are the elaborate dining areas and the Houdini Seance Room. There are five dining rooms, decorated with posters and lithographs of famous magicians, their century-old etched-glass windows look out over Hollywood. Dining is a feast, the food prepared by a French chef and grandly served by butler-like waiters wearing tail-coated evening suits, white ties, and gloves. During an average evening there are three hundred or more dinner guests. A private close-up magic show, presented at the table,

Ornate glass-domed ceiling combined with the wall-framed posters of famous magicians set the mood for elegant dining and magic fun at the Castle, where guests enjoy a bountiful feast of both good food and good conjuring.

The chef seems to be doing a little magic of his own as he prepares a flaming dish beside the table for a private dinner party at the Magic Castle. In the background is a display of handcuffs, the likes of which failed to restrain Houdini, whose spirit comes back twice a night to produce spooky spiritualistic happenings in the Houdini Seance Room. But that make-believe haunting is strictly for entertainment.

is often requested by a dinner party, and people frequently arrange to have some favorite performer entertain them.

The very special Houdini Seance Room, for dinner parties of exactly twelve people, is booked months ahead for its two seatings a night. The dozen diners are seated at a large round table set with crystal stemware and fine silver, and are attended by a special steward and his staff. The food is prepared at the side of the table, where the executive chef cooks it to individual order. Wine and liqueurs are served, and when the mood has been properly set, actor-magician Sandy Spillman joins the dinner group, acting as a medium to involve them in a Houdini seance. Spillman creates a series of fantastic pseudospiritualistic effects in which the spirit of Houdini seems to haunt the table.

From the second floor dining area a connecting corridor leads to the Castle's showrooms, a full entertainment unit reconstructed from a garage and completed in 1976. It includes two small theaters, a museum, a bar, and an area for impromptu close-up magic. Interior design and furnishings are in the same style and atmosphere as the mansion: stained glass windows, crystal chandeliers, attractive ceilings, and richly carpeted floors.

In the impromptu area a big felt-covered table is available for magician members to entertain their guests by presenting their own close-up magic. A Castle performer is also on hand to amuse guests with

magic while they are waiting for the scheduled shows to begin. Guests may also visit the Robert-Houdin Museum room with its displays of old apparatus and automata.

The Palace of Mystery, an intimate little theater that seats one hundred people, provides a perfect setting for the presentation of stage magic: a large stage, colored velvet curtains, full theatrical lighting facilities, a good sound system. Top magic acts perform there, presenting three 45-minute shows a night, with three acts working each week.

The show also changes weekly, beginning Tuesday and ending on Sunday. On Monday nights, new acts are auditioned or "regulars" try out new material, perform for agents and talent buyers. Four dressing rooms are available and there is a permanent stage manager to take care of curtain and music cues.

The Parlour of Prestidigitation, a smaller theater that seats sixty people, has four shows a night, featuring one performer. Basically this room is designed for stand-up magic acts, but the seats are elevated so that some close-up table magic of the larger kind also can be shown.

Magic lectures by visiting lecturers are given for members only in the Palace of Mystery or the Parlour of Prestidigitation once or twice a month, and there is a complete video system with monitors that can be set up if a lecturer is explaining close-up tricks or sleights that need better viewing.

All the shows presented throughout the Castle start exactly

on schedule and the programs for each evening are posted so guests will know what is happening next and where. The scheduling is planned so that during the course of an evening a person can see all the shows with ease, and there is ample seating in all the rooms. Even on crowded nights one usually waits on line less than ten minutes. Each show has a host who greets the guests and seats them to the capacity of that room. There is no smoking in the showrooms, which are comfortably air-conditioned or heated as required.

From the second-floor dining area of the old building there is another staircase leading up to a third floor of the mansion, but a sign on the door says: "Authorized Persons Only." That third floor, which houses the Castle offices and library, is off limits to associate members and their guests; only the Academy's magician members are admitted.

The library is extensive, one with hundreds of numbered and indexed books, files of magic magazines and lecture notes, and an audio library with cassettes of the lectures that have been given at the Castle. New books are regularly purchased, as are older ones to be added to the reference shelves. No books are to be taken out, but they are always available to members for reading and study in the library. A copying machine permits reproduction of printed material at no charge to members. There are also felt-topped tables for the magician who wants to practice newly learned sleights, and mirrors so he can watch his own hands closely as he runs through the moves.

On the same floor are the offices of Bill and Milt Larsen and the Castle's reservation and booking offices. Bill Larsen's office houses hundreds of videotapes of almost everything having to do with magic that has been shown on television in recent years. The Castle also videotapes some of its own shows, as well as interviews with famous magic personalities for viewing by members in future years.

The Academy's annual awards, magic's version of the film industry's Oscars, are presented at a gala awards show at the Variety Arts Theater in downtown Los Angeles. It is a formal dress affair, with searchlights outside the theater sweeping the skies, Hollywood film and television celebrities making the presentations, and luminaries of the magic world prominent among the nearly one thousand guests who attend. Outstanding magic acts perform on stage between the presentations for the year's best magician, best stage magician, best close-up magician, best lecturer, and a dozen other categories of performing, creative and literary accomplishment. Special fellowships and awards of merit are also presented.

Information. The Academy of Magical Arts, Inc., 7001 Franklin Ave., Hollywood, CA 90028. Phone: 213-851-3313, Monday through Friday after 11 A.M. The Magic Castle is the private clubhouse of the Academy's members, associate

The spell of the Magic Castle extends even beyond the mansion's walls, as famed magician Mark Wilson demonstrates by floating this young woman in space in the Castle driveway. The Castle is often used as a setting for television-show episodes, pictorial advertising, and fashion photography.

members, and their invited guests. Visiting magicians who live two hundred or more miles from Los Angeles are always welcome, but should phone to identify themselves and make dining reservations. Those who visit in the evenings must be over twenty-one; younger magician visitors are admitted for brunch on Sundays. The Castle is open evenings seven days a week and for lunch Fridays.

9

CLUBS AND CONVENTIONS

There are magic hobbyists who don't belong to magic clubs and who seldom attend conventions, for many practical and personal reasons, but they are a minority. Magic is the kind of a hobby that almost demands company, sharing its fun, its learning and common knowledge, and enjoying the friendship of those who also love doing magic and seeing it done.

The first convention of magicians anywhere in the world was held in June 1926, at Kenton, Ohio, by the International Brotherhood of Magicians, with about three hundred members attending. By 1978 the fiftieth IBM convention, held that year in San Diego, had a registration of more than fifteen hundred, and the annual conventions of the Society of American Magicians have

drawn almost equally large numbers. Among other big yearly conventions are those of the Pacific Coast Association of Magicians, the Texas Association of Magicians, and two that are sponsored by magic dealers: Abbott's and Tannen's.

Somewhat smaller regular conventions, which some magicians prefer because they *are* smaller, include the Midwest Magic Jubilee, the Mid-American Magic Conclave, the New England Magicians Convention, NyCan (New York State and Canada), and the convention of the Magicians Alliance Eastern States.

From early March to late November there are magic conventions somewhere in the country almost every month, with the peak convention-going seasons in midsum-

The little backroom theater at Martinka's magic shop in New York where the oldest of the magic societies, The Society of American Magicians, was founded in 1902. COURTESY FLOSSO-HORNMANN MAGIC CO.

mer and early fall, when they are often held only days apart. Many magic hobbyists attend two or three, with wives and children often joining in the combined convention trip as the family's vacation. Avid conventioneers, with the free time and the money to do so, may travel the whole circuit, flying from city to city. Others settle for one of the big national conventions, usually the one that is being held that year in a city nearest to home.

There are also one-day conventions—sponsored by magic clubs or by dealers—in Boston, the Philadelphia area, New Jersey, Connecticut, Ohio, Kansas, Los Angeles, and elsewhere. Auctions, in addition to lectures and shows, are often a feature.

Thousands of dollars' worth of magic is offered at auction every three months in New York at the one-day conventions that Larry Weeks has regularly held four times a year. Weeks, a magic dealer, collector, popular comedy magician, and famed juggler, has organized some fifty of the one-day conventions. He was the first to run these on a continuing basis and to establish the auction market as part of them. His conventions include showings of historic magic films, live shows, and lectures; prominent magic personalities appear as his guests of honor.

The annual conventions of the magic societies are held in different cities each year, with the affiliated club of the convention city acting as host. Usually they are four-day affairs, normally from Wednesday through Saturday. Almost all the major magic conventions follow what has become a traditional pattern of events.

There are big stage shows of magic each night, an annual banquet with speeches, awards and presentations on the final night preceeding a last gala all-star show, and all through the four days from morning until long after midnight there is magic happening everywhere and constantly. Depending on the arrangements, the nightly shows may be in a hotel grand ballroom, a huge convention auditorium, or nearby theater. But wherever held, they generally are elaborately staged productions to present magic at its glamorous best.

Shows are planned to provide a variety of every type of stage magic: famed illusionists surrounded by assistants and dancers; the scenery and spectacle of their touring shows; professional nightclub acts; pattering or pantomimic magic comedians; headliners brought in from Europe or Japan; polished sleight-of-hand manipulators; surprising novelty acts; well-known performers who are perennial convention favorites. There is also much "for magicians only" fun in sketches and slapstick satire.

Convention mornings frequently start with contests, which may begin right after breakfast and continue until noon. Junior and senior contestants compete on the basis of presentation, originality, and other criteria. While the contests are going on, other groups may be holding meetings devoted to their specialized magic interests. There may be business meetings of the society's officials, a dealers' meeting, a get-together of collectors; and for the women a special magic show, fashion show, or a guided tour of the city's smart shops and other places of sightseeing interest.

By mid-morning the dealers' display rooms probably will be open, and the constant promenading and crowd-gathering that goes on here all during the convention will begin. At the large conventions some fifty dealers may set up display booths with demonstrators. The aisles between the booths become the convention's busy cross-walks where old friends are rediscovered, new friends are made, magic is talked, projects and magic business deals are discussed—and where the greats of magic mingle with the crowd, signing autographs.

Afternoons usually start with some special event in the grand ballroom: the first of several shows of their products by the dealers, a kid show forum, performances by club-show magicians. Featured lecturers then take the stage, one after another, throughout all the afternoons. Close-up shows are presented too. These are always among the convention's most popular events, and present viewing problems that are overcome in various ways so that the sort of magic intended for showing to only a few people right at the table may be seen comfortably by all convention-goers. Sometimes convention groups move from one special close-up room to another, with high-banked bleacher-like seats installed so the group can look down at the table. At other times the close-up performers move from room to room, repeating their routines for each assembled group; or closed-circuit television cameras may be focused on a performer and viewing screens spaced around one large room.

After the nightly big stage shows, there are likely to be other, smaller shows that start at midnight and go on for as long as anyone can stay awake. Sometimes a star lecturer or famous performer will take over the stage at midnight, or hold a special-admission lecture in one of the hotel parlors—showing some of his magic, revealing some of his secrets, reminiscing about his experiences, answering questions, and giving advice. Meanwhile private parties will be going on; gatherings of friends in somebody's room for the doing of tricks and the talking of magic, or for the relaxation, gags and horseplay of social fun.

Night and day, magic happens all over the convention hotel—in the bars, coffee shops, restaurants, lounges, lobbies, and even in elevators between floors. By the second day, hotel waitresses become used to having coins for tips magically plucked out of the air, or to seeing

dinner rolls float in space. They take it for granted that spoons can be bent by the "power of the mind" or that a selected card is likely to be discovered in a ham sandwich. Bartenders hardly blink when drinks are turned upside down without spilling, and chambermaids are no longer surprised to find a live rabbit in a bureau drawer or a dove perched on the shower rod in the bathroom.

A convention that is unusual in its surroundings is the annual fall Magic Jubilee sponsored by the New York magic dealer Louis Tannen, Inc. Instead of a big-city location, it is held at Brown's Hotel, a luxurious Catskill mountain resort at Loch Sheldrake, New York. The magic is given showcase settings in a fully equipped theater and a nightclub, and when the weekending magicians are not doing magic they can enjoy the vacationing pleasures of a swimming pool, sauna, dance studio, and other attractions. The room rates include three full meals a day.

The jubilees, which started in 1962, are attended by well over a thousand magicians. There are the morning-long close-up shows, daytime and midnight lectures, and Tannen's also brings in some twenty-five other dealers to set up displays and demonstrate their magical merchandise. The nightly stage shows frequently star European performers making their first American convention appearances.

But the most unusual of all the magic conventions are the "Get-Togethers" that have been sponsored since 1934 by Abbott's Magic Manufacturing Company in its little home town of Colon, Michigan. A farming village surrounded by woodland lakes, Colon calls itself "The Magic Capital of The World," and during the week of the annual Abbott's Get-Together the whole town puts out the welcome mat for the convening magicians, who outnumber its slightly more than one thousand population.

Colon has no hotels or motels and there is no public transportation into or out of town. But magicians who don't arrive by automobile are picked up by the magic company's staff at bus depots or airports fifteen miles away. Villagers open their homes to the magicians as paying guests; some lake cottages and houses can be rented. There are also church dinners, and meals at a grill and other eating places. Local merchants have sidewalk sales and there is a Saturday arts fair.

Abbott's sets up a factory showroom in an elementary school gymnasium. Afternoon lectures and other events as well as the big evening magic shows are held in a high school auditorium. The days and nights are filled with magic at one of the biggest and busiest of conventions.

In the United States, there are about 375 local magic clubs affiliated with either the International Brotherhood of Magicians or the Society of American Magicians, and probably another hundred or more independent clubs of one kind or another. They vary in size from those with several hundred members to clubs with a dozen members or less.

Other countries throughout the world, particularly in Europe, also have their scores of affiliated or independent clubs, and the fraternity is very much an international one. A magician who travels almost anywhere will find himself a welcome visitor at club meetings.

In the big metropolitan areas where there are likely to be a dozen magic clubs within the city and nearby suburbs, there is some sort of a club event almost every week, and many magicians belong to several different clubs. Clubs are fewer in smaller cities, and some magicians who live in rural areas regularly drive a hundred miles or more to attend club meetings.

The average American magic club meets once a month, although some clubs recess during the summer. Small clubs often meet informally at the home of one of the members, rotating meeting places according to which member volunteers to be host that month. Others have fixed meeting places at magic shops, restaurants, hotels, church or school auditoriums, or other available community halls. Stage facilities vary from club to club, as does the formality of meetings.

Entrance requirements for new members also differ. There are clubs that require prospective members to perform for the club or for a committee before their applications will be approved, while others accept any magic enthusiast who wants to join. Some knowledge of magic is expected, but few clubs expect a newcomer to display expert skill.

Many clubs set minimum-age limits, but they may also have youth programs to teach and encourage junior magicians so they can become members when they are old enough. During the year clubs generally have some meetings that are open to younger hobbyists, as well as to invited adult guests.

Club members perform at meetings and have a chance to try out new tricks and routines. There are often meeting nights devoted to performing tricks of a particular category: cards, silks, ropes, mental effects, comedy magic. Members attend lectures by visiting speakers and by other club members who talk about their specialties. Some clubs have workshop nights of instruction and constructive criticism, as well as group question-and-answer sessions to discuss specific magic problems.

Collector members show exhibits from their collections and display and demonstrate old apparatus. There are talks about magic history and magic books, showings of films of famous magicians. Sometimes a magic dealer is invited to present a show of new effects being marketed. There are auctions and swap nights.

Many clubs stage annual public shows, to raise club funds or for charity benefits, some of them elaborate big-theater affairs and others more modestly staged in high school auditoriums. Members join in programs to entertain in hospital wards, senior citizen centers, and other institutions. One club may put on a show for another nearby magic club in exchange for having members of that club stage its own show for the original performers. The exchanges may involve several clubs in the area. During National Magic Week in October there are often special club performances and public events to promote and publicize magic. Socially the clubs have annual banquets, award ceremonies, summer picnics, ladies' nights, family nights, and holiday magic parties.

In addition to the two large national magic societies, there are regional and state associations of magic clubs such as the Pacific Coast Association of Magicians, the Magicians Alliance Eastern States, the Southwestern Magicians, the Texas Association of Magicians, Florida State Magicians. Women have a national society, the Magigals, and there are also the Magic Collectors Association, the Magic Dealers Association, and many other special interest organizations. Magic Youths International, now an affiliate of the Society of American Magicians (whose assemblies are helping MYI organize new local chapters), is the oldest of the young magicians' societies; it was first formed in 1935. Dedicated to bringing together young magicians around the world, MYI has long published its own magazine, *Top Hat,* and maintains a lending library of magic books which its members may borrow by mail.

By far the largest of the independent magic societies is the Academy of Magical Arts, with its nearly four thousand members and associates. (See Chapter 8: "Showplaces of Magic.") Not on that scale, but with several hundred members, are some of the independent groups in other cities, many of which have been active for a quarter of a century or longer.

Several cities have what amount to magic clubs without regular members, elected officials, dues, or programmed meetings. They are simply informal gatherings for lunch, dinner, or late snacks and drinks at some spot that has become a traditional place for get-togethers. San Francisco, Minneapolis, and Cleveland are among them, and in Las Vegas magicians playing in the hotel showrooms gather with others on Wednesdays after midnight at a Chinese kitchen.

The most famous of the luncheon groups is the New York Magic Table; its daily meetings that draw visiting magicians from all over the country and the world have made it the subject of newspaper publicity, national magazine articles, and television news shows. Nobody knows from day to day who will turn up, but sooner or later most of the big names in magic do, along with stars of hit Broadway shows, films, and television, sports champions, best-selling authors, college presidents, or state supreme court judges. On the other hand it may be a day when nobody shows up but a few of the "regulars" and a would-be card trickster or two.

Larry Arcuri, a magic-magazine editor and columnist and former New York newspaperman, started it in the early 1940s. At that time, Chicago had a well-known Magicians' Round Table (now no longer active) and Arcuri and a few others thought New York should have one. He established its first home at the Dixie Hotel, where the luncheon sessions were held for over twenty years. More recently the New York Magic Table has moved through other locations, with Arcuri helping to assure that it always has a good meeting place.

The Table now gathers its magicians at the Gaiety West Restaurant at 224 West 47th Street, off Broadway in the heart of the Times Square theatrical district, Mondays to Fridays from noon to 2 P.M. Anyone interested in magic is welcome, and the management gives

The New York Magic Table, where magicians gather every day for lunch with visiting magicians from around the country and the world, and often entertain famous guests with table magic as they have for more than thirty years. Seated, back row at left, is Larry Arcuri, who started it in the 1940s; in back row at right is Joe Barnett, unofficial host and Table reporter.

magicians a discount on their luncheon checks. Arcuri is there nearly every day, ready to prime the flow of close-up magic with tricks of his own. Also on hand is another charter member of the group, attorney Joe Barnett, who genially acts as the Table's unofficial host and reports on its happenings in *M-U-M* magazine.

Here are capsule descriptions of the "big three" of magic clubs.

The Society of American Magicians

Oldest of the magic associations, the Society of American Magicians was born in 1902 in the back room of a New York magic shop where magicians got together on Saturday nights. Two doctors and the shop's owner were largely responsible for its birth.

Dr. W. Golden Mortimer, who was to become the society's first president, was a native New Yorker and a professional magician in his youth before turning to the practice of medicine. The other physician, Canadian-born Dr. Saram B. Ellison, had also set up medical practice in New York; he was not a performer but a collector of conjuring books and a true lover of the magical arts. The dealer was Francis J. Martinka; born in Prague and manager of a famed magic theater in Vienna, he came to the United States in 1872 and a year later

opened his first magic shop, in which he was joined by his brother Antonio, a builder of illusions and magic equipment. With its little back-room theater and stage, the Martinka Magical Palace on Sixth Avenue near 14th Street became a center of magic activities.

Amateur and professional magicians who gathered there and sometimes performed for one another often discussed the idea of forming a magic society. In April 1902, thirteen of them met in Martinka's back room and set up a temporary organization with Dr. Mortimer as chairman and Dr. Ellison as secretary. They named it the Society of American Magicians and appointed a committee to draw up a constitution and bylaws. Shortly afterwards a permanent society was formed. There were twenty-four charter members and Dr. Mortimer was elected president.

The two doctors did most of the planning and Mortimer claimed the honor of having devised the structure of the organization, its title, seal, bylaws, and catchy motto: "Magic-Unity-Might." In a written statement of the group's purpose, he declared: "This is an organization intended to unite those interested in magic, not only professionals but amateurs, manufacturers of conjuring apparatus, collectors, and all who are in any way interested in the art."

Within a year the society had 129 members, including some from other cities and a few from foreign countries. Among the more prominent were U.S. magicians Harry

Kellar and Howard Thurston, Britain's, David Devant, and the first woman member, Madame Bedan of Boston. Harry Houdini, who became president in 1917 and served for nine years, enthusiastically helped to build up what by then had become a considerable number of affiliated clubs, called "assemblies," across the country. Thurston also built membership when he was president in 1927.

The SAM now has about six thousand members, approximately two-thirds of whom belong to its 126 assemblies, and the rest associate members. Although basically a U.S. society, it has become increasingly international in recent years, with many associate members in foreign countries and a number of foreign assemblies, from Canada and South America to Europe and Asia.

The society's constitution provides that "any reputable and desirable person, seventeen years of age or older, genuinely interested in magic as an art" is eligible for either active or associate membership. Junior membership is open to those fourteen to seventeen, with all rights and privileges except voting or holding office. Women are admitted on the same basis as men.

Applications for active membership must be made through one of the affiliated assemblies, subject to the bylaws of that assembly, and require the endorsement of two members of the society as well as a vote by the particular assembly concerned. Applicants are urged to join one of the assemblies as active members whenever possible.

However, associate membership, which does not require belonging to one of the assemblies, is available to anyone who cannot attend assembly meetings for personal reasons or lives too far away. No endorsement is needed for associate membership, and applications can be obtained directly from the office of the society's secretary. Membership dues include a subscription to the monthly magazine *M-U-M*. (See Chapter 6: "Books and Magazines.")

Information. Society of American Magicians, Herbert B. Downs, International Secretary, 66 Marked Tree Road, Needham, MA 02192. Phone: 617-444-8095.

The International Brotherhood of Magicians

Back in 1922 three teenaged magic hobbyists started a mail correspondence club, so that those interested in magic could share friendship and ideas. They called it the International Brotherhood of Magicians, since one of them lived in Canada and the other two in the United States. It has become the largest of all the magic societies, with members and affiliated clubs in nearly every country in the world.

The Canadian who became its first president and officially IBM member Number One was Len Vintus. The second member was Gene Gordon, later a leading magic dealer as well as a professional magician, and the third was Ernest Schieldge, who took the stage name of Don Rogers. The Brotherhood caught on almost immediately, enrolling four hundred members in a dozen countries within a year. The membership directory was supplemented by a mimeographed newsletter named *The Linking Ring* to symbolize the linking together of the Brotherhood—as in the classic trick of linking steel rings together. By the time the IBM was in its third year, *The Linking Ring* had become a regularly printed magazine. (See Chapter 6: "Books and Magazines.")

Within two years more the International Brotherhood of Magicians had been built into a flourishing society of more than fourteen hundred members—not only amateurs but many well-known professionals.

The man largely credited for IBM's growth from those foundations into a fully organized worldwide fraternity of magicians and affiliated clubs was the dynamic W. W. Durbin.

Bill Durbin was a magician by preference, a lawyer by profession, a successful businessman and politician by occupation, and an organizer by inclination. He had performed magic professionally at times and it remained his first love. But he had also built a floundering sign-manufacturing company into a profitable nationwide business. As Ohio Democratic chairman, he had built up the Democratic organization in his state, helped to put its candidates into office, and in the early 1930s served in Washington in a top-level position with the United States Treasury.

Durbin was also determined to put his organizing talents behind the International Brotherhood of Magicians. He arranged its first convention in 1926 and held it on the grounds of his home in Kenton, Ohio, in the Egyptian Hall, the little private magic theater he had built there for himself. (See Chapter 8: "Showplaces of Magic.") The IBM elected Durbin president and he took office in April, 1927, and was duly reelected over the next ten years until his death in 1937.

As IBM president, Durbin shifted the Brotherhood's headquarters to Kenton, where it has remained ever since. Durbin gave it a firm working base and a constitutional body, and pretty much accomplished for it what he had done for the sign-making company and his political party. Certainly not IBM's founding father, he was undeniably its greatest builder and booster. But many others, before him and after, also contributed much to its continuing growth.

The International Brotherhood of Magicians now has about eleven thousand members in North and South America, Europe, Africa, Asia, Australia, and New Zealand. There has even been enrollment behind the iron curtain—in East Germany, Bulgaria, Czechoslovakia, Hungary, and Poland. The IBM has two hundred and fifty affiliated clubs, called "rings," in the United States, thirty five in other countries.

230

Among the larger overseas rings are those in Belgium, France, Italy, Holland, Sweden, Switzerland, Australia and New Zealand, Buenos Aires, and Singapore. But the largest ring anywhere is the British Ring, which includes members from England, Scotland, and Wales, and is practically a full magic society within itself. It has its own publication, the *Budget,* and holds annual conventions as big as those of the parent organization, with an attendance of fifteen hundred magicians.

Applications for membership in the International Brotherhood of Magicians can be obtained directly from its headquarters in Kenton. Candidates must be sponsored by two members, and must submit information on the official application as to their experience in magic and their special interests. Junior memberships are available for those from ages fourteen to eighteen. Those who join affiliated rings must be IBM members and are subject to the admission requirements and by-laws of the ring. But it is not necessary to join one of the rings to become a member of the IBM itself. Membership dues include subscription to *The Linking Ring.*

Information. The International Brotherhood of Magicians, Mary T. Dowd, Executive Secretary, 28 N. Main Street, Kenton, OH 43326.

The Magic Circle

The Magic Circle, the most prestigious of magic clubs, has its headquarters in London, complete with permanent clubhouses, theater, museum, and library. Among its fifteen hundred amateurs and professional magician-members are Prince Charles, Earl Mountbatten of Bur-

A truly royal magician, His Royal Highness Prince Charles, performing at The Magic Circle's clubhouse in London for his fellow members of the magic club and a party of royal visitors. The Prince of Wales presented an entertaining routine with the Cups and Balls, combining his sleight of hand with the comic use of a collapsing wand, and was accepted into membership in The Magic Circle on October 28, 1975. SYNDICATION INTERNATIONAL-PHOTO TRENDS

ma, and several magicians from both houses of Parliament, as well as others in high position in government, the arts, the academic, professional and business worlds, publishing, films and television. But enrollment is international, and includes many members from the United States.

The Circle was founded in 1905, at Pinoli's restaurant in London, by a group of twenty-three magicians organized by enthusiastic amateur Neil Weaver. David Devant, Britain's greatest magician, became its first president. In 1906 the new club began publishing its magazine, *The Magic Circular*. (See Chapter 6: "Books and Magazines.") By 1907 membership had swelled to more than one hundred and fifty, the Circle had given its first annual dinner and public show, and was holding regular weekly meetings.

As it continued to grow it moved through a succession of meeting places: a famous Fleet Street tavern, a railway inn, a plushy West End hotel, a vast basement clubroom, a Bloomsbury ballroom. Finally the present clubhouse was built in Chenies Mews, and opened in 1968.

The doors of the Circle open into a lobby where there is a large round magic mirror, from which the visitor's reflection gradually vanishes to reveal a display of club trophies. To the left is the impressive and mysterious main clubroom, with a black circular carpet in the middle of the floor. A great canopy is surmounted by a monstrous witch's hat, again with a mirrored reflecting device that gives a person standing in the center of the circle the impression that it is slowly rotating around him.

Built into the clubroom walls are illuminated showcases displaying some of the Circle's museum's treasures. The museum itself is on a second floor, along with the reference library of magic books going back through the centuries. Downstairs beneath the museum is the lending library, with its thousands of more recent books. Off to one side of the clubroom is the theater, an intimate showplace where an audience of more than one hundred can sit in comfort to watch shows or hear lectures from the fully equipped stage.

Members meet every Monday night, except holidays, for lectures, shows, other events, and the examinations of those who seek to advance through the various degrees of Circle membership. The meeting nights are for members only and guests may not be invited except by special permission.

But the Circle also opens its doors to the public, welcoming club groups and parties of up to one hundred people to unique magical evenings called "at homes." These are held as often as three nights a week—with admission only by ticket purchased in advance—and have become so popular that there is a long waiting list. The special evenings of public entertainment present a history of magic, as well as stage and close-up performances. Each year the Circle also hires a West End theater for a week or more to present a big public Magic Circle Show.

For members there are auction sales, collectors' days, many other events. In the autumn there is a banquet, cabaret, and dance, to which members and associate members may bring guests, and in the spring a less formal supper and entertainment.

The Magic Circle has no women members, although in the dim past there have been four women associate members. Applications for associate membership may be made by anyone with a genuine interest in magic. Full membership is limited to men over the age of eighteen, who have a knowledge of, and practical ability in, the art of magic. All meetings and events are open to full members and associates alike; all receive *The Magic Circular*.

A newcomer first becomes an associate. From there, he can proceed by examination to full membership, and then may advance to become an associate member of the Inner Magic Circle. Finally he may win recognition as a full member of the Inner Magic Circle, but that last degree is conferred only by a call of the president and council, and is a most coveted honor.

Information. The Magic Circle, Secretary John Salisse, 12 Hampstead Way, London, N.W. 11, England.

10

THE DEALERS

More than just a store where tricks and equipment are sold, the magic shop traditionally has been a social gathering place of magicians, an information center about magic activities, an informal theater of magic, and very often a creative workshop, learning hall, and booking office for magic acts. It is also, at least to its owners, a place of business, although the hobbyists who frequent magic shops sometimes tend to forget that fact and consider the shop a happy clubroom where purchases are merely incidental to the fun.

The larger shops, as well as some smaller ones, often operate a combined business of retail sales, manufacturing, publishing, wholesaling, and mail-order merchandising. Others sell only retail, only whole-sale, operate no shop at all but sell only by mail, or specialize in supplying tricks of one particular category, such as those with silks, cards or coins.

For a few big dealers, magic is a business with sales of well over a million dollars a year, but for most the income is more modest. Some dealers have been in the business half a century, and others venture into it and fade out of it again in a month.

There are many more who are part-time dealers, selling magic as a sideline to their full-time occupation, making a profitable hobby of a nights-and-weekends magic business. It may be a mail-order business, with a spare bedroom or garage serving as stockroom and office, or a small retail magic shop set up in the dealer's home to cater to area magic enthusiasts. Even the family station wagon may be converted into a traveling magic shop, to make the rounds of nearby magic clubs on meeting nights, or to visit some distant group of hobbyists by appointment. Quite a few new flourishing full-time magic companies began as part-time hobby businesses. A good proportion of all marketed tricks and apparatus comes out of home workshops—where articles are made or assembled by hobbyists who are also skilled craftsmen—either to be sold through other dealers or directly retailed by advertising in magazines.

In addition to the standard tricks and equipment that nearly all magic shops and companies offer, most dealers have some things that are exclusively their own, or at least not readily available everywhere. Even more or less standard equipment varies greatly in details of construction, design, or decoration, to suit it for use under various performing conditions or for different routines and presentations. Old things are forever being "improved," and new effects are advertised by the dozens a month.

There are magic buyers who eagerly shop the world for whatever is new, buying by mail from foreign dealers as well as from those closer to home. Much domestic buying of magic is now also done by phone. Some dealers maintain twenty-four-hour answering services so callers from various parts of the country can take advantage of night phone rates. The purchaser can order

The shipping room of the biggest of the magic dealers around the start of the century, Martinka & Company in New York, as pictured in an old catalogue engraving. COURTESY FLOSSO-HORNMANN MAGIC CO.

from the company's catalogue, charge the tricks to his major credit card account, and get immediate delivery.

The magic dealers described here are only some of the very many, selected as representative of various kinds of shops, companies, mail order concerns and manufacturers.

Abbott's Magic Manufacturing Co.

It takes a five-hundred-page catalogue as big as a telephone directory to list the tricks, apparatus, illusions, publications, and products the Abbott's company sells by mail order and through other dealers. In a modern factory in the farming village of Colon, Michigan, which is about as far removed from big-city centers of magic activity as any place could be, twenty-five people work full time at supplying the world's magicians with whatever they need.

Percy Abbott, an Australian magician, Sydney magic shop owner, and vaudeville performer, came to Colon in 1927 to stay with his friend, the celebrated American big-show illusionist Harry Blackstone, who had a summer home there. The two started the Blackstone Magic Company and worked together for a year and a half, but after some disagreements Abbott took to the road again as a performer. Abbott meanwhile had married a Colon girl, Gladys Good-

rich, and after their first child was born they decided to give up roadshow trouping and settle down in Colon.

In 1934 Abbott founded the magic company that bears his name, rented a room for it above the village grocery store, and borrowed the money to have his first twenty-page list of tricks printed. The company dangled for a time at the end of a shoestring, but Abbott's inventive brand of magic caught on. One of his first big reputation-builders with magicians was a still-popular trick called "squash," the almost visible vanish of a filled whisky glass from the bare hands.

Abbott brought Ohio magician Recil Bordner into the company as a partner, and they moved its expanding operations into what once had been a carriage factory. Here, they built an office and workshop on the first floor and a small theater upstairs for demonstrations. The Get-Togethers that were to bring hundreds of conventioning magicians to Colon for a week's magic fun each year were begun (See Chapter 9: "Clubs and Conventions,") and publication of *Tops* magazine soon started. (See Chapter 6: "Books and Magazines.")

For a time Abbott's had its own branch retail magic shops in New York, Chicago, Detroit, Indianapolis, and Los Angeles, but eventually closed them, continued wholesaling its products to other dealers, and concentrated its retail sales on the worldwide mail-order merchandising from Colon.

When Percy Abbott retired in

1959, a year before his death, his share of the company was bought by Bordner, who continued to build it into one of the biggest of magic businesses. Abbott's moved to a new building in 1974, and the plant now fills 42,000 square feet of floor space, equipped to provide all the makings of hundreds of make-believe miracles.

Address: Abbott's Magic Manufacturing Co., Colon, MI 49040.

The Flosso Hornmann Magic Company

Probably the oldest continuously operated magic company in the world is the Flosso Hornmann Magic Company on 34th Street in New York. It can trace its ancestry back to a magic shop started in 1856.

The Martinka brothers bought it

Where the magic was made at Martinka's in the early 1900s, before the oldest of American magic companies passed through a succession of famous owners (Martinka-Carter-Houdini-Hornmann-Ducrot-Flosso) to become the Flosso-Hornmann Magic Company. COURTESY FLOSSO-HORNMANN MAGIC CO.

in 1877 and became the leading American magic dealers of their time, and it was in their back-room theater that the Society of American Magicians was founded in 1902. (See Chapter 9: "Clubs and Conventions.") In 1916 the Martinka company was purchased by famed illusionist Charles Carter, who—when not touring the world as "Carter the Great"—stored his equipment in the shop's back room. This apparatus included his most sensational illusion, "The Lion's Bride." Legend has it that at times Carter also kept the lion itself in the back room and that it roared so threateningly that the magic shop customers would buy anything in a hurry just to get out.

Carter announced plans to expand the business into a whole chain of branch magic shops across the country, but the plans fell through and the company soon had an even more famous owner, Harry Houdini. Houdini became proprietor in 1917, put some of his staff in to run the Martinka shop, and managed the business between performances and feature-film making in Hollywood. As a magic shopkeeper it was said that Houdini particularly enjoyed demonstrating tricks for the youngsters who came in to buy, and that he was never too busy to give a word of advice to any aspiring youthful magician. Reportedly, Houdini's advice was: "Practice!"

In 1920, Houdini merged Martinka's with the Hornmann Magic Company, which had been operated for many years by Professor Otto Hornmann at 304 West 34th Street,

still the location of the company's present shop. The next in line of its well-known owners, after Houdini, was Frank Ducrot. Under his real name of T. Francis Fritz, Ducrot had edited and published the influential magic magazine *Mahatma* (See Chapter 6: "Books and Magazines"), and was a popular private-party entertainer in New York.

Rotund, genial, and well-liked by magicians who made his shop a favorite rendezvous, Ducrot was famed among them for his "thumb tie" routine, his presentation of the "linking rings," and skilled manipulation of billiard balls. He was also the creator of the now standard method for a trick used by almost every performer who does magic with silk handkerchiefs: the "twentieth century silks."

Ducrot ran the shop from the late 1920s until his death in 1938, when the Martinka-Carter-Hornmann-Ducrot succession became the Flosso Hornmann Magic Company, after being bought by Al Flosso. Known as the "Coney Island Fakir," Flosso was beloved in the world of magic, not only as a unique performer but as a unique individual who claimed to have come from the mythical "Isle of Malagoola," a place of wonderful make-believe inhabited by him alone.

Born in New York in 1895, Al Flosso bought some of his own first tricks as a boy at Martinka's, and was a friend of all the store's various owners, including Houdini. A professional magician from the age of thirteen, he trouped the circuses, carnivals, sideshows, graduated into the big-time vaudeville circuits and top resort hotels, and kept his audiences everywhere belly-laughing over his delightful style of Coney Island hokum combined with unusual magical skill. No other magician ever has, or possibly ever will, extract as much pure fun as Al Flosso did from his coin-catching Miser's Dream routine with a boy volunteer from the audience. He had performed for Thomas Edison, for Franklin Roosevelt, was later seen by television's viewing millions on the old Ed Sullivan show, had worked with **Eddie Cantor** and teamed with comedian Bud Abbott when they were unknowns, was honored by the world's magic societies, and continued his active performing until his death in 1976 at the age of eighty-one.

Flosso was also a collector and seller of antique magic apparatus, and under his proprietorship the age-old 34th Street magic shop be-

One of the displays of rare apparatus and memorabilia, part of the Al Flosso collection, exhibited in the Flosso-Hornmann Company magic shop. COURTESY FLOSSO-HORNMANN MAGIC CO.

Another of the shop's museum cabinets displaying old magic equipment and puppets.
COURTESY FLOSSO-HORNMANN MAGIC CO.

came a place bulging over from its counters, shelves, and cabinets with spilling stacks of magic literature and equipment from the past. Hundreds of old gadgets and gimmicks were unfamiliar to many contemporary magicians; only Flosso himself remembered their use. He could always dig out anything that couldn't be found anywhere else, and perhaps reluctantly part with it for an honestly bargained price. But

---

Jack Flosso, owner of "the world's oldest new magic shop," the Flosso-Hornmann Magic Company, still in continuous operation at the same 34th Street location in New York as it was even before Houdini owned and ran it, and with an ancestry it traces back to a magic shop started elsewhere in Manhattan in 1856.

the shop's customers were his friends and there was never any pressure to buy. The understanding was that everything was there to be asked for, would be sold if you insisted, but Flosso would just as soon sit next to you in one of the chairs out in front of the counter, send out for coffee and sandwiches, and talk magic. The kid debating how to spend a dollar would get as much of Flosso's attention as the famous magician who came to spend the afternoon and search for magic treasure.

Al Flosso's son Jack, a world-traveled performer himself and long associated with his father in operating the shop, is now its owner. Jack Flosso has managed to preserve much of the century-ago atmosphere, while converting the establishment into "the world's oldest *new* magic shop." He has created museum-like displays, in glass-fronted wall cases, of some of his father's magic collection. But all the latest in modern magic, along with the best of the old and good, is available for today's magicians.

Address: The Flosso Hornmann Magic Co., 304 West 34th Street, New York, NY 10001.

Johnson Products

The Johnson Products company specializes in the manufacture and sale of precision-made coin tricks and other small apparatus and secret devices for close-up performers. With Johnson trick coins, and the added skill of the magician who uses them, seemingly ordinary quarters, half-dollars, and various other coins can be made to do all sorts of things money never does except by magic.

The business was started as a hobby in 1968 by retired magician Charles Johnson. He found a skilled machinist, Sam LaPorte, had him make up some gimmicked coin tricks and sold them under the company name of Johnson Precision Products. LaPorte presently bought the company and kept the Johnson name. Over the years the company's reputation for producing high-quality coin magic grew until Johnson became the largest wholesaler of that type of magic.

But although LaPorte was an expert machinist, he knew very little about the art of magic, so in 1972 he hired the magician Mike Caveney. Interested in magic from the age of nine, Caveney had worked at odd jobs around a magic manufacturing company as a boy, had started winning magic convention awards as a performer while still in his teens, and after college had become a successful professional trade-show magician. He first took the job with Johnson Products in 1972 to fill in between trade-show engagements.

After Caveney learned how to manufacture the Johnson products, he developed the retail side of the business, wrote a mail-order catalogue and monthly advertisements for the various magic magazines. He also created and wrote routines to go with the equipment, displayed and demonstrated the company's effects at magic conventions around the world, and helped locate new items to add to the expanded line.

The company that had started as a hobby grew into a prospering retail mail-order business, as well as a wholesale operation. "The secret word," Caveney says, "is 'Quality.'" Proud of that quality, Johnson backed its products with a money-back guarantee, unusual in magic because the purchaser of a trick can hardly expect a refund after he learns its secret. But Johnson received few requests for refunds.

In addition to its widely marketed products, the company also does custom work for many top professional magicians who have special things made to order. Its line now includes not only coin tricks, but tricked poker chips, leather work, card and mental magic, and a variety of magical accessories. The unique company keeps eight full-time employees busy.

Address: Johnson Products, P.O. Box 734, Arcadia, CA 91106.

Magic, Inc.

Owned by two of magic's best-liked and best-informed people, Jay Marshall and his wife Frances, Magic, Inc., is geographically located in a building of its own in Chicago, but spreads its business and the Marshalls' activities out over the whole world of magic. It is not just a magic shop, new and used bookshop, magic factory, publishing house, and retail and wholesale mail order company with an international trade. It is also a meeting place for magic clubs, a creative production center, a haven for collectors and visiting greats of the magic world, something of a private museum, and the home of Mr. and Mrs. Marshall. (See Chapter 3: "Women in Magic"; Chapter 6: "Books and Magazines.")

The business was started, in another Chicago location, as the Ireland Magic Company in 1926, by magician Laurie Ireland, and about five years after it began the now Frances Ireland Marshall went to work there and later married the owner. After Ireland's death, she married the multi-talented Jay Marshall. They incorporated the business in 1963, with Jay Marshall as company president and Frances Marshall as secretary-treasurer, renamed it simply Magic, Inc., and have continued to operate it together.

Jay and Frances Marshall, whose company in Chicago, Magic, Inc., deals in nearly everything that has to do with magic around the world, pictured here at a convention of the Norway Magic Circle.

At one time or another most of the Chicago area's estimated ten thousand young and older magic hobbyists and more professional magicians probably have passed through the shop's doorway, and on busy days a good proportion of them seem to be there all at once. Visiting magicians from around the country and the world often fly in mainly to go there, and those who plan visits in advance can send for a map to guide them through Chicago to the shop.

The retail magic shop on the building's first floor, managed by Walter Gydesen, is the display and demonstration room. On one wall is a news bulletin board of area magic activities and announcements of who is performing where and when. The first floor also houses the Punch and Judy Bookshop, filled with hundreds of new and old volumes of magic, puppetry and related performing arts; it is personally managed by Jay Marshall. It buys and sells books by mail, deals directly from the shelves, and conducts a book-search service to fill customers' want lists for old magic books. Himself a noted collector of books and other magic memorabilia, Marshall is an avid and experienced book searcher. Walter Gydesen, when not store-managing the retail magic business, is a devoted magic collector, specializing in posters, and is executive secretary of the Magic Collectors Association.

Farther back are the offices, manufacturing, assembly and shipping rooms, and at the rear a busy printing plant and bindery. The building extends into a small theater, which in addition to providing a stage for a variety of magic events is the regular meeting place of two independent magic clubs and a junior magicians' group. It is also the place where collectors get together each year for the Collectors' Weekend mini-convention jointly sponsored by The Magic Collectors Association and Magic, Inc.

There are those who pun that the "Inc" of the company's name should rightly be "ink" because it publishes so many new magic books, booklets, routines, specialized instruction manuals in particular categories, and numerous other items including an annual calendar of world magic events. Its own general magic catalogue of several hundred pages is designed so sections can be added to keep it up to date, and there are also available a series of well-annotated book catalogues, brochures describing new books and products, and *Trick Talk,* a periodically issued bulletin of what is new.

Address: Magic, Inc., 5082 N. Lincoln Ave., Chicago, IL 60625.

Paul Diamond's Magic and Fun Shop

A skilled magician and in love with magic from boyhood, Paul Diamond always dreamed of having a magic shop of his own. In 1964 he gave up another profitable sales

Paul Diamond, who started a small magic and fun shop in Fort Lauderdale, Florida, and found himself with a mail-order and manufacturing company that keeps him constantly traveling the country and the world as a popular lecturer, convention performer, and demonstrator of the magic he creates.

business and started Paul's Magic and Fun Shop in a busy Fort Lauderdale, Florida shopping center. It flourished as a center for Florida magicians—and for magicians visiting the state from everywhere. Diamond meanwhile developed it into a large mail-order, wholesale, and manufacturing business. He still enjoys demonstrating tricks across the counter when he has the time. But he is constantly traveling the world, promoting and showing his magic, and performing at magic clubs and conventions.

He is also among the busiest and most popular magic lecturers. In one recent year alone, he lectured across the United States, in Mexico, Canada, Hawaii, Singapore, Hong Kong, Thailand, Taiwan, Japan, Germany, Sweden, and England. For magicians, he presents four different lecture programs: on impromptu and close-up magic, silks, coins, and stage magic. Each hour-and-a-half lecture is followed by a demonstration of exclusive effects he offers for sale. Diamond combines the appearances for magic groups with another career—working as a magician at trade shows, conventions, and promotions for large corporations.

But the Florida shop remains his headquarters, and although it manufactures a variety of tricks and supplies, its main specialty is coin magic, on which there is a five-year guarantee against defects. Paul's Magic and Fun Shop also publishes a number of books on coin and close-up magic.

Much of Diamond's retail mail-order business is based on a "club" of regular customers. To become a "member" a person buys a "lifetime catalog." The company promises that it will be kept up to date perpetually with regular mailings of new pages about the latest magic, and that the purchaser "will never have to buy another catalog." There are frequent special offers, discounts, and clearance sales for those on the permanent mailing list.

Address: Paul Diamond's Magic and Fun Shop, 903 North Federal Highway, Searstown, Fort Lauderdale, FL 33304.

Phil Thomas Yogi Magic Mart

Built upon nearly half a century of personalized service to magicians, the Phil Thomas Yogi Magic Mart in Baltimore has been called a "supermarket of magic." A visitor steps from a smartly modern mirror-walled elevator directly into an enormous 35,000-square-foot-room—once an Arthur Murray dance studio ballroom. On the long rows of shelves is an array of magic and books from more than four hundred different manufacturers and suppliers—probably the biggest display of magic ever assembled in any magic shop in the world.

It is three and half times larger than a previous shop, a block away, that was destroyed by fire in 1978.

Saved from the fire (although much was lost) are some of the rare memorabilia of the old shop's museum, to which Thomas has added from his own lifetime collection of props personally given him by famous magicians. The new shop's museum also is larger than before, filling thirteen glass-fronted cases.

Among the things saved was part of the little old eight-foot stage on which Thurston, Blackstone, and other magic immortals performed gratis, to entertain members of the Yogi Magic Club. At the back of the present shop's big room is a fully equipped modern stage. The Yogi Club, with more than three hundred active members, is among the largest and oldest of independent magic clubs. It still meets regularly at the Mart the first Saturday of every month, as it has for thirty-seven years. Separately, two magic schools are conducted there, with classes for juniors on Saturdays, for adults on Thursday nights.

"Baltimore has always been a big city for magic," Thomas says. "It has produced an unusual number of amateurs—an unusual number of whom have become professionals."

When he was a boy, Thomas's church minister showed him a few tricks with coins that first got him interested in magic. He soon discovered that down the block from where he lived there was another boy magic fan, and the two became young magic pals, performing some of their first public shows together. His boyhood friend was Milbourne Christopher, who went on to become one of the most celebrated of

modern magicians. (See Chapter 2: "Performing Magic.") Thomas combined his own successful performing with his career as a most successful magic dealer.

He started in the business by selling tricks and equipment from a little magic den set up in his own home. In 1935, he established his first real magic shop on Baltimore's downtown Charles Street, and several years later moved it to a new location on the same street, where the business grew through some forty years, until the fire in 1978.

For a very brief time, it seemed to Thomas that all he had built through the years was in ruins. But Baltimore's magicians were at the scene almost before the firemen had left, rallying around to help salvage what could be saved from the wreckage, and hundreds of phone calls and letters from friends and customers all over the country reinforced his conviction that he hadn't lost a business, only the shop. Within days plans were under way to build the new and bigger Yogi Magic Mart "supermarket" right down the street.

Business went on as before, in the shop, by mail, and wholesale to other dealers, based on the policy Thomas had adopted, nearly a half-century earlier, of providing "personalized service." He believes this has been the keynote of his success. "We honestly strive to serve, through the mails, as conscientiously as if the customer were right in the shop," he explains. "Because of our much larger facilities and augmented staff, we will now be able to serve magicians and magic shops throughout the world more effectively."

He and his wife Ann still put in full days at the shop, but Thomas has never lost his love of performing magic as well as selling it, and Ann is also his partner in the many magic shows they give. David Roemer, the full-time shop manager, takes charge of the staff when Phil and Ann Thomas are off "gallivanting around the world," as Roemer puts it, presenting their magic on luxury cruise ships to the Mediterranean and to Europe.

Address: Phil Thomas Yogi Magic Mart, 217 N. Charles Street, Baltimore, MD 21201.

Rings 'N Things Magic Company

Michael Brazill, president of the Rings 'N Things Magic Company, who conjured up out of a basement workshop an American success story, magic version. His flourishing manufacturing firm now wholesales thousands of sets of Linking Rings and many other things to 350 magic shops and dealers.

The Rings 'N Things Magic Company grew in half a dozen years from a one-man business in a basement workshop—with an investment of fifty dollars—into a wholesale manufacturing firm supplying its quality metal-crafted magic products to more than three hundred and fifty magic shops and dealers.

Mike Brazill, a Jennings, Missouri, magician who had some hobby knowledge of metalwork and ran a tool rental business with his brother, decided that what his fellow magicians really needed were some good sets of Linking Rings. So

he put fifty dollars into buying a motor for a metal lathe he had restored to working condition in his basement shop. That was in 1969, and before the year was over he and a helper had turned out and sold

248

more than a thousand sets of his "new design" rings.

The next year the basement shop produced three thousand sets of rings, a thousand dove pans (used by magicians not only for conjuring up doves but for such effects as magically baking birthday cakes), and six hundred sets of newly designed metal cups for the ancient Cups and Balls trick. With orders flooding in, Brazill needed somebody to handle the mail, do the packing, shipping, and billing, and he hired Sandra Byrne to run the office while he ran the shop. She handled the business side of the shop so well that he offered her an interest in it, and she became a partner and vice-president when the fledgling company was incorporated in 1972 with Brazill as president. Because by then they were making a lot of other "things" as well as linking rings, they named it the Rings 'N Things Company. Three years more and it was firmly enough established to move into its own spacious plant, the present location in Jennings.

With Brazill directing the manufacturing and Sandra Byrne capably managing the company's business as probably the only woman executive of a wholesale magic-making firm, the Rings 'N Things Magic Company also employs about a dozen metal craftsmen and other employees. The product line has been expanded to more than thirty different items. All are sold with a lifetime guarantee against defects in workmanship.

Address: The Rings 'N Things Magic Company, P.O. Box 3982, St. Louis, MO 63136.

Probably the only woman executive of a wholesale magic manufacturing corporation, Sandra Byrne, originally hired to do the office chores for the then still small Rings 'N Things Magic Company, managed the company's business so well she became a partner and vice-president.

Silk King Studios

The Silk King Studios of Harold and Thelma Rice in Cincinnati provide the world's magicians not only with the finest of silks that are specially woven, designed, and made for magical uses, but with the secret devices, tricks, and routines of silk magic.

Rice started the specialized business as a hobby in 1929, and although it has grown over the years into the largest producer of silk magic—sold directly by mail and through other dealers—he and his wife have never considered the volume of sales as important as "the satisfaction gained from works of art well done." The business, says Rice, is still "a labor of love." It has been a successful and profitable enterprise, in which his wife has been an active partner since their marriage in 1937, but their greatest reward has been "the realization that our personalized creations are giving others pleasure."

In his non-magic life, Rice is a prominent educator. After majoring in art at the University of Cincinnati and starting as a public-school-system art supervisor, he earned his education doctorate at Columbia, became head of Alabama University's art department, then dean and later president of America's oldest professional college for women, Moore Institute in Philadelphia. He returned to the University of Cincinnati in 1963 to become dean of its College of Design, Architecture and Art, and in 1973 became coordinator of the university's graduate school studies in art education.

But his magic education began as a boy in his home town of Salineville, Ohio, with the feeding of a disappearing goat, an animal that the then well-known magician S. S. Henry vanished from a box twice a day during his Chautauqua circuit tent-show appearances in Salineville. In return for feeding the goat, young Harold Rice got in free to see Henry's magic shows, and that made him an aspiring magician. By the time he was in college, he had become an accomplished performer, with a specialty act built around silk magic. As an art major, he designed and created his own brilliantly colored silks, which attracted the attention of other magicians who saw him perform. "Some local magicians persuaded me to make a few colored squares of silk for them," he explains, "and before I knew it I found myself in business as a magic dealer."

Rice's silks became recognized by magicians not only for their brilliant and permanent colors and theatrically eye-catching designs, but for their durability, careful hand-workmanship, and the woven-to-order texture that would allow them to be tightly folded into small secret places in magic apparatus, from which they would expand fresh and unwrinkled. An excellent performer himself, Rice also created practical routines others could use, including many novel effects with specially designed and patterned

250

silks, large squares and streamers with rainbow bursts of color, comedy silks, and a series of artistic "picture" silks—exclusive products he supplied. He became the leading expert on the care and handling of silks, and invented new apparatus for silk magic.

Rice has written half a dozen books on the subject and publishes books about silk magic written by others. He is the editor of the definitive *Rice's Encyclopedia of Silk Magic,* each of whose three volumes runs to more than five hundred pages. (A fourth volume is in preparation.) Their detailed instructions, explanations, and several thousand illustrations cover just about everything there is to know about silk magic.

To magicians, the name "Rice" has long been synonymous with "silks" and they long ago started calling him "The Silk King," which accounts for the name of the business he started fifty years ago as a hobby.

Address: Silk King Studios, 640 Evening Star Lane, Cincinnati, OH 45220.

Supreme Magic Company

Located in the small Devonshire town of Bideford, among the hills and hedges of southwest England, the Supreme Magic Company does a major part of its business with customers in the United States. Among the biggest of mail-order magic companies, Supreme is a maker of everything in magic, 70 percent of which it ships out of England to twenty-five thousand magicians and dealers around the world, the largest number of them Americans.

Supreme makes buying easier for its U.S. customers by eliminating the perplexities of computing foreign currency and postage. All of its lists and catalogues price everything in dollars, with mailing costs included in the price. Orders are immediately

---

American magicians, shopping the world by mail for their magic, buy thousands of their props, tricks, and books from the Supreme Magic Company in the small Devonshire town of Bideford in England. Americans account for a major part of the business done by the firm, which is one of the largest mail-order dealers and manufacturers.

251

acknowledged by airmail and goods are shipped the day the order is received.

The company handles an estimated ten thousand different magic props, tricks and books, strives to keep them all in stock and in production. On the average the staff invents about one trick a day, not all of which are added to the line, although many are. The daily mail brings more than two hundred letters, including probably a dozen from new customers. Although the business is conducted by mail, Supreme also demonstrates its products internationally at some fifty magic conventions and gatherings a year.

Edwin Hooper started Supreme in his native town of Bideford in 1954—against the advice of those who told him a magic dealer couldn't prosper outside the big-city London area, and of those who thought he should have kept his job

Edwin Hooper, leaning over counter at center, started the Supreme Magic Company with nobody's help and against almost everybody's advice that it was too far from a big city for a magic business. He proved again that if you build a better magic service, magicians will beat a mail-order path to your door. At left, his son Michael Hooper; right, Ian Adair, prolific magic writer, creator, and dove-magic expert.

with a wholesale grocery company. He had given up the grocery job—where he learned much about packaging and stock control—to perform magic in resort hotels, and then in London as a children's entertainer. He had also worked for a time for an established magic manufacturer, where he learned something about making and selling tricks to magicians.

He returned to Bideford with savings of about six hundred dollars, persuaded his father to lend him a like amount, and launched his magic business as a one-man operation in one room of a house at the top of a steep hill on High Street. He had an initial line of some twenty tricks to sell, and the energy and enthusiasm to work eighteen hours a day. But the going was hard and the capital not enough, so for one whole long summer he gave six-a-day Punch and Judy shows on the sands of a nearby seaside resort, and sold homemade Punch puppets to youngsters at the end of each show. The takings kept him going until he had the new Supreme Magic business on its feet.

As the business grew, Hooper expanded it from the one room through the whole house, added a shed in the back garden, and then hammered through to the house next door. Gradually, with more renovations and extensions, it became a large and modern magic factory. Fifteen people work on the premises and twenty more in cottages scattered throughout the Devonshire countryside, where Supreme's magic business has revived the ancient tradition of cottage industry. The cottage shops that supply the company's needs include a full-time woodworker with his own small staff, a silk-screener, a family that turns out hundreds of brightly hued goose-feather flowers every week, and other single craftsmen or man-and-wife teams.

Townspeople have become accustomed to the fact that some rather unusual products are shipped out or received by Supreme. But now and then there is a complaint from the Bideford post office. A particularly loud one was heard on the day an incoming parcel burst open, sending hundreds of spring-loaded green-cloth vipers leaping all over Her Majesty's mailroom.

Hooper himself still starts work at 7:30 A.M., but usually finds he can now get home by 10:30 P.M.—although some nights he takes work home with him. Inventor-magician and dove magic expert Ian Adair, a prolific writer of books and routines and creator of tricks, has been with the company since its one-room days, and Hooper's son Michael, who grew up in the business, has become part of its management team.

In addition to publishing many magic books, Supreme publishes two popular magic magazines, *Magigram* and *The New Pentagram*. (See Chapter 6: "Books and Magazines.") The company has no public magic shop and a sign on the Bideford door reads: "Not Open to The General Public." But there is a modern factory showroom, open to magicians only, and visiting magicians are always welcomed.

Address: The Supreme Magic Company, 64 High Street, Bideford, Devon, England.

Louis Tannen, Inc.

Atop a Broadway skyscraper that overlooks Times Square, seventeen stories above Loew's State Theater where magic's vaudeville headliners once played, the modern magic shop, storerooms and offices of Louis Tannen, Inc., are as busy as a perpetual magic convention.

On any Saturday and all through the day, seventy or more magic enthusiasts at a time, amateur and professional magicians, men and women and kids, fill the penthouse shop six deep in front of the counters where half a dozen demonstrators simultaneously display the latest big and small miracles.

Weekdays the front shop is somewhat quieter, allowing the company's partners and present owners, Tony Spina and Jack Ferero, to get on with their major business. Tannen sells magic by mail to thousands of individual customers all over the world and wholesales it to three hundred and fifty dealers. The company also manufactures, imports and exports magic, and pub-

Any Saturday at Tannen's penthouse magic shop, high above New York's Times Square, magicians line up in rows six deep to see the latest tricks demonstrated and wait their turn for a chance to buy.

lishes new magic books to add to the several hundred it has already published.

The Tannen annual catalogue, a big hardbound volume itself, runs to more than seven hundred pages. Four times a year, to supplement the catalogue with news of the newest tricks and books, *Top Hat Topics* is mailed out free to customers. It has a circulation of nearly three times that of the most widely circulated magic magazine.

Tannen also rents illusions for use in television, trade shows, and advertising, plans and conducts Tannen's annual summer-camp magic school and the Tannen Jubilee conventions at Brown's Hotel. When inventory time comes, employees check out an estimated seventeen thousand different items, from tricked pennies to stage equipment for floating a lady—or for harmlessly dissecting her into three equal parts.

At work in Tannen's back rooms and offices are eighteen full-time employees; out front are the counter demonstrators and clerks. But the business also provides outside work for many suppliers of the varied things that go into the assembling of tricks. The company has two additional warehouses, one in New York, one in New Jersey. Annual sales amount to more than one and one-quarter million dollars.

Even a fire that swept through Tannen's in the summer of 1978, doing considerable smoke and water damage, couldn't keep out the customers long. While the mopping-up operations were under way,

magicians waded through ankle-deep debris, almost as anxious as the owners to have the place quickly put back to business as usual. Tannen's emerged from the fire: completely renovated, freshly restocked, its offices and storerooms restructured for greater efficiency, and bigger than before.

Lou Tannen, who founded the company, built it, and transformed it into a friendly corporate giant, had become a touring professional magician while in his teens, had worked for a New York magic manufacturer, and had also started selling magic when he was still so young he couldn't legally sign a lease for his first shop in 1929. A genial, red-haired, polished young performer of magic, Tannen made a host of friends among magicians as he ventured into every phase of the magic business. He was joined in some of his earlier ventures by his brother Irv.

He had magic shops at various times in Brooklyn, Atlantic City, and on Broadway, as well as storefront street-level joke, fun and trick shops, and several small manufacturing companies. At one of the shops, he employed a one-armed demonstrator-magician who, despite his handicap, was an expert with a pack of cards. When someone at the counter asked if a demonstrated trick was easy to learn, the man would hold up his one hand and say, "If I can do it, you should be able to." That usually clinched the sale.

In May 1944, Lou Tannen opened his first big magic shop upstairs in the Wurlitzer Building on 42nd Street near Times Square. This was a somewhat risky enterprise since there would be no off-the-street walk-in customers and the shop would have to attract a following of magicians willing to search it out. But the area had other successful magic shops, and Tannen's gradually became the most successful of all. It had grown into a prospering big business by the time the 42nd Street building was torn down and Tannen moved the company into its present Broadway location.

One of the young magicians who had found his way into the 42nd Street shop about a month after its 1944 beginning was the then fourteen-year-old Tony Spina. Admiring Spina's skill, genuine devotion to magic, and ambition to make a career of it, Tannen guided the young man. Spina performed at hospitals and for the American Theater Wing; within two years, at the age of sixteen, he became a professional magician, breaking into vaudeville just as vaudeville was dying out.

Although the bookings were sometimes lean, Spina married his assistant and pursued his professional magic career until 1957, when his growing success in the automobile business forced him to put his performing on a semi-professional basis. He had never planned to go into automobile sales; it was only to supplement his income from magic, as a "temporary thing," that he took a job driving a parts delivery truck for General Motors. Thirteen years later he was

general manager of the largest Chevrolet dealership in the New York City area.

During all those years he had gone on developing his magic, studying stage dramatics, working to build a top professional act, and creating many effects that his close friend Lou Tannen put on the market. He continued to perform whenever he could, at trade shows, resort hotels, major magic conventions in the United Sates and Europe. Magic was still what Spina most wanted to do, more than selling automobiles.

One day Lou Tannen mentioned to Spina that he was thinking of retiring to Florida, so he would finally have the free time once again to enjoy performing magic. That led to further discussions, and in 1969 Spina joined the firm with Tannen and his brother Irv. Lou Tannen finally retired five years later and Irv Tannen and Spina bought the entire business.

Back in the 1940s, when the Tannen shop had been on 42nd Street, another of its frequent visitors was young New Jersey magician Jack Ferero, a busy club-date performer even while attending high school. After his Army service and graduation from Seton Hall University, Ferero continued his performing, but also became an accountant. During the twenty years he worked for industrial firms in that capacity, he spent all his free time presenting many magic shows, but never as many as he wished he could do.

For thirteen of those years Ferero was with ITT. As its special accountant, he also performed trade and industrial shows for the company. But magically these were sometimes frustrating years, because as Spina had found with automobiles, Ferero also found that no other success is entirely satisfying when magic is what a man most loves.

Ferero and Spina talked about that one night, when Spina was still selling automobiles and Ferero was still an accountant. They had been to a New York magic lecture together and afterwards stood on a street corner, wishfully thinking aloud. As they now recall, one of them joked that what they ought to do was buy a magic shop so they could spend all their time with magic, and the other said, never dreaming it would happen, "Sure, let's buy Tannen's."

That was nearly ten years before Ferero decided that he had finally had enough of industrial accounting and really did want to get into the magic business. He was convinced that this field would allow him to combine his knowledge of magic with his years of practical big business experience. It was the same combination that had worked well for his friend Tony Spina, by then a partner at Tannen's. So Ferero talked to Spina and Irv Tannen, and in 1976, Tannen's had a third partner, Jack Ferero. Meanwhile Irv Tannen had been considering his own future plans, and in 1978 retired.

Tony Spina and Jack Ferero now became the owners and directors. They have divided the work be-

Jack Ferero (left) and Tony Spina (right), who own and operate Louis Tannen, Inc. Years ago, when they never dreamed it would happen, they joked that someday they should buy Tannen's so that they could spend all their time doing magic. And they did.

tween then, with Ferero handling the inventory control, dealer contacts, and wholesaling, and Spina in charge of retailing, development of new tricks and products, advertising, and publicity. It *is* work and it is big business, but both are doing what they like, and what they like is magic.

Address: Louis Tannen, Inc., 1540 Broadway, New York, NY 10036.

11

A SHORT DICTIONARY OF MAGIC

A

Alphabet Cards—cards with letters of the alphabet on their faces and with backs that match standard playing cards; used for various tricks in which words are spelled out by the choice of cards, etc.

Anti-Gravity Effects—effects in which objects magically remain suspended or balanced against the pull of gravity, as when a wand or a spread-out pack of cards clings to the tips of the overturned fingers.

B

Back and Front—such terms sometimes become confusing when used to describe the performance of tricks. From the performer's viewpoint, *back* is the side toward him or behind him. *Front* is the side toward the audience, and a *front view* is what the audience has when seated facing the performer. Thus if a magician holds the back of his hand toward the audience, the back of the hand is toward the front, and while it is in that position if he drapes the top end of a rope over the back of his hand, that end hangs over to the front. The related terms "right" and "left" usually mean the *performer's* right and left. Thus if he turns his body left, his right side is toward the audience.

Back Palming—hiding cards, coins, or other small objects clipped between the fingers at the back of the hand so the palm of it appears empty. The hidden objects may be manipulated from one side of the hand to the other while turning the hand to show first one side and then the other, as in the stage production of cards or coins from the air. (See also palming.)

Ball Glass—see glasses.

Bank Night—a mental magic effect (sometimes also called "Just Chance") for which they are many methods and routines. The performer explains that there is something valuable, such as a twenty-dollar bill, sealed in just one of three or four identical envelopes he is holding. He then gives spectators a choice of any of the envelopes, allowing them to change their minds or trade envelopes as they desire. But they find nothing of value in any of the envelopes they choose, and at the end the performer has the one remaining envelope—which contains the money.

Bar Magic—(1) magic performed by a bartender-magician for patrons seated at his bar; (2) apparently impromptu tricks shown to companions by a magician who happens to be visiting a bar.

Billiard Balls—small wooden or plastic balls used in manipulative magic, originally made in imitation of billiard balls, but usually smaller and lighter for performing purposes.

Bill Tube—a small metal tube with a tightly screwed or padlocked cap in which a borrowed dollar bill, signed playing card, mental prediction, or something else (such as a small handkerchief) may be made to appear when the previously empty and locked tube is opened by a spectator.

Black Art—the use of black against black for concealment in stage tricks and illusions, as when assistants dressed totally in black or an object covered with black cloth cannot be seen against a black backdrop. A *black-art act* is one using the principle, usually combined with luminous and lighting effects.

Blank Cards—playing cards with standard backs but nothing printed on their faces.

Blendo—a long-popular silk handkerchief effect in which handkerchiefs of various colors are tied together and visibly changed into a large multicolored silk scarf.

Blindfold Effects—effects in which a magician or mentalist performs various feats while his eyes are securely blindfolded or taped shut, or his vision apparently sealed off in some other manner. His head may be covered with a hood or a metal or wooden shield; his eys can also be sealed with bread dough, surgical pads, thick windings of cloth, or bandages.

Body Clips, Droppers, Holders—small devices with safety-pin attachments that may be fastened under the jacket to conceal coins, cards, balls, handkerchiefs, and other objects, so that the performer can secretly get them into his fingers when his hand rests at his side.

Book Tests—mental magic effects in which the performer is able to reveal words or sentences printed on a page of some book chosen by a spectator and unseen by the performer. Similar tests involve revealing what is on apparently unseen pages of magazines or what is printed in a newspaper headline, news item, or classified ad. There are also book tests with telephone directories, in which the mentalist reveals a spectator-chosen phone number; and tests with large dictionaries, in which one selected word out of thousands is revealed.

Box Jumper—a female assistant in an illusion show: one of the pretty girls who jump in and out of cabinets, trunks, boxes, and other equipment as she vanishes, reappears, floats in the air, or is sawn in two.

Brain Wave—a card trick with many variations in which the card merely thought of by any member of the audience is found to be the one card face up in the pack and the only card with a back that has a different color from all the rest.

Break-Away—a comedy prop that seems to break apart when a spectator handles it. There are break-away wands, fans, spoons, candles, and boxes.

C

Calculator Magic—a fast-developing magic specialty in which mathematical and mental effects and other types of tricks are performed with pocket calculators.

Candle Magic—tricks with lighted candles have been a popular form of magic since at least the nineteenth century, but modern stage magic and the creation of new mechanical candles have given such tricks renewed popularity. Candles are not only produced, vanished, and multiplied from one to eight at the performer's fingertips, but they also visibly change color, or are transformed into other objects, or from solid to liquid. They penetrate sheets of glass and other solids, handkerchiefs are pulled through their flames undamaged; and the flames alone can be taken from the candles to be manipulated in the hands.

Canes—more popular with modern stage magicians than once traditional magic wands, canes are floated in air, danced through space, visibly vanished, produced, and transformed to silk handkerchiefs and other objects. Although mechanical in operation, their handling requires skill for effective presentation.

Card Magic—in recent years card trickery has advanced far beyond most other types of magic to become for many enthusiasts a highly sophisticated specialty that embraces a wide range of subtle methods and expert sleight of hand. Its ardent followers—who often delight in devising effects to baffle fellow magicians as well as the public, and in solving card magic problems put to each other—have a terminology, jargon, and literature of their own. Each year, dozens of new card tricks and even more variations of older ones fill the pages of magic magazines, books, and pamphlets. But there are also innumerable entertaining and baffling card tricks that are comparatively easy to do, and many of the subtleties originated by the "cardicians" gradually become part of general magical knowledge.

Change Bag—a small cloth bag, either flat or circular and attached to a handle used to switch, force, change, vanish, or produce various objects placed inside it.

Choppers—the apparatus that slices a solid metal blade through some part of a person's body. There are "head choppers," "wrist choppers," "leg choppers," and "finger choppers," among others.

Cigarette Magic—once enormously popular and a specialty that brought fame to some skilled magicians, the production and manipulation of lighted cigarettes and the many tricks and routines performed with them have somewhat faded in popularity in recent years because of smoking bans and antismoking campaigns.

Close-Up Case—an attache case or other small case used by the close-up performer for carrying his props. Usually divided into compartments, each of which contains the props needed for a particular routine, the case also serves as a means of secretly getting objects into his hands, or disposing of them while reaching into the case to pick up something else. If he performs seated at a table, he may have the case on a chair beside him or on the floor at his feet. Those who stand or walk from group to group while performing sometimes use shoulder-sling bags or wear aprons with large pockets at the front. Some elaborate close-up cases include equipment for playing taped music or other sound effects.

Close-Up Magic—tricks that are performed close to a small group of viewers, rather than those shown on a stage or at some distance from a larger audience. It is magic done "right under the eyes" of the spectators, often but not always with the magician seated at a table and with one or two close spectators participating in the tricks. But there are also close-up magicians who perform while standing, or while seated on a floor or bench, surrounded by spectators.

Close-Up Pad—a thick cloth, felt, or rubber-cushioned mat, about the size of a table place mat, used by some close-up magicians to give them a proper surface for performing their tricks.

Club Date—a term covering the whole field of magic shows that might be given by a local magician: for clubs; civic, fraternal or business organizations; church societies; youth groups; private parties; public dinners; or for various other associations in his area. It was first used by theatrical agents to mean a booking for a single performance at such a place rather than a contract to play a nightclub or theater. The majority of magicians who perform for a fee are *club show* performers, appearing before all types of audiences in all sorts of places. Some work through agents, but most book and sell their own shows.

Coins Through Table—a coin magic classic for which there are many routines. Basically four or more coins are magically passed through the top of a table, one at a time.

Color Changing—tricks in which the color of handkerchiefs, balls, cards, or other objects is magically changed.

Commercial Effect—a trick or routine that goes over well with the public—one that "pays off" with an audience, even though it might not puzzle or interest fellow magicians.

Commercial Magic—the hiring of a magician by some business or industry to promote its products and sales at industrial or trade shows, sales meetings, parties, dinners, and other gatherings, or in public performances sponsored by the company, in television commercials, and for other purposes of advertising and promotion. A lucrative field for some magicians but one that also demands specialized talents and often long hours and hard work under difficult performing conditions.

Copper-Silver—a coin trick with many different routines, in which a silver coin tightly held in a spectator's hand magically changes places with a copper coin held in the performer's hand.

Cups and Balls—probably the most ancient of all magic tricks, a close-up classic in which small balls vanish, reappear, multiply, and change places under a row of inverted cups. For a climax, the cups may be tipped over to reveal such things as a lemon, an onion and a potato, large balls, wine or other liquid, or live baby chicks. Metal, plastic, china, and plain cardboard cups have been used. There are also *one-cup* routines, with a single cup and one visible ball, which usually also have some surprise ending. The history of the trick has been traced

back several thousand years and explanations of it were printed in the earliest of magic books, with endless variations ever since.

D

Dancing Cane—a trick in which a walking stick is made to float in air and to dance back and forth and around the performer, usually while he dances with it.

Dealers—those who deal in the sale of equipment, devices, books, and instructions for magicians. Some *retail* dealers have magic shops or showrooms open to the public. Others operate mainly mail-order businesses, and many combine both. There are *wholesale* dealers, who supply standard or exclusive tricks and equipment to retailers, and *specialized dealers,* who sell mostly the tricks or props in one particular category, such as cards, coins, silks, etc. Although most dealers of all kinds also sell magic books, pamphlets, and magazines, there are magic *booksellers* who specialize in new or used magic books, many of which are not generally available in public bookstores.

Devil's Handkerchief—a pocket handkerchief made to be used as a changing bag for the vanish, production, switching or forcing of various objects.

Diminishing Cards—a trick in which a full-sized pack of cards gradually grows smaller each time they are fanned out, until the magician finally reduces them in size to cards no bigger than this thumb nail.

Dinner-Table Magic—tricks performed for friends or fellow guests at a dinner table, usually after the meal when everyone is relaxed and in the mood for a little informal entertainment. Such tricks often make use of articles to be found on the table: cups, saucers, water glasses, forks, spoons, matches, salt, sugar, dinner napkins, etc.

Display Stand—a small easel-like stand the magician may have on his table to display a row of coins, cards or other objects to the audience.

Ditch—to get rid of something secretly, as to *ditch* a coin hidden in the hand by dropping it into a pocket while reaching into the pocket to remove a pencil.

Do As I Do—routines in which the magician attempts to "teach" a spectator how to do a trick by giving him an identical set of props so the spectator can imitate the doing of it, move by move, but with comic or surprising results.

Doll's House—an illusion with a small doll house, raised from the floor on four legs mounted on casters so it may be swung completely around to show it from all sides. The illusionist opens the front and the house is seen to be filled with miniature furniture, which he removes. He then shows a small costumed doll and places that into the doll house, closing up the little house again. Suddenly the roof bursts open and the front swings wide as a beautiful young woman appears, as though the doll house were much too small to hold her within it. The doll has vanished and the woman is costumed as the doll was.

Double-Backed—a playing card with a back design on both front and back, so that whichever way it is turned it always appears to be back upward. There are also *double-faced* cards, printed with a face both front and back; sometimes the same face on both sides but more often with two different faces, such as an ace of spades on the front and a three of diamonds on the back.

Double Lift—lifting two cards together from the top of the pack to show them as a single card.

Dove Pan—a deep metal pan with a covering lid that has long been used by magicians, not only for the production of a live dove but also to produce a rabbit, silk streamers, a birthday cake, or almost anything else that will fit inside it.

E

Effect—how a trick looks to the audience; not what really happens but what *seems* to happen.

Egg Bag—a classic trick with an egg and small cloth bag that has gained fame for some of its celebrated performers. Simple in method and direct in effect, its success depends on its entertaining presentation, and there are many routines and variations. Basically, the bag is turned inside out to show it empty and an egg is then produced from it. Dropped back into the bag, the egg vanishes. A spectator may put his hand inside and feel around to convince himself the bag is empty, or the bag may be twisted into a knot, laid flat and stamped on. Even after such convincing "proof" that the egg has vanished, it is discovered once more inside the bag.

Egg Magic—various types of magic using eggs. Magicians frequently change handkerchiefs into eggs or eggs into handkerchiefs, and sometimes pretend to explain how they do it in a way that leaves the audience more than ever puzzled. Another popular trick is one in which a scrap of white paper, bounced up and down on a fan, visibly turns into an egg, which is then cracked open to prove it is real. The yolk and white may be poured into a folded newspaper from which they vanish. Eggs also are multiplied from one to four at the fingertips and lend themselves to many of the manipulations done with billiard balls. Wooden, plastic, and very thin or thicker rubber eggs are available for various magical purposes.

Envelope Card—a double card made like an envelope or half-envelope, usually open at the top or along one side, so another card or cards can be slid down inside and all can be shown as a single card.

Escapes—tricks in which the performer frees himself from various physical restraints such as handcuffs, chains, ropes, straitjackets, sealed boxes, safes, jail cells, etc.

ESP Cards—used in serious scientific experiments for the testing of extrasensory perception, they are also widely used by magicians for mental effects and other tricks. Each card has a standard playing card back and one of the five ESP symbols printed on its face: a circle, cross, three vertical wavy lines, a square, or a star. There are five cards of each symbol in the usual pack of twenty-five cards.

F

False Count—occurs when a number of cards, coins, dollar bills, or other things seem to be fairly and openly counted from hand to hand, hiding the fact that there really are fewer or more than the number apparently counted.

Fanning Powder—a talcum-like powder sometimes used on playing cards to smooth their surfaces and make them easier to fan during card manipulations.

Feather Flowers—brightly colored imitation flowers made of dyed feathers in bouquets that compress into a small space and then spring out to full size when produced.

Finger-Flinger—one whose interest is more in the ability to perform expert sleight of hand, or in intricate and difficult methods, than in entertaining the public with magic. Often said of those who endlessly show card, coin, and other close-up moves to each other: they are constantly "flinging their fingers."

Finger Palm—hiding a small object within the loosely curled lower fingers, so that the first finger and thumb are free to be used naturally to pick up, hold or display other things while the back of the hand is toward those watching. (See also palming.)

Flash Wand—a wand that shoots a flash of flame from one end, often with an explosive sound; used by stage magicians to dramatize a magical effect or to distract the attention of the audience from some secret move or device.

Floating in Air—since the earliest times magicians have made persons and things seem to float in the air: themselves, their assistants, spectators from the audience, rabbits and other animals, balls, balloons, crumpled sheets of paper, wands, canes and golf clubs, glasses and bowls of liquid, tables and chairs, lighted candles and electric bulbs, musical instruments, microphones, dancing dolls and skeletons, hats, shoes and coats, and of course playing cards and handkerchiefs. There are two basic kinds of floating effects: when a person or object remains in space without any visible support it is called a *suspension;* when the person or object rises up through the air it is a *levitation.*

Foo Can—a metal can used for the production or vanish of liquid in many magical effects and comedy routines. Merely by the way it is handled in tipping it over, it can be shown empty or full of liquid as the performer desires.

Force—to make a person choose a particular card, color, number, or object the magician wants him to choose, even though he is given an apparently free choice. Hundreds of methods of forcing have been devised.

Forcing Packs—the *standard* or *one-way* forcing pack, used to make a spectator choose the card a magician wants him to choose, consists of fifty-two cards that are all alike, so that it makes no difference which one is chosen. If two or three different cards are to be forced, a *two-way* or *three-way* pack may be used, the entire pack made up of groups of two cards or three cards all alike. There are a number of other forcing packs tricked in various ways so the pack can be riffled through or fanned out to show the faces apparently all different before a card is forced.

G

Gimmick—a hidden device used for accomplishing a trick.

Glasses—tricked drinking glasses, now often plastic rather than glass to avoid breakage, serve various magical uses. A *ball glass* has a round hole in one side so that a ball or other small object dropped into it may be secretly tipped out into the hand when the glass is covered. A *bottomless glass* may simply be one without a bottom, or it may have a temporary removable bottom in the form of a disc. A *slit glass* has a small slot out near the bottom of one side so a coin may pass through. A *mirror glass* has a mirrored partition across the middle, which creates the illusion that the glass is empty of whatever may be hidden behind the mirror. There are many more types of tricked glasses, some general utility props, others designed for specific tricks.

Glide—secretly drawing back the bottom card of a face-down pack so as to remove the second card from the bottom instead of the bottom one.

H

Hand Washing—sometimes said of a magician who goes through prolonged and unnecessary moves in showing his hands this way or that while performing manipulations. He "washes his hands in the air."

Hank Ball—a hollow metal or plastic flesh-colored ball with a large hole in one side, used for the production or vanish of a silk handkerchief. Attached to the ball is a loop of catgut or monofilament, which is hung over the thumb so that the ball, with a handkerchief inside, may be manipulated to show both front and back of the hand empty.

Hat Tricks—the many tricks once done with borrowed hats are not as easy to perform as they once were, simply because there are few if any hats available to borrow from members of the audience. Few men now wear hats or carry them with them to their seats when they come to watch a magic show. If a magician wants to bake a cake in a hat or produce a rabbit from one, he usually has to use a hat of his own. Colorful paper or plastic party hats are sometimes used, and some of the old hat tricks are still performed with paper bags, cereal or detergent boxes, women's pocketbooks, and other containers instead of hats.

Holdout—see pull.

I

Illusion—all magic tricks are illusions, but to a magician, "illusion" means a big stage trick, as when a person appears or disappears from a cabinet, floats in the air, or is sawn in two. Illusions generally involve the use of assistants, large apparatus, and effects in which the magic happens to people or to big animals such as horses, tigers, or elephants. But illusions are not always confined to stages or platforms where elaborate theatrical and mechanical devices are available. Many modern illusions have been adapted for use in nightclubs, trade shows, outdoor fairs, television studios, and places where audiences almost surround the performer.

Injog—see jog.

Invisible Thread—a term that includes several types available from magic dealers. Some are very fine and strong black or colorless thread, others plastic monofilaments. Used for a variety of tricks, they are almost invisible against a proper background.

J

Jog—while shuffling a pack of cards, to put one card down so it sticks out a little beyond the rest and serves as a place-marker. When a card is *jogged* so it sticks out from the front end of the pack, that is an *outjog;* at the rear end, it is an *injog.*

Jumbo Cards—sometimes also called giant cards, these are playing cards about seven inches high and about twice the width of ordinary bridge-size cards.

K

Kid Show—a magic show for an audience of young children.

L

Lapping—a close-up magic technique in which objects are secretly dropped into the lap or taken from the lap by a performer seated at a table.

Layman—what a magician calls a person who is not a magician.

Lecture Show—a public performance of magic combined with a lecture on some subject, with the magic used to make the lecture more entertaining, or to illustrate it or to dramatize or emphasize the points the speaker wants to put across.

Linking Rings—the visible linking together and unlinking of large and apparently separate and solid metal rings, a centuries-old classic. The gleaming flash and clanking sound of the silvery rings theatrically heightens the effect, which is one that can be presented almost anywhere, under any performing conditions. Toy sets of linking rings have been included for years in magic sets for children, but to perform the trick entertainingly requires good routing and considerable practice and skill.

Liquid Magic—tricks in which various liquids are used, such as the production or vanish of liquid-filled glasses or bowls, the penetration of liquids through solid objects, the repeated pouring out of liquid from an apparently empty vessel, etc.

Liquid Suspensions—tricks in which water, milk, or some other liquid remains suspended inside a bottle, cup, or tube, and does not spill out when it is tipped upside down.

Lota Bowl or Vase—a metal, plastic, or ceramic bowl or vase from which liquid is repeatedly poured even though it apparently is drained empty after each pouring. It is often used as a continuing effect throughout a magician's act, with the performer pouring water from the bowl after each trick to the increasing amusement of the audience as water keeps flowing from the "empty" bowl.

M

Magic Emcee—a magician who acts as master of ceremonies (M.C. or *emcee)* for a variety show or other program, by performing a trick or magical comedy bit before introducing each act or speaker. As part of the program, he usually also performs a brief act of his own.

Magic Lecture—talk given by a magician to other magicians, usually including a demonstration of tricks and an explanation of how to do them.

Magicians' Wax—a pliable, putty-like adhesive which dries hard but remains tacky so that a tiny pellet of it may be used to attach thread to something, or to stick two objects together and yet allow them to be instantly separated by a slight pull.

Magnetic Devices—cards, coins, balls, dice, cups, boxes, wallets, rings, ropes, and all sorts of other seemingly ordinary objects, in which magnets or thin straps of steel responsive to magnets, are used for many magical purposes.

Manipulative Magic—magic done to display the skill of the hands in manipulating cards, coins, or other small objects.

Mirrors—despite popular belief to the contrary, today's magicians seldom use mirrors to accomplish their tricks, although they are still used in some forms of stage magic.

Misdirection—the planned strategy of distracting the thoughts and attention of spectators in order to hide the secret of a trick by leading their minds away from the truth of what is happening and influencing them to accept what the magician wants them to believe. Misdirection embraces the whole psychology of deception, and mechanics, moves, facial and vocal expression, patter, and convincing presentation.

Miser's Dream—the classic trick in which the magician seemingly "catches" a large number of coins, one after another, by reaching into the air for them and dropping them into a pail or other container.

Monte Effects—magical versions of the old gambling game in which the viewer tries in vain to guess which of three face-down cards is the queen, or which of three walnut shells a dried pea is hidden under, or which of three matchboxes contains a coin, etc.

N

Nest of Boxes—a set of boxes, one of which fits inside another, which are opened up one at a time until a borrowed coin, ring, watch, or other object is discovered inside the smallest of the boxes. In stage versions, a rabbit or other animal may be produced from the smallest of the nested boxes, with the borrowed ring tied to a ribbon around its neck.

Noah's Ark—an illusion with a horizontal cabinet built to resemble a small ark. The front and back doors are dropped open so the audience can see through the empty cabinet, then the doors are closed, and the illusionist produces ducks, geese, chickens, and other birds and animals by reaching into the "ark" through window-like openings cut in the front door. He finally drops open the door and a girl appears inside the ark.

Number Cards—cards with standard playing-card backs but with only large numerals printed on their faces. There are two kinds, packs with nubers from 1 to 52 and packs numbered 0 to 9, the latter containing duplicate numbers to make a full pack and to allow for combination of the single digits into any larger number.

O

Okito Coin Box—a small round metal box and lid used in close-up coin magic. There are many routines for its use and a variety of different boxes. Combined with skilled sleight of hand, the Okito box permits a wide range of effects in which coins put into it vanish, change, multiply, or penetrate.

Out—the way a magician gets himself out of trouble if something goes wrong with a trick. An experienced performer usually is aware of the possible outs, so he can cover a mistake, switch things around or quickly devise some substitute means of bringing the trick to an acceptable conclusion.

Outjog—see jog.

P

Paddle Move—a way of manipulating a small flat-surfaced wooden or plastic paddle for a variety of close-up effects. With the handle of the little paddle held between the thumb and fingers of one hand, the magician can make wooden pegs put through holes in the paddle jump about from hole to hole, make spots change color, or seem to change pictures, numbers, chalk marks, etc.

Palming—hiding something in the palm side of the hand to conceal it from those looking at the back of the hand. (See *back palm, finger palm, thumb palm.*)

Paper Coils—long and tightly wound coils of narrow colored paper, designed so the magician can produce them as streamers. There are big *hat coils,* originally made to fit just inside the bottom of a top hat; *hand coils,* made to fit within the hand; smaller *mouth coils* for the production of paper streamers from the mouth; and several other kinds, including the *throw-out coils* commonly used as party streamers.

Paper Magic—newspapers, tissue, paper napkins, and almost everything else made of paper has been put to use by magicians in the creation of a vast number of tricks that cover the whole range of possible magical effects. The props are inexpensive, and although some of the tricks require considerable advance preparation as well as practiced skill in handling and presentation, they have the appeal of seeming to be done with something ordinary and familiar.

Pass—(1) secretly shifting the two halves of a pack of cards to bring a card from the center to the top; (2) pretending to put something from one hand into the other, or to put it under a cup or somewhere else, while really keeping it hidden in the hand.

Passe-Passe—tricks in which two objects—such as a bottle and a glass that have been covered with tubes—are made to change places.

Patter—the words spoken in presenting a trick.

Penetration—tricks in which one apparently solid object seems to pass through another solid object.

Pet Effect—some trick or routine that is a favorite of a particular magician, one that he is known for performing well, perhaps an old or standard trick that he has greatly improved.

Pocket Tricks—the kind done with props that may be carried around easily in the pockets for informal showing almost anywhere to one or two people or a small group. Although they often seem impromptu, good pocket tricks usually are as carefully routined, rehearsed, and presented as any other tricks.

Prediction—a mental magic effect in which the performer seemingly predicts something that is about to happen, such as, for example, choices or decisions that spectators are on the verge of making.

Production Items—objects specially made to conceal in a small space and look big when produced. Some, such as hollow alarm clocks or imitation bottles, are made to nest together, to be produced singly. Others are of compressible latex or sponge rubber, molded to the shape of fruits, vegetables, frankfurters, pies, cakes, ice cream cones, skulls, etc. There are also similar items, made of cloth with shaped metal springs inside, known as *spring goods*. In addition, there are telescoping barber poles and flagstaffs, birdcages that squeeze together, large dice that fold flat, and a variety of objects made of colored paper—flowers, garlands, pop-up balls, etc.

Pull—a cord or elastic arranged to pull objects secretly from the hands up the sleeve or in under the jacket to vanish them. There are different pulls for various purposes, with attachments at one end designed to take a handkerchief, coin, pencil, dollar bill, or other article. Some are worked by the pull of the elastic or the movement of the arms; others are spring activated. A *holdout* is a related up-the-sleeve device to deliver hidden objects into the hand; sometimes it is combined with a pull to take things from the hand.

R

Reel—a small flesh-colored device, similar to a reel-type tape measure, with a spring-activated spool inside, upon which is wound a length of thread or monofilament, so that the drawn-out thread is automatically pulled back again inside the reel. Used for tricks with handkerchiefs, cards, ropes, and other objects.

Repeat Effects—routines in which the presentation and patter are built around the repeated showing of the same trick, usually with some surprise twist at the end after it has been shown several times.

Restoration—a basic magical theme on which hundreds of effects have been built. Rope, ribbon, string, electric cords, balloons, bicycle tires, lengths of cloth, handkerchiefs, and other things are cut and restored; strips of paper, newspapers, magazine covers, paper money, and playing cards are torn or burned and restored; wands, eggs, dinner plates, borrowed rings and watches are broken and restored. Many stage illusions, such as that of sawing a woman in two, are basically restoration effects.

Rice Bowls—an oriental magic effect, presented for years by magicians around the world, in which two china or metal bowls are used. One is filled with rice, the other put mouth-to-mouth on top of it. When the bowls are parted the rice has doubled in quantity and spills out from the bowls. The emptied bowls are then put together again and instead of dry rice, they are found filled with water.

Rising Cards—making a chosen card or cards seem to rise up out of the pack, a classic trick with hundreds of methods and variations.

Rope Tricks—penetration, linking, vanish, production, transposition, color change, and almost every other possible basic magic effect has been performed with rope. There are scores of magical knot-tying tricks, and hundreds of routines have been devised for the cut and restored rope effect, which nearly every magician has performed at one time or another. What magicians generally use for rope tricks is not really rope, but a type of white cotton cord, similar to clothesline but softer and more pliable. Magic dealers supply it in two standard thicknesses, the larger kind intended for greater visibility in stage presentations.

Rough and Smooth—cards are brushed or sprayed with a *roughing fluid* on their faces or backs so that they cling together in pairs but can be smoothly separated to show them individually when desired.

Routine—the step-by-step presentation of a trick, or of a series of tricks blended together as a unit.

S

Safety-Pin Tricks—the close-up tricks in which safety pins are made to link, unlink, penetrate one another, shrink, multiply, or change while being manipulated by the performer.

Self-Contained—referring to a trick in which everything needed for the effect is within the apparatus used, so that nothing needs to be secretly added or attached.

Self-Working—a trick that works automatically, either mechanically or by some arrangement of the objects being used.

Shell—a hollow imitation of a solid object such as a billiard ball, bottle, cube, coin, or wand, sometimes exactly fitting over the object itself so the two may be shown together as one.

Shiner—a small mirror or button of polished metal hidden in the palm or clipped to the inside of the fingers so that a magician or mentalist can see the reflection of suits, numbers, or designs on cards that are passed across the hand.

Short Card—one card trimmed slightly shorter than the rest to serve as a locator in the pack, so the pack can be cut to lift away all the cards above the short one and thus locate a chosen card or group of prearranged cards at that place in the pack. A *short-corner* card is one with only a single corner slightly trimmed; a *narrow card* is slightly narrower at the sides than the rest. There are also *long cards* and *wide cards,* but they are less commonly used.

Silent Act—a magic act or routine without patter.

Silk Dyeing—magically changing the color of silk handkerchiefs as they are passed through the hand or through a tube.

Silks—what magicians call the

brightly colored handkerchiefs and scarves they use, even though in recent years they are not always made of pure silk as they once were.

Sixth Finger—a hollow flesh-colored and finger-shaped tube that fits between the other fingers so the hand casually may be shown empty; used for the production of a silk handkerchief, a small roll of dollar bills, or other objects that may be hidden inside the extra finger.

Sleeving—manipulating coins or other small articles so as to drop or propel them secretly from the hand into the sleeve to hide them. Sleeving is used mainly in close-up tricks, although some tricks with larger objects also make use of the sleeves. But magicians generally do not hide things "up the sleeve" as often as the public seems to suspect.

Sleight—a particular method of accomplishing some specific deceit with sleight of hand, such as one of the sleights that might be used to secretly switch one coin for another.

Sleight of Hand—tricks done mainly by the skills of the hands rather than by other means. The magician who learns basic sleight of hand is always equipped to perform a little magic almost anywhere with a few coins from his pocket, a borrowed pack of cards, or whatever else may be available; and is less dependent on manufactured or specially prepared props. Learning sleight of hand also teaches him misdirection and gives him a grounding in the other principles on which good magic is built.

Sliding Die Box—an old but still popular comedy trick in which the magician attempts to vanish a large die from a box that has two side-by-side compartments, each with a front and top door. The audience thinks it hears the die slide back and forth from one side to the other as the performer tips the box and opens one set of doors at a time—which leads to shouts of protest that the die is hidden in the opposite side from the one shown empty. After leading the audience on, the magician finally opens all the doors at once, to show that the die really has disappeared.

Slit Glass—see glasses.

Small Magic—the kind done with small props, such as cards, coins, thimbles, rope, and the like—in contrast to stage illusions. Refers only to the size of the objects used, since much small magic is "big" in its effect.

Sponge Balls—balls of soft sponge rubber that are made to appear, vanish, or multiply while in the hands of the performer—or of any member of the audience who may be asked to hold them.

Spook Show—a stage magic show built around pseudospiritualistic effects, planned to startle the audience with the fun of strange and supposedly supernatural happenings. The theater often is darkened while ghostly forms and "terrifying" monsters appear and spirits apparently frisk about in the audience. Presented less frequently in recent years than they once were, touring spook shows usually combine a stage performance with the screening of a "horror" movie.

Spring Fowers—brightly colored

paper or plastic flowers, made to compress into a flat bundle for concealment, with spring-activated steel bands inside that suddenly open the flowers wide when they are produced.

Spring Goods—see production items.

Square Circle—among the most popular of all production props, the square circle consists of a square tube with see-through slots in the front, and a round tube. After each is shown empty, the round tube is nested inside the square tube and a large production is made.

Stacking—(1) arranging cards, coins, or other objects one atop another in a certain order; (2) sweeping an inverted dice cup back and forth on a table so as to pick up dice separately and stack them up inside the cup one on top of another.

Stand-Up Magic—the kind performed while standing before an audience, rather than by a close-up magician seated at a table.

Stooge—a plant or confederate posing as a member of the audience. The stooge may be invited to the stage, as though he were a spectator, to assist in some trick or comedy routine. There are also times when a magician may arrange before a show to have some member of the audience prepared to lend a handkerchief, dollar bill, or something else when there is a need to borrow it without delay during the performance; or he may arrange with such a volunteer stooge to call out a particular number, the name of a card, etc.

Streamer—a long multicolored silk banner, often produced from a box, tube, or other apparatus previously shown empty.

Strippers—a tricked pack of cards slightly tapered at the side edges so that a card or several cards put into the pack the other way around can easily be located and "stripped out" by pulling them from the pack with their side edges gripped between the thumb and fingers.

Substitution Trunk—an illusion in which the magician and an assistant almost instantly change places after the former has been shackled, tied in a cloth bag, and locked up inside an examined trunk, where the assistant is found seconds later, shackled and tied in the bag as the magician had been. Houdini, who didn't invent it but who greatly improved its presentation, called it "metamorphosis" and performed it almost from the start of his career throughout much of his life.

Sucker Trick—one that deliberately leads people to believe they have guessed the secret, until a final twist proves them wrong and leaves them fooled at the end.

Switch—the secret exchange of one thing for another, either by sleight of hand or by the use of apparatus or some mechanical device.

T

Table—Hopping—performing of close-up magic by going from table to table to entertain guests seated at the various tables in a restaurant, nightclub, or at some public luncheon or dinner.

Thimble Tricks—manipulative stage or close-up magic originally done with ordinary sewing thimbles, but often performed by magicians with brightly colored, jeweled, or large thimbles for greater visibility.

Thread Puller—a stage magician's backstage helper; the term dates from the era when tricks frequently were accomplished by the pulling of threads or strings from behind the scenes.

Three-Way Pack—see forcing packs.

Thumb Palm—manipulating a coin, thimble, folded paper, or other small object to hold it in the crotch of the thumb, gripped between the bottom edge of the thumb and top edge of the palm, when the back of the hand is toward the audience. (See also palming.)

Thumb Tie—an "escape" trick in which the performer's thumbs are tightly tied, strapped, taped, or shackled together so that it seems impossible for him to separate his two hands—although he does so instantly, passing his hands and arms through various solid objects, and yet showing that his thumbs remain bound.

Thumb Tip—a flesh-colored metal, plastic, or rubber cap shaped to fit over the tip of the thumb so various small objects can be hidden within it while the hand appears to be empty.

Time Killer—some trick or routine that takes considerable time to perform, or some form of specialty entertainment related to magic, which the magician may use to stretch out his show when he is required to give a longer performance than usual. Despite the term "time killer," the experienced magician usually chooses such routines for their proven entertainment values as well as their time-consuming function.

Transformation—the changing of an object's shape or appearance, as when a cube is changed into a ball, a handkerchief into an egg, or when an illusionist changes a skeleton into a living person or a lady into a tiger.

Transposition—the disappearance of a person or object from one place and reappearance somewhere else, as when an assistant is "fired" from a cannon and appears again in a previously empty trunk, or when a handkerchief disappears from a tube and then appears in a glass.

Trap—a (usually) spring-hinged door or panel in a stage floor, platform, cabinet, trunk, box, table top, or elsewhere, allowing people or objects to be passed through it secretly, after which it springs back into place to close the opening.

Trick—one magical happening.

Twentieth-Century Silks—a classic silk handkerchief trick in which a vanished handkerchief reappears between two others that previously have been tied together.

Two-Way Pack—see forcing packs.

V

Vanishing Birdcage—a reputation-maker for many famous magicians of the past and still featured by some of today's best-known performers, this is the instant vanish of a solid-looking metal cage and its canary from the magician's fingertips.

Visible Magic—the kind that happens in full view, usually instantly and without any covering, as when a balloon suddenly bursts and a live dove appears, or when all the cards in a pack suddenly start shooting up into the air like a fountain.

Volunteer—a person invited from the audience to help with a trick.

W

Wand—symbol of the magician, which also is frequently used to help conceal small things hidden in the hands. Many special wands have been devised as mechanical aids for various magical purposes and comedy effects. There are mechanical wands for the vanish or production of handkerchiefs, coins, and playing cards; and a variety of wands that fall apart, droop, spin, explode, or shoot out a stream of water.

Well—a hole in the stage magician's tabletop with a hidden cloth bag suspended beneath it so that objects may be dropped into it or removed from it secretly. Although some wells are artfully concealed by the way the tabletop is ornamented, they generally are practical only for platform use.

Z

Zig-Zag—the most frequently performed illusion of recent years: a girl stands inside a slender upright cabinet and the illusionist pushes the middle of her body far out to one side, apparently dividing her into three parts. The zig-zag is one of the inventions of the late British magician, Robert Harbin.

INDEX